The Story of "Me"

Frontiers of
Narrative

SERIES EDITOR
Jesse E. Matz, *Kenyon College*

The Story of "Me"

Contemporary American Autofiction

MARJORIE WORTHINGTON

University of Nebraska Press | Lincoln and London

Introduction

Autofiction in an American Context

It is not that the Author may not "come back" in the Text, in his text, but he then does so as a "guest." If he is a novelist, he is inscribed in the novel like one of his characters, figured in the carpet; no longer privileged, paternal, aletheological, his inscription is ludic. He becomes, as it were, a paper-author: his life is no longer the origin of his fictions but a fiction contributing to his work.

—Roland Barthes, "From Work to Text"

As the scare quotes in the title indicate, *The Story of "Me"* analyzes novels that feature a character who shares his/her name with the author, a phenomenon of contemporary American fiction that took shape in the late 1960s and early 1970s and continues in earnest today. Beginning with works like Ronald Suckenick's *Up* (1968) and *Out* (1973), John Barth's *Chimera* (1972), and Kurt Vonnegut's *Breakfast of Champions* (1973), the trend has grown in scope and popularity until the present day when it has become a postmodern trope, found in works like Richard Powers's *Galatea 2.2* (1995), Arthur Phillips's *The Tragedy of Arthur* (2011), and Ben Lerner's *10:14* (2014). To refer to these novels in which the author appears as a fictionalized character, I use the term "autofiction," which has had a long and somewhat contentious history in French literary circles but is not yet widely known in a U.S. context. Regardless of what they are called, however, autofictional texts have been proliferating for decades, and they evoke a variety of cultural anxieties. In a manner similar to actors' ironic self-portrayals in film and television, autofictional author-characters often provide a satirical commentary on authors' real-life personae.[1] Autofiction's continual reference to the extratextual person of the author suggests that, while his/her cultural power may have diminished, the author still shows definite signs of life. Furthermore, the purposeful elision between the author and the author-character draws attention to the impossibility of fully delineating the difference between fiction and nonfiction.

The autofictional trope has become so common in American fiction that it almost seems a requirement for contemporary authors to engage in it, yet not only has there been little critical discussion of this trend but there has yet to emerge a consensus about what such works should be called. Raymond Federman's idea of "surfiction" and James Rother's "parafiction" are two examples of terms coined to refer to the metafictional novels I discuss in this book. However, while both of these terms made brief, notable appearances, they have since largely disappeared from the critical conversation. French writer Serge Doubrovsky's term "autofiction" best suits these texts in no small part because it has gained traction in ways other terms have not. Doubrovsky coined the term to refer to a particular type of narrative that exhibits elements of both fiction and autobiography. The primary defining trait of autofiction as I define it is the inclusion of a characterized version of the author, usually as the protagonist. I say characterized version of the author because as autofictional narratives unfold, it becomes patently clear that, although they share a name, the protagonists and the authors are not identical to one another.

For example, the character "Bret Easton Ellis" within the novel *Lunar Park* is married with a son, while the actual Ellis has never been married and has no children. As my use of quotation marks suggests, *Lunar Park* toys with readers' sense of reality by depicting a "Bret" whose biography is simultaneously similar to yet often distinct from that of the extratextual Ellis. The two become divergent yet metaleptically interconnected entities: this is the defining characteristic of autofiction.[2]

Admittedly, of course, the same could be said about the subject of a memoir or autobiography, in that the person represented in such a text is not identical to the author him/herself but is a narrativized version of that person rendered into writing. What sets American autofiction apart from memoir or autobiography is that while "Bret" and Ellis share some biographical similarities, they are also markedly different in ways both mundane (one is married and the other is not) and extraordinary ("Bret" spends much of the novel battling the ghosts of his fictional characters who come to life to attack him—an experience I can only assume the real Ellis has not had). Unlike memoir or autobiography, autofiction often depicts its author-characters in clearly fictional situations, thus blurring the already hazy boundaries between fiction and nonfiction.[3] While an autobiography or memoir is meant to be read as a true story, autofiction is meant to be read primarily as a novel. For this reason, the meaning and power of an autofictional text resides more in its plot and themes than in the biographical or historical accuracy of the story it tells. Thus the thematic significance of *Lunar Park* arises from the depiction of "Bret" as a writer literally haunted by his creations, particularly by Patrick Bateman, the murderous protagonist of Ellis's much-reviled 1991 novel *American Psycho*. Thus *Lunar Park* makes literal the figurative notion that *American Psycho* continues to cast a shadow over its author's career. The onomastic connection between "Bret" and Ellis makes that point more vividly than a purely fictional character could, for it lends a patina of "reality" to an otherwise patently fictional situation. Autofiction highlights the extent to which the link between an autobiographical character and his/her author is undeniable but somewhat tenuous at the same time. (I use both pronouns here, but by far most American autofiction is written by white men.) In keeping with that point, *The Story of "Me"* maintains the critical tradition of referring to the author-character in quotation marks to differentiate him/her from the author-figure who exists outside the text. This practice serves as a reminder that, despite their onomastic connection, there is always a distinction between an autofiction's author-character and its author.

Although autofiction is a highly metafictional genre, and although metafiction in general has been the subject of countless critical examinations, it is somewhat striking that American autofiction has yet to receive much critical attention, given the lively and contentious international discussion that has surrounded the topic. This is particularly the case in France, where autofiction has been accused of "representing nothing more than a lucrative 'plan marketing' through which to sell books, a cynical loophole through which to sidestep any legal responsibility for the more painful revelations it might make, or a simple confusion with the long-standing genre of the autobiographical novel" (Elizabeth Jones 2009, 3). Indeed, the term "autofiction" generates such heated debate in France that the discussion has been characterized as "a theoretical soap opera comprising numerous episodes and many twists and turns" (Jeannelle and Viollet 2007, 18). Hence it becomes necessary for me to engage somewhat with those twists and turns to arrive at the definition of autofiction that I think best reflects the contemporary American literary context.

The critical inattention to autofiction in the United States is also somewhat strange because the employment of an author-character has become so prevalent in recent years as to serve as a kind of authorial rite of passage, although the term "autofiction" is rarely applied to these works. Indeed, one could echo Jones's argument that the authorial intrusions of autofiction have in some cases devolved into an American "plan marketing." The lengthy but by no means exhaustive list of contemporary American autofictions that is included in this book's appendix demonstrates that autofiction is a full-fledged fictional mode in American literature. This book will examine several of these autofictions qua autofiction, discussing their historical development, particular characteristics, and narrative effects. To do this, I will alternate between close readings of the texts in question, discussion of their historical and theoretical contexts, and analyses of relevant cultural movements. In other words, because it is the first entry in the critical discussion of American autofiction, this book is necessarily synoptic in scope, painting a panoramic portrait of the development of a fictional tradition sixty years in the making. My focus, except for a very few examples, is on American fiction and the particular social and cultural elements that have fomented and shaped the steady rise of autofiction in the contemporary period.

One aspect of my argument is that, because of its liminal position between fiction and memoir, autofiction exerts a greatly different narrative influence than the so-called autobiographical novel, which features characters who resemble their authors but do not have an onomastic relationship with them. To clarify, autofiction differs from autobiographical novels like *David Copperfield* and *A Portrait of the Artist as a Young Man* which contain some biographical information about their authors but which are meant to be viewed unambiguously as fictions. By contrast, autofiction revels in ambiguity by evoking the name of its author and including nonfictional information about him/her, while quite consciously fictionalizing the author-character at the same time.

Thus autofiction is distinct from traditional autobiography or memoir because, while autofiction is partially factual or, to use the narratological term of art, "referential," it is not entirely so. Rather, much of it is fictional by design, and by that I mean that it is not simply fictional in the sense that any event rendered into language is inherently fictional, but fictional because the text portrays events that simply did not happen. Autofictions are primarily novels, but they straddle the line between fiction and nonfiction by concocting fictionalized versions of their authors. By doing so, autofiction demonstrates that a narrative has a different valence depending upon whether it is perceived to construct a fictional world or whether it is directly connected to the extratextual one. By playing with the boundary between fiction and nonfiction, autofiction demonstrates that, while that boundary may not be clearly demarcated and can be breached, it does exist nonetheless. As such, autofiction provides an argument against the poststructuralist notion that all language should be seen as a fictional construction: the constantly shifting reading strategies that autofiction requires demonstrate that we have decidedly different expectations for fiction than for nonfiction. This in-depth study of American autofiction will illuminate the differences between how we read fiction and nonfiction and what those differences reveal about contemporary conceptions of authorship.

In American literature, the rise of autofiction can be traced to several different catalysts. One is the increasing focus in literary modernism on techniques that attempt to portray the intricacies of human consciousness. Autofiction also arose partially from the "death of the author" debates that began in the late 1960s and that have continued in various forms since then. Furthermore, the flourishing of American autofiction can be read as a symptom of authorial anxieties that stemmed from the literary gains made by women and writers of color, gains that challenged the heretofore prevalent image of the author as a creatively powerful white male. In our contemporary moment, the primacy of this image is further challenged by the proliferation and increasing popularity of confessional memoirs written not by accomplished writers but by "everyday people." And authorial anxieties are further exacerbated by the democratization of authorship made possible by the myriad new-media outlets that allow anyone with access to a computer to write for a potentially wide audience. In other words, new-media technologies have allowed nontraditional lay writers to challenge the notion of what it means to be a creative genius—to be an author. By focusing on these various anxieties, contemporary autofictional narratives force a reconsideration of the privileged place historically afforded the author in the early twentieth century. The autofictional phenomenon writ large can therefore be read as a symptom of the declining cultural capital of the traditional figure of the author. Furthermore, because it is fictional and yet maintains an undeniable connection to the extratextual world, autofiction demonstrates the possibilities for and limits on language as a means to portray real-life experiences with any accuracy.

It is important to mention that the definition of the term "autofiction" with which I am working is only one of many in circulation. There is as yet little consensus about the term's exact meaning, and it is the subject of fairly constant debate, particularly in the French literary circles from which the term derives. Originally, Serge Doubrovsky invented the term "autofiction" for the back-cover blurb of his 1977 novel *Fils*, which reads: "Fiction, of facts and events strictly real, if you prefer, autofiction, where the language of adventure has been entrusted to the adventure of language in its total freedom" (Doubrovsky 2013, i). According to this definition, autofiction is a factual autobiographical narrative about events that did happen to people who actually do exist, yet it is a narrative told with the intimate directness in keeping with "language in its total freedom." When pressed to elaborate upon the term in a 1997 interview, Doubrovsky expanded his definition to indicate a narrative that is mostly factual but whose author should be afforded a certain amount of leeway to rearrange or even alter actual events in the service of presenting more fully the "true" identity of the protagonist/author:

> The meaning of one's life in certain ways escapes us, so we have to reinvent it in our writing, and that is what I personally call *autofiction*. . . . *Fils* is an attempt to write, not an account of, but an experience of analysis within one day of the narrator's life. It is obviously fictitious, because it is a forced totalization, it is totalized only by the text, it is not a recapturing of my whole life in one day. So the essence of the book is already fictitious although all the details in it are strictly correct and referential as we would say (Doubrovsky quoted in Celestin 2001, 400).

Here, Doubrovsky articulates a common poststructuralist argument about the nature of written narrative in any form: to put something into words is to shape it by choosing which details to depict and how to depict them.

According to this school of thought, to narrativize is inherently to fictionalize, for all writing is merely a representation of reality, not reality itself. Or, as Hayden White so famously put it in regard to historical writing, "What is at issue is not, 'What are the facts?' but rather, how are the facts to be described in order to sanction one mode of explaining them rather than another" (1976, 44). Proponents of this view of writing use the term "referential" to describe a narrative that attempts to depict extra-textual events, since no narrative can be fully "true." For Doubrovsky, autofiction describes a narrative that arranges facts in a creative way and, in so doing, strays at times from strict adherence to historical accuracy or referentiality. Autofiction, to Doubrovsky, is therefore not *fictional* but *fictive*, in that it embraces the creative possibilities inherent in the act of writing but does not fabricate events. In a translation of a 1988 essay, Doubrovksy goes on to say that his text actually adheres quite closely to narrative referentiality: "I wrote 'novel' on the cover simply because I felt obliged to, thus instituting a novelistic pact by asserting fictitiousness, in spite of the tireless insistence of historical and personal reference. . . . As in a good and scrupulous autobiography, everything that is said and done in the narrative is drawn literally from my own life. Places and dates have been verified with maniacal insistence" (1993, 33). Thus for Doubrovsky, autofiction refers to a verifiably referential text that simply engages in the shaping and alterations necessitated by the process of rendering an event into language.

Doubrovsky developed his idea of autofiction (and wrote the novel *Fils*) in more or less direct response to Philippe Lejeune's famous definition of autobiography, published in his seminal essay "The Autobiographical Pact" (1973). In this essay, Lejeune defines an author of an autobiography this way: "Straddling the world-beyond-the-text and the text, he is the connection between the two. The author is defined as simultaneously a socially responsible real person and the producer of a discourse" (1989a, 11). That an author must have a biographical or historical existence outside the text he/she has written is, for Lejeune, the crux of autobiography. He argues that the author of an autobiography enters into an unwritten but well understood pact with the reader: "a contract of identity that is sealed by the proper name" (19). That is to say, this contract "supposes that there is *identity of name* between the author (such as he figures, by his name, on the cover), the narrator of the story, and the character who is being talked about" (12). An autobiography, to Lejeune, is defined as a narrative in which the author, the narrator, and the protagonist share a name. Notice that Lejeune does not say that the *figures* of the author, narrator, and protagonist are identical, but rather that they operate under the same moniker: they share "identity of name." Lejeune recognizes, then, what Doubrovsky has mentioned above: that the act of narrativization necessarily causes the separation of the written from the writer. But to Lejeune, the connection between the protagonist and the author of an autobiography can be made through the equation of the name of the protagonist within the book to the name of the author on its cover.

It is this onomastic connection, according to Lejeune, that differentiates autobiography from fiction because autobiography, through the proper name, represents an intersection between the inter- and extratextual worlds. Lejeune argues that an author of autobiography attempts to "neutralize" the "indetermination of the first person" "by grounding it in the proper name" (1989a, 20). This emphasis on the connection between the autobiographical protagonist and the proper name of the author is Lejeune's intervention into the way autobiography had previously been discussed: before his argument that autobiography makes direct reference to the proper name of its author, the primary characteristic of autobiography had been considered to be its use of first-person narration. This equation does not hold up very well, however, given the large number of fictions that use the first person yet are in no way autobiographical. In order to accommodate the poststructuralist idea that saying or writing "I" does not refer unproblematically to a person existing outside language, Lejeune points out that autobiographers yoke the enunciation of "I" to their own proper name, thereby making clear that the autobiographical text is referential, not fictional.

These ideas are what Doubrovsky was responding to—even rejecting— in his novel *Fils*, in an attempt, as he said in a letter to Lejeune, to "fill up that 'square,' which your analysis left empty" by writing a *fiction* in which the "I" simultaneously did *and* did not refer to the author. (Note here that Doubrovsky has shifted his definition of autofiction from referring to a purely referential text that has been fictively shaped, to a text that contains elements of both referentiality and fiction.) Thus autofiction refutes Lejeune's argument that the onomastic connection between author and protagonist is constitutive of an autobiographical narrative. In other words, autofiction often depicts an author-character in fictional, not referential, situations, suggesting that while the author and the protagonist may share a name, the narrative itself may not be purely referential. Lejeune himself came to recognize the potential for a text to be both fictional and nonfictional in a 1982 essay reworking his previous ideas about fiction and autobiography: "I am thinking about the possibility of *neither one nor the other, but I forget both at the same time!*" (1989b, 134). In other words, Doubrovsky's autofictional experiment drew Lejeune's attention to the myriad texts that already break his pact by using the author's name in a fictional narrative that contains autobiographical elements as well or "both at the same time." In other words, Lejeune came to recognize the effect an autofictional text might have on his autobiographical pact.

What autofiction thus demonstrates is that autobiography—even with its gesture toward the proper name—is no better situated to "prove" its referentiality than is fiction. Autofiction makes this idea manifest by engaging the name of the author in order to construct a character who differentiates him/herself from, yet undeniably still refers to, the person outside the text. In this way, the elemental difference is revealed between a textual character and a real person, even when the textual character and the real person share a name and elements of biography. While autofiction maintains a correlation between the extratextual author and the eponymous author-character, that correlation is always slippery at best.

To Doubrovsky, autofiction represents an attempt to convey an accurate, intimate, and completely factual representation of a self in connection with late twentieth-century theories of the self that view it as always incomplete, fragmented, and coalesced by memory (which is by its very nature flawed and often false). Doubrovsky's brand of autofiction is meant to serve as a narrative portrayal of his psychotherapeutic process: "Autofiction represents the fiction that I have decided, as a writer, to make of myself and for myself, incorporating therein, in the fullest sense of the term, the experience of analysis, not just thematically but in the very production of the text" (1993, 41). This is one reason why Doubrovsky differentiates autofiction from autobiography, which he defines as a narrative that "retraces a life from its beginning to its end at the time of writing in chronological and logical order" (2013, i). For Doubrovsky, autobiography retraces a *life*, while autofiction presents a *self*. Because the postmodern conception of self is not logical or orderly, Doubrovsky's autofiction aims to represent the self truthfully, even if doing so requires taking liberties with pure referentiality. In autofiction, as in all fiction then, narrative "Truth" is distinct from historical or biographical factuality.

American writer Tim O'Brien argues something similar when he says: "A thing may happen and be a total lie; another thing may not happen and be truer than the truth" (1990, 79). Thus a truthful representation of a self sometimes requires taking fictional liberties with the reconstruction of events that would not be acceptable in autobiography. Of course, it should be noted that autobiographies also frequently reorganize events temporally, often indicating the writer's knowledge of things to come or things past (prolepsis: "I had not yet had this experience" or analepsis: "This event reminds me of an earlier one"). However, even if events are temporally reorganized in an autobiography, they must still refer accurately to events that occurred in the extratextual world. Similarly, although autofiction has perhaps more license to fictionalize than autobiography, Doubrovsky's definition of autofiction dictates that it must not stray too far from the accurate representation of extratextual events. In possible contradiction of that mandate, Doubrovsky publishes his texts under the rubric of *novel*, a term traditionally used to refer to fictional narratives. His insistence that autofiction tell a referential story belies the label of novel; in fact, I would posit that, in the United States, an autofiction adhering to Doubrovsky's definition (of a highly intimate yet referential portrait of a narrativized self) would be classified not as a novel but as a *memoir*.

Indeed, the current popularity of memoir in the United States is probably one reason why the term "autofiction" has yet to catch on with any strength here, even though autofictions themselves have proliferated in recent American literature. It could be argued that Doubrovsky's kind of autofiction has traditionally focused on the "auto" half of that term, featuring texts focused more on portraying a self in all its complexity than on crafting a fictional narrative. To complicate matters, Philippe Gasparini and others have expanded Doubrovsky's definition of autofiction to claim that, rather than being a purely referential narrative, autofiction is more of a "hybrid" genre that constantly shifts between the referential and the fictional. As one adherent of this hybrid definition puts it, autofiction is "a frontier area, where body and writing take on the fantasies, illusions, aspirations, rooted cultural imagery of the writer" (Robin as translated by Ferreira-Meyers 2012). Vincent Colonna is perhaps the strongest advocate of this second definition: "According to Colonna, the term autofiction encompasses all the processes of fictionalization of the Self . . . insofar as the author is fantasizing his own existence, a project in which imaginary characters are more or less close extensions of his/her Self" (Ferreira-Meyers 2012, 106). As Colonna himself says: "We would do well to restrict the neologism 'autofiction' to authors who invent a personality and a literary existence for themselves" (2004, 198). To put it yet another way: "In some of its hues, *autofiction* involves authors writing the self without concern for what they perceive it to be, but rather, as they fantasize it" (Boyle 2007, 18). In this conception, autofiction is still centered around the narrative construction of the truth of a self, but it is free to employ any fictional elements necessary to do so. So this definition gives equal weight to both elements of the term "autofiction," conceiving of the self as a fictional creation of its author. The resulting texts are by turns both referential and fictional, with little attention given to separating fact from fiction. Dervila Cooke sums up the difference between the two definitions when she says: "Colonna's view of autofiction seems to suppose a predominance of invention, while the practice of Doubrovsky is closer to objectively verifiable fact" (2005, 80). Adherence to referentiality is, however, important for both definitions.

But it is a third definition that I employ for the most part in this book, for this third definition, coined by Gérard Genette, most accurately describes the particular way autofiction has emerged in American literature. In contrast to both Doubrovsky's and Gasparini's ideas, Genette's definition more overtly embraces the "fiction" part of the term "autofiction." Genette differentiates *"true* autofictions," "whose narrative content is, if I may say so, authentically fictional" from "false autofictions, which are 'fictions' only for legal purposes: in other words, veiled autobiographies" (1993, 77n31). Or as E. H. Jones puts it, "Autofiction is what results when the realms of the impossible, of the more than possible, are entered into" (2010, 179). True autofictions, for Genette, are those which are more fictional than not, but which maintain the onomastic connection between author and protagonist. He evokes *The Divine Comedy* as a quintessential example of an autofictional text, in which the eponymous author-protagonist named "Dante" implies: "I, the author, am going to tell you a story of which I am the hero but which never happened to me" (1993, 76).[4] Thus for Genette, autofictions are *fictitious* despite the nominal relationship between their authors, narrators, and protagonists. Autofictions are not autobiographies or memoirs by another name but *novels* that play with the expectations evoked when the protagonist and the author share a name and some biographical information, but when that protagonist engages in clearly fictional endeavors. It is this third definition that most closely describes novels like Philip Roth's *Operation Shylock* (1994) in which "Philip" embarks on a secret mission for the Israeli Mossad, or Arthur Phillips's *The Tragedy of Arthur* (2011) in which "Arthur" inherits an authentic but previously undiscovered play by William Shakespeare, or Mark Leyner's *Et Tu, Babe?* (1992) in which "Mark" undergoes "visceral tattooing" to imprint an image of himself surfing directly onto his heart. American autofiction combines the clearly fictional with the seemingly accurate biographical history of its authors.

Yet at the same time, the rise and continued escalation of American autofiction demonstrates that the differentiation between fiction and nonfiction still retains an enormous cultural significance. My purpose in this book is not to engage in the continuing attempt to draw a clear line of demarcation between literary fiction and nonfiction, but rather to argue that the proliferation of autofiction illustrates that, although that line cannot be clearly drawn, neither can it be completely erased. American autofiction is *both* fictional and referential: it involves texts featuring a character who shares the author's name and who resembles the author in some respects, but who becomes embroiled in clearly fictional situations. Most American autofictions are published as novels, not simply because they employ creative narrative technique or because they aim for the legitimacy that accompanies the category "fiction," but because they are indeed highly fictional. They are not *completely* so, however, because they deploy eponymous author-characters who share a tenuous biographical connection to their authors.

In that sense, American autofiction resembles what Linda Hutcheon called historiographic metafiction: "novels which are both intensely self-reflexive and yet paradoxically also lay claim to historical events and personages" (1988, 5). Historiographic metafiction refers to fictions that feature historical figures as characters and historical events as plot points, but which also take fictional liberties with these figures and events, depicting nonfictional people in fictional situations. A classic example of historiographic metafiction is Robert Coover's novel *The Public Burning*

(1977), which fictionalizes the trial and execution of Julius and Ethel Rosenberg. Hutcheon coined her term in order to elucidate how postmodern literature contributes to the conception of history as a narrative rather than a purely referential account: "Historiographic metafiction self-consciously reminds us that, while events did occur in the real empirical past, we name and constitute those events as historical facts by selection and narrative positioning" (1988, 96). In a related manner, whereas historiographic metafiction addresses the constructed nature of historical accounts, autofiction addresses the constructed and constantly changing nature of authorship: although an autofictional author may have an empirical existence outside an autofictional text, the primary image we as readers have of the author is presented through the text's narrative positioning.

Much as historiographic metafiction makes its connection to the world outside itself by referring to historical events and figures, autofiction makes that connection by deploying an onomastic author-character. Thus autofiction is similar to historiographic metafiction, in that it exposes the problematic nature of "both any naïve realist concept of representation and any equally naïve textualist or formalist assertions of the total separation of art from the world" (Hutcheon 1989, 6). But while historiographic metafiction and autofiction both use the strategy of depicting nonfictional events and people in fictional narratives, the former does so to challenge received notions about historical discourse and the latter does so in a simultaneous repudiation and defense of authorial authority.

Autofictions grapple with contradictory textual and extratextual factors. On one hand, they are clearly novels: they are published, promoted, and categorized as fiction, and they depict situations that are unmistakably and consciously fictional (e.g., the ghosts and demons of *Lunar Park* and the conscious computer construct of *Galatea 2.2*). However, they also exhibit some undeniable nonfictional traits: their protagonists have an onomastic and biographical connection with the extratextual author. Doubrovsky's words are helpful here, for although he adamantly insists that autofiction is a "false fiction which is the story of a true life," he goes on to describe it by saying, "Neither autobiography nor novel in the strict sense, it operates in a no-man's-land, in a ceaseless cross-reference, in a space which is impossible and elusive everywhere but in the operation of the text itself" (as quoted in Spear 1991, 357). This "no-man's-land," this liminal position between autobiography and novel, is the key element here, for it gestures to one reason why autofiction has become such a popular genre among contemporary authors: it exemplifies the linguistic self-consciousness that characterizes the postmodern literary period.

By contrast, a nineteenth-century author like Dickens was satisfied to name his protagonist David Copperfield, a decision that freed him both to draw upon his own life story and to fictionalize at will; the result is a narrative that contains many autobiographical elements but that is undeniably a fiction. In this contemporary period, by contrast, autofiction has emerged as a common strategy, for while autofiction features a combination of fictional and autobiographical elements similar to autobiographical novels like *David Copperfield*, the implied equation between author and protagonist forges a very different relationship with the reader than an unalloyed fiction does. Alex Hughes argues that autofiction denies the reader some of the pleasures associated with reading autobiography: "The autofictional work, then, is a generically 'bastard' narrative artefact that, in contrast to the classically autobiographical confessional *recit*, refuses to incite or allow us to exploit it in order to seek definitively to know, to decipher the existential 'truth' about, to pin down the particularity of, and thus to individualize (and objectify), its 'real-life' creator" (1999, 112). Readers cannot read autofiction as they do a traditional autobiography. Nor can they read it as they might read a traditional work of fiction. By purposefully and metafictionally gesturing outside itself to the extratextual author, autofiction renders narrative suture impossible, as it constantly reminds the reader of the "real" world outside the text, even if only to demonstrate its own imminent departure from that reality.

Thanks to their eponymous author-characters, autofiction is neither entirely fictional nor completely referential: "Neither autobiography nor novel, then, strictly speaking, it exists in a perpetual oscillation between the two, inhabiting a space that only the operation of the text makes possible or accessible" (Doubrovsky 1993, 33). Autofictions draw upon and toy with the expectations and traditions of both fiction and memoir writing and in doing so they demonstrate that, regardless of poststructuralist notions that all writing is a re- and therefore mis-representation of reality, there is a readerly difference in weight or value between fictional and nonfictional texts. To demonstrate, I would point to G. Thomas Couser's definition of memoir as a text which "presents itself, and is therefore read, as a nonfictional record or re-presentation of actual humans' experience" whose primary function is "to make identity claims" (2012, 15, 13). Like Doubrovsky's idea of autofiction, memoir has traditionally been thought of as a referential narrative told from a highly particularized and personal perspective. It represents one person's side of a story perhaps, but is a nonfictional story nonetheless. However, as both autofiction in France and memoir in the United States have become more and more widespread, the definitions of both have evolved to include more creative and often fictive, if not fictional, elements. Couser notes, "Today, memoirs often incorporate invented or enhanced material, and they often use novelistic techniques" (2012, 15). In this sense, the term "memoir"—at least here in the United States—seems to encapsulate the kind of narrative Doubrovsky means when he speaks of autofiction. He has noted that autofiction often assembles events "in a radically altered presentation disorderly or in an order which deconstructs and reconstructs the narrative according to its own logic with a novelistic design of its own. It can recount, and I personally do so constantly, past events or feelings, long gone situations, in the present tense, as if they were just happening" (2013, i). The fact that the incorporation of "enhanced material," "novelistic techniques," and "radically altered presentation" are now allowable in both genres demonstrates the extent to which autofiction and memoir have shifted away from being purely factual narratives toward a closer relationship with fiction. This comparison of autofiction to memoir also illustrates that in the United States, what Doubrovsky refers to as autofiction would probably be considered memoir, and that the American novels that I discuss here adhere more closely to the definition of autofiction espoused by Gérard Genette.

Some American autofictions feature an author-character described in the third person: Paul Auster's *City of Glass* (1985), Jonathan Safran Foer's *Everything Is Illuminated* (2002), Salvador Plascencia's *The People of Paper* (2005), and Ruth Ozeki's *A Tale for the Time Being* (2013) are four important contemporary instances, while *The Autobiography of Alice B. Toklas* (1933) is perhaps the first example. But a far more common form of autofiction features the homodiegetic author-character who also serves as the novel's narrator and who, therefore, employs first-person narration.[5] In this form, the onomastic relationship between the author and narrator/ protagonist in autofiction is for Genette an "intentional contradictory pact" (1993, 76). Genette refers here, of course, to Lejeune's autobiographical pact, which is violated in autofiction because the equation between author and protagonist-narrator cannot consistently be drawn with any certainty. In other words, autofiction's combination of the biographical and the fictional is deliberately equivocal: sometimes the author-character is depicted referentially, sometimes fictionally. It becomes difficult, if not impossible, to determine which aspects of the autofiction are "true" and which are "false," and for me, this kind of definitive determination is not the point. Rather, the constant narrative code-switching that reading autofiction necessitates raises important questions about the nature of authorship and of reality in narrative. Because these novels contain some autobiographical elements and are simultaneously and avowedly fictional, they not only defy the autobiographical pact but give the lie to it by demonstrating that all autobiographical texts rely upon a narrativization process that is by definition not transparently referential.

This "intentional contradictory pact" tended in earlier decades to elicit confusion among some American readers about the place of autofiction on the spectrum between fiction and nonfiction. Indeed, Philip Roth even contributed to this confusion by publishing a letter in the *New York Times* asserting that the outlandish events depicted in *Operation Shylock* actually took place (Roth 1993). Just as in the eighteenth century "readers had to be taught how to read fiction" as an emergent genre (Gallagher 1994), twentieth-century readers could be said to have had to learn to read autofiction as an ironic representation of an author-character standing on the borderline between fiction and autobiography. But in the current moment, most contemporary readers are not confused by the autofictional nature of a text because they are equipped—perhaps through frequent practice—to comprehend the liminal nature of autofiction and, for that matter, of fiction and memoir as well. Indeed, I will argue here that the proliferation of autofiction has had wide-ranging effects on readers' relationship to more traditional fictional and referential texts.

As Genette has said, the contradictory autobiographical pact is intentional because readers are not meant to take the author-character as the "true" extratextual author, any more than they are meant to believe that Dante actually traveled to the underworld, purgatory, and heaven. Or as Linda Hutcheon says in a similar discussion of Daniel Defoe, "most readers today (and many then) had the pleasure of a double awareness of both fictiveness and a basis in the 'real'" (1998, 107). In contemporary terms, the presence of the eponymous author-character in autofiction implies that the events in the novel actually happened, not just in the world of the text but in the world external to it as well. A primary pleasure of the autofictional text arises from the double awareness of knowing that many of those events are actually fictional; the reader is in on the ironic joke of the autofiction. Furthermore, an examination of autofiction provides insight into the current popularity of memoir by limning what it is about a nonfictional account that is so attractive to contemporary reading audiences, despite poststructuralist arguments about the inherently non-referential nature of language.

In fact, it could even be argued that autofictions represent the extent to which poststructuralist ideas about written narrative have been accepted by mainstream audiences. Poststructuralist narrative theory decreed that any and all writing was by its very nature merely a representation of reality and, therefore, a fiction. The well-known argument goes like this: whenever words are arranged in order to convey information, the shaping of events into a verbal format and a narrative structure necessarily requires the reconstruction, and therefore the fictionalization, of those events. Language and narrative are not transparent modes of communication; rather, they inherently impose a screen between the audience and the reality being depicted. Raymond Federman, consummate author of Doubrovsky-esque autofictions such as *The Voice in the Closet* and *Return to Manure,* puts it well when he says: "If one admits from the start (at least to oneself) that no meaning pre-exists language, but that language creates meaning as it goes along, that is to say as it is used (spoken or written), as it progresses, then writing (fiction especially) will be a mere process of letting language do its tricks. To write, then, is to *produce* meaning and not *reproduce* a pre-existing meaning" (1981, 8). This theory has led to the idea that all writing is fiction, a phenomenon that Marie-Laure Ryan has called "panfictionality" as a result of Derrida's designation of the binary opposition between fiction and nonfiction as a socially constructed "hierarchical axiology" (1988, 236). It has been debated which side of the hierarchical binary is the privileged side, however, as Derrida argues that fiction has often been viewed as nonfiction's "parasite," while Arnaud Schmitt has posited that, in artistic terms, fiction is the privileged side of the binary hierarchy. Certainly, both have a point, especially in the current moment where fiction may have more cultural cachet (as per Schmitt), while the publishing market values nonfiction more and more: memoir sales increased 400 percent between 2004 and 2008 (Yagoda 2009, 7).

Indeed, part of my argument will echo Schmitt's: just as Doubrovsky may embrace the designation of "novel" for his memoir-esque work in order to lend his autofiction a more literary patina, some authors of American autofiction parody the memoir form in order to appeal to the prurient interests of the contemporary American reading public who have a seemingly insatiable appetite for ripped-from-the-headlines stories about prominent or otherwise interesting people. By playfully crossing and recrossing the admittedly hazy dividing line between fiction and nonfiction, autofiction demonstrates that such a line does indeed exist— at least in the minds of contemporary readers. Autofiction thereby provides a formidable challenge to the notion of panfictionality.

Furthermore, the proliferation of contemporary autofiction demonstrates that poststructuralist ideas about the nature of language have entered the cultural mainstream. The rise of autofiction in concert with the rise of memoir (a development I discuss in further depth in chapter 5) suggests that, while readers still yearn for a factual story, they have accepted the poststructuralist notion that narrative is a reconstruction, not a transparent representation, of events. Thus readers can recognize the simultaneous yet contradictory idea that an autofiction might be *both* factual and fictional. That readers are willing and able to read a novel in which a historically extant character engages in clearly fictional situations indicates that they understand that a written representation cannot accurately represent an actual person. This distinction remains clear even when the character being described has the same name as a person in existence outside the text. Paradoxically, autofiction also demonstrates two very different connotations conveyed, on the one hand, by a purely fictional protagonist and, on the other, by a protagonist who shares a name with an extratextual figure.

Autofiction, then, becomes a vehicle through which to discuss the different modes of reading employed with fiction as opposed to memoir. Although some writers and theorists would agree with Federman that good fiction "exposes the fictionality of reality" (1981, 7), the increasing popularity of contemporary memoir suggests that not only is reality not viewed as fictional but that there is some quality in an ostensibly factual account that distinguishes it from fiction. On the other hand, metafiction's suggestion that real life is also a fiction has persevered for so long because the primary focus of most metafiction has had little to do with the extratextual world and more to do with the world constructed by narrative. In other words, the literary metafictional project has typically not been to call into question the ontological reality of the extratextual world but to explore the limits of what a text can accomplish within the narrative world it constructs. My point here is that neither the "all writing is fiction" nor the "clear demarcation between fiction and nonfiction" approach has sufficed for the metafictional experiments that have proliferated in the postmodern period. This is where a study of autofiction is useful: because it is both fictional *and* referential, a focus on autofiction helps illuminate what the distinction between them is and why, in our current cultural moment, factual autobiographical accounts seem poised to overshadow fictional ones in the popular imagination.

Autofiction serves myriad narrative functions, and this book attempts to enumerate them in order to demonstrate the larger cultural anxieties they expose. Although the increasing levels of self-consciousness in postmodern fiction emerge somewhat organically from the textual experiments of high modernism, the rise of autofiction in the United States was nudged in particular directions by specifically American cultural, philosophical, and historical trends.[6] For example, chapter 1 addresses the fact that by far most American autofiction is written by white men. This chapter argues that the authorial intrusions of autofiction could be read as both emerging from and as a reaction against modernist ideas of impersonality and universality. I will argue that the element that unites both impersonality and authorial intrusion as literary strategies can be traced to a perceived "crisis of masculinity" that emerged several times in various ways over the twentieth century and continues to do so today. The highly particularized representations of authors in autofiction emerged in concert with and as a counterpoint to feminist arguments that what had been considered the literary and human "universal" was in fact a very specific and limited white male perspective.

Chapter 2 illustrates how autofictions thematize the creative power of their authors by simultaneously demonstrating that power and calling it into question. In this sense, autofiction can be seen as a salvo in the continuing death of the author debate: how can an author be dead if he appears as the controlling narrative voice in his novel? Simultaneously, however, writerly authority is challenged by these very novels, which often take as their theme the diminished authorial power of their protagonists. For example, "Arthur" in *The Tragedy of Arthur* is a successful writer unable to enjoy his success out of the shadow of his lifelong competition with the work and reputation of William Shakespeare.

Chapter 3 continues the discussion of authorial intrusion by connecting the development of American autofiction to the trend known as "the New Journalism," which was often characterized by reporters writing themselves into their stories in order to provide a fuller and more vivid account of events. This form of journalism had its heyday in the early 1970s, but its effects can still be felt in the current proliferation of the experiential memoir. Certain forms of autofiction can be traced directly back to this journalistic movement, which eschewed the traditional journalistic objectivity in which the reporter effaced his/her presence in the story in favor of a style of reportage that admitted and even encouraged the involvement of the reporter in the action being reported. Just as the emergent autofictional traditions I discuss in chapter 1 can be read as a recognition that any single perspective is necessarily partial, not universal, the New Journalism makes evident that pure journalistic objectivity is not possible for the same reason. I argue that the autofictional New Journalism of writers such as Tom Wolfe, Hunter S. Thompson, and Norman Mailer aim for a greater level of accuracy by admitting and even overtly thematizing the partiality of an individual author's perspective; they accomplish this accuracy by inserting their own avatars into their narratives.

Chapter 4 elaborates upon how the experimental nature of autofiction provides another strategy for writers grappling with the difficulties of portraying trauma. By affording trauma survivors the means to "tell it slant" yet still remain somewhat connected to a referential storytelling strategy, autofictional strategies are consistent with the tradition of trauma fiction to employ narrative experiments to depict events that are difficult if not impossible to represent with any accuracy through language.

Chapter 5 addresses the simultaneously adversarial and symbiotic intersections between autofiction and the contemporary memoir. I argue that the increasing proliferation of autofiction and the recent explosive popularity of the contemporary memoir both demonstrate the wider cultural acceptance of poststructuralist theories of how language works to construct perceptions of reality. At the same time, however, these genres also expose the limitations of the cultural absorption of those theories. That is to say, contemporary readers are capable of comprehending the ironic representation of the author-character in autofiction, but there still exists a strong yearning among contemporary readers for a factual account, or a "true story."

In general, autofiction makes manifest the following poststructuralist ideas: (1) That the context—in this case the paratext (the title page, the extratextual factual information)—is essential to reading. We cannot and do not simply look to the world of the text to give it meaning; rather, we always draw meaning from outside, from context, as Derrida has argued. (2) The fact that readers require this context resuscitates the figure of the author who, rather than being dead, has proven to be a pervasive concept in imbuing a text with meaning, as Foucault has argued. (3) On the other hand, American autofiction departs from poststructuralist ideas about the inherent fictionality of all writing by walking the line between fiction and nonfiction, sometimes falling on one side of the line, sometimes on the other. What this liminality demonstrates is what nonacademic readers have always known: there is a difference in valence between a factual and a fictional story, and each elicits very different expectations and reading strategies.

Roland Barthes famously argued that there has been a shift in cultural authority over the centuries from author to reader. This is, however, only one of many shifts in authority taking place in contemporary culture. Autofiction emerges as a response to those shifts: it has proliferated in this contemporary moment in reaction to the diminishing cultural authority of the novel and of authors in general and the white male author in particular. The overt presence of an author-character in autofiction marks an attempt to reassert authorial authority while simultaneously demonstrating the limits of that authority. Subsequently, autofiction serves paradoxically as a postmodern challenge to traditional notions of authority and truth and as a somewhat conservative attempt to reassert those traditions. Just as it both blurs and reaffirms the boundary between fiction and nonfiction, autofiction asserts and calls into question traditional authorial authority, as it is often marked by gender, race, and class.

1 Masculinity, Whiteness, and Postmodern Self-Consciousness

Vladimir Nabokov, John Barth,
Kurt Vonnegut, and Richard Powers

> *The "serious" contemporary hetero-male novel is a thinly*
> *veiled Story of Me, as voraciously consumptive as all of*
> *patriarchy. While the hero/anti-hero explicitly* is *the author,*
> *everybody else is reduced to "characters."*
>
> —Chris Kraus, *I Love Dick*

The copious theoretical work done in recent years on the history of maleness and masculinity reveals one thing quite clearly: white masculinity
has apparently been "in crisis," either continually or serially, since the
turn of the nineteenth century. These "crises" have been given various
names and arise in response to movements demanding women's suffrage,
demands for civil rights for people of color, rising immigration rates, and
increasing numbers of women in the workplace. As a result, the traditional view of what it means to be a man has been evolving rapidly, often to the chagrin of the men involved. Indeed, historians of masculinity have argued that some of the greatest resistance to the demands of
the various women's and civil rights movements of the late nineteenth,
twentieth, and early twenty-first centuries has arisen from the realization that if women and people of color were to be granted greater representation in personal, public, and professional life, a complementary adjustment would have to be made on the part of white men. Hence
dominant masculinity is continually perceived to be in crisis.

My focus for this chapter will be primarily on the effect feminist movements have had on these masculine crises and the significant historical
scholarship on twentieth- and twenty-first-century masculinity that has
emerged to describe them. For example, David Rosen posits that before

World War I, white men "suffered psychic conflict from the softening of gender lines under the influence of urban middle-class domestication" (1993, 181). In response, men's and boys' groups emerged to "remasculinize" men; arguably, World War I itself emerged as the primary means by which this remasculinization was to occur. According to Kaja Silverman's *Male Subjectivity at the Margins*, the idea of "masculinity in crisis" continues into postwar America. David Savran builds upon Silverman's argument by tracing the effects of this crisis in contemporary white American masculinity, while Alice Ferrebe argues that, in the decades following World War II, masculinity "fail[ed] to pay the traditional dividends" in a world of men "anxious over its waning influence" (2005, 1, 8). Sally Robinson's *Marked Men: White Masculinity in Crisis* chronicles what she calls a "white male decline in post-sixties America" (2000, 2). And today even boys are facing a supposed crisis, and their struggles to fit into contemporary American educational structures are outlined in books like Michael Kimmel's *Angry White Men: American Masculinity at the End of an Era*. Discussions of race and gender are vital to understanding these male crises because, Kimmel argues, they involve white men's feelings of "aggrieved entitlement" as they fail to achieve or be granted the economic and social power which they have been acculturated to see as their due.

It is interesting to note that words like "crisis" become the common terms of art when an empowered group is faced with having to relinquish some of that power. Tellingly, such terms are not used in discussions of women or people of color negotiating new ways of defining their identities and engaging with the world. Rather, a situation becomes a "crisis" when entrenched concepts of supremacy might be on the chopping block. Moreover, the term provides a certain rhetorical cover for the reactionary and often repressive actions of those on the potentially losing end. A backlash against feminist advancements is understandable— even defensible—when such a backlash is couched in terms of a "masculinity crisis." How else ought a population in crisis to respond to changing circumstances but to quash those changes as completely as possible? Such reactionary responses have emerged again and again as various civil rights and women's movements have arisen.

For this reason, I agree with Sally Robinson when she says, "The question of whether dominant masculinity is 'really' in crisis is, in my view, moot: even if we could determine what an actual, real, historically verifiable crisis would look like, the undeniable fact remains that in the post-liberationist era, dominant masculinity consistently *represents itself as in crisis*" (2000, 11, emphasis mine). In other words, what is important for both Robinson's and for my argument is not whether these crises of masculinity actually exist, but rather how the perceptions of those crises are made culturally manifest and reflected in the literature of their time. A variety of compelling arguments about the repercussions to literature of the masculinity crisis have already been made. For example, Rita Felski argues that the repudiation of femininity became one of the central metaphors of modernism; Sandra Gilbert and Susan Gubar trace the crisis of modernism and modernist art and literature to an "ongoing battle of the sexes that was set in motion by the late nineteenth-century rise of feminism" (1988, xii); and Kathleen Fitzpatrick evaluates the potential obsolescence of the novel in the age of television through its effect on mostly male-authored works. My particular argument will focus on the ways in which the "crisis in masculinity" (whether it be a single, long-lasting crisis or a series of differentiated ones) has given rise to an increased self-consciousness in fiction by men, leading ultimately to the trend I have been calling autofiction.

From the late nineteenth through the twentieth century, countless public figures viewed the influence of the various women's movements as an overt threat to traditional manhood. Many were the exhortations to reassert male authority in the household and to reaffirm traditional masculinity—however it was currently defined—in the greater world. As this chapter will discuss, however, it was not common to discuss—or even to recognize—the effects of masculine privilege on literary endeavor until the latter part of the twentieth century, with the advent of feminist literary criticism. While male modernist writers thought and wrote a great deal about their artistic philosophies, they usually did so without recognizing the extent to which their ideas were inflected by masculine-gendered concerns. As a corrective, late twentieth-century scholars of modernism pored over historical artifacts in order to prove linkages between gender and events like World War I and particular artistic innovations. But the modernist artistic figures themselves seem patently unaware of any influence the international suffrage movement or changing perceptions of women's societal roles might have had on the artistic events of the day. It has taken the profoundly important work of scholars such as Sandra Gilbert, Susan Gubar, and Bonnie Kime Scott to point out the extent to which modernist literary texts and philosophies are steeped in gender concerns, namely, in the shoring up of masculine power and privilege.

Following in these scholars' influential footsteps, I want to turn my attention to the subsequent era of literary self-consciousness, when many so-called postmodern writers were responding to the perceived loss of centrality of the traditional male authorial figure by resorting to self-conscious narrative experiments, often involving the inclusion of characterized versions of themselves. Early in the postmodern period, male writers inserted onomastic avatars of themselves into their works, but, like the modernists, often without an apparent awareness of the gender issues inherent in doing so. During the latter half of the twentieth century, gender consciousness began to be raised, at first mostly focused on the effects and limits of femininity as a social construction. More recently, of course, critical and theoretical attention has been turned to the effects, limits, and very real privileges of masculinity as well.

At this point, however, it remains for me to make the connection between the perceived crisis of masculinity and postmodern self-consciousness. The time from the late twentieth century to the present was and remains an extremely self-conscious period, both artistically and philosophically. A primary argument of this book is that the artistic self-consciousness found in metafictional texts is linked in a variety of ways to the philosophical self-consciousness of the times, which focused on the nature of subjectivity and the place of the subject in the world. One important component of a subject's place in the world is, of course, gender, and the mid- to late-century rise of feminist theory was in part responsible for writers' increased awareness of the impacts gender has on subjectivity.

Thus it is my contention that the self-conscious nature of postmodern literature can be seen in part as a reaction to the rise of feminism, particularly the second-wave feminism of the 1960s and 1970s in which feminist writers made inroads into the arenas of literary study. Read this way, many of the postmodern writers of the time, such as John Barth, Kurt Vonnegut, and Ronald Sukenick, are reacting to the trope of the disempowered masculine author figure with increasing self-consciousness, even if their work evinces little to no recognition of a perceived "crisis of masculinity." Later in the century, however, self-conscious autofiction by such writers as Philip Roth and Richard Powers do manifest a distinct sense of the predicament caused by the waning power of masculine authorship.

This chapter will discuss the connection between the increasingly self-conscious fiction of the twentieth and twenty-first centuries and the burgeoning awareness of the exigencies of male privilege. I will limn the ways that the growing cognizance of how masculinity develops and evolves as a social construct affected contemporary American fiction. As feminist literary theory emerged in the 1970s and beyond to challenge the notion that our conception of "the author" is unquestionably male by default, the so-called "literary fiction" of white male writers took a decidedly self-conscious turn. This development directly contrasts (and also, paradoxically, arose from) the high modernist mandate that the author's "self" should be far removed from the work of art. And while the self-less-ness of the modernist period has been ascribed to the attempt to maintain for literature an objective, masculine identity, my argument is that the growing awareness of masculine privilege brought about by second-wave feminism's forays into literary theory fomented the increasing self-consciousness of postwar American fiction.

Of particular interest here is Kathleen Fitzpatrick's notion that "the anxiety of obsolescence both requires social privilege to be mobilized as a discourse and conceals the repressed anxiety that the threatened disappearance of that privilege engenders" (2006, 20). In other words, when a cultural trope (such as "the author") is deemed to be in danger of becoming obsolete (or "dying"), the resulting anxiety actually masks a deeper anxiety about the potential loss of social privilege. The emergent anxiety that self-conscious fiction evinces of a loss of authorial authority actually provides cover for the deeper-seated anxiety of loss of male privilege. Furthermore, this self-consciousness is one of the primary markers of difference between modernist and postmodern fiction. A fruitful means by which to understand this literary self-consciousness as it relates to masculinity is through a study of autofiction, in which the male author makes a charactorial appearance in his text in order paradoxically both to demonstrate his waning authorial power and to reassert his decidedly masculine authority.

It would be instructive here to elaborate very briefly on the emergence of the concept of masculinity as a social construct. Depending upon one's point of view, traditional concepts of masculinity have supposedly either been under continual siege or have had to withstand many discrete yet repeated attacks from forces that would try to weaken American manhood. For example, the increasing industrialization at the turn of the twentieth century rapidly transformed male workers from individual master crafts-men and business owners to factory or office employees involved in repet-itive, often disempowered work. This development brought about the end of what historian Michael Kimmel has called "the era of the Heroic Arti-san" and ushered in the era of the faceless "Company Man" (2013, 84).[1] At this time, the immigrant population was exploding in the United States and the dawn of first-wave feminism saw women entering higher educa-tion and the workforce in greater and greater numbers and, of course, de-manding suffrage rights. These developments caused anxiety in some white men who believed that their primacy was being threatened (Kim-mel 2013, 85–87). An oft-cited literary example of male reaction to these developments is the character Basil Ransome from Henry James's 1885 novel *The Bostonians*. Although Ransome is portrayed rather equivocal-ly, at once both hero and villain, his perspective was shared by many in the late nineteenth century when he said: "The whole generation is wom-anized; the masculine tone is passing out of the world . . . which, if we don't soon look out, will usher in the reign of mediocrity" (1984, 293).

This sense of imminent threat to American manhood, and subse-quently to American society writ large, was prevalent throughout the twentieth century (and remains fairly widespread now). Increasing pre–World War I demands for women's suffrage and other rights stemmed from the first wave of the women's movement and resulted subsequent-ly in a call for the remasculinization of men. According to Kimmel, the possible remedies that were suggested to stem the feminization of men took many forms, from games and sports to men's clubs like the Free-masons and even the Ku Klux Klan. Indeed, Gilbert and Gubar posit that the militarization of the western world that led eventually to two world wars was the ultimate means by which national manhood could be re-asserted or constructed in the first place.

With the postwar rise of the women's liberation movement in the 1960s and 1970s, masculinity was once again ostensibly thrown into "crisis." This attitude is perhaps typified by novels such as *One Flew over the Cuck-oo's Nest* (1962) in which a group of white male patients in a psychiatric hospital are victimized by a powerful female nurse and her African American orderlies, or *The Stepford Wives* (1972) in which a group of aggrieved white suburban men resist the women's movement by replacing their wives with subservient animatronic robots. This sense of a masculinity crisis caused, among other things, the 1980s "backlash" against feminist advancements that was so well documented by Susan Faludi (1991). In response to second-wave feminism's women's liberation movement, some men called for a corresponding "men's movement," bringing about reactions as wide-ranging and varied as the "Wild Man" retreats run by Robert Bly in the 1970s, the militia movement of the 1990s, the Tea Party activists of 2009, and the "Make America Great Again" mantra of Trump supporters of the present day. Without a doubt, the perceived diminishment of masculine authority throughout the twentieth century had profound effects on the literature of the period, but those effects differ greatly from the beginning of the twentieth century to the twenty-first.

The influence of first-wave feminism on modernist literature has been detailed by Sandra Gilbert and Susan Gubar in their three-volume work, *No Man's Land*, in which they argue that literary modernism was to a large extent the artistic response—from both male and female writers— to the rapidly changing values and roles for women in late nineteenth- and early twentieth-century society. To demonstrate the resulting fears of the loss of male authority, Gilbert and Gubar point to the large number of modernist characters evincing male impotence in the face of perceived female derision or feminine sexual power (Leopold Bloom, Lord Chatterley, and Jake Barnes, to name only a few). Gilbert and Gubar beautifully demonstrate how modernist writers reacted to changing gender mores by misogynistically scapegoating women, both in life and through their representation in literature. The thematic repudiation of women and the feminine became de rigueur for writers in this period, exemplified perhaps by Ernest Hemingway's desire to entitle his 1927 short story collection *Men without Women*.

One example Gilbert and Gubar provide strikes me as particularly important for my argument: they posit "The Love Song of J. Alfred Prufrock" as an example of modernist male disempowerment by pointing out how the poem "emphasizes the ways in which the absurdly self-conscious modern male intellectual is rendered impotent by, and in, the company of women" (1988, 31–32). For my argument in this chapter, the important aspect of this sense of conflict between the sexes is the extent to which male impotence is portrayed in concert with Prufrock's crippling self-consciousness—self-consciousness that makes him unable to act, to speak, or to live a full life. For Prufrock, for Jake Barnes, for Leopold Bloom, the very consciousness of their own impotence in the face of women's perceived powerful sexuality is the greatest threat to their masculine authority.

Whereas Gilbert and Gubar focus on thematic misogyny, Andreas Huyssen provides a similar argument about the very structure of modernist literature. He points out that, in late Victorian and modernist periods, mass culture had come to be associated with and even equated to the feminine: "Time and again documents from the late nineteenth century ascribe pejorative feminine characteristics to mass culture—and by mass culture here I mean serialized feuilleton novels, popular and family magazines, the stuff of lending libraries, fictional bestsellers and the like" (1986, 49). Women, Huyssen argues, were characterized as readers of mass cultural material that was, therefore, characterized as feminine. In order to repudiate mass culture—and especially the feminine—modernist (mostly, but not always, male) literary writers produced literary structures and instructions on how to read literature that attempted to differentiate their work from those widely popular genres (hence the term "high modernism"). According to Huyssen, the "Great Divide" literary writers attempted to construct between high modernism and popular culture is indicative not only of an elitist intellectualism on the part of writers like Eliot and Pound but also of an attempt to distance their work from influences deemed feminine and therefore inferior, or inferior and therefore feminine. As a result, "high modernist" texts take forms that are highly erudite, allusive, complex, and self-contained. "Only by fortifying its boundaries, by maintaining its purity and autonomy, and by avoiding any contamination with mass culture and with the signifying systems of everyday life can the art work maintain its adversary stance" (Huyssen 1986, 54). In this sense, modernist texts are meant to refer only to themselves and to the great western literary tradition: they do not attempt cultural commentary or critique, for that would place them in the realm of the worldly and popular and, by extension, the feminine.

From the modernist writer's point of view, this decree that the text be purely unified and self-contained also prohibited any depiction of authorial self-consciousness. In other words, modernist texts exhibit what Huyssen terms "the erasure of subjectivity and authorial voice" (1986, 54). And while contemporary scholars like Aaron Jaffe and Jonathan Goldman have pointed to the myriad ways in which modernist authors self-consciously constructed their authorial personae, often through performances of ostentatious literary virtuosity, these authors did not indulge in the autofictional authorial intrusions that became so common later in the twentieth century.[2] A modernist author, Goldman argues, wanted to be viewed "as not only the art object par excellence, but also the master choreographer of the culture that contains him as such an object" (2011, 7); however, he goes on to point out that "modernist technique conceives of the author as an idealized, incorporeal entity" (11). In other words, the self-conscious metafictional elements that would assert themselves in the second half of the twentieth century are not in evidence in modernist texts, for self-conscious reference to the world outside the text goes against the artistic philosophy articulated, for example, by T. S. Eliot. Eliot's famous essay "Tradition and the Individual Talent" (1919) asserts, "The progress of an artist is a continual self-sacrifice, a continual extinction of personality" in the service of the artistic voice which was to speak through the poet but was to represent the vastness of literary tradition. Thus the poet was responsible, not for representing his own feelings and experiences, but for acting as a conduit through which the greater (western) literary tradition could be conveyed and advanced. Therefore, according to Eliot, poetry should not be "personal" but rather "an escape from emotion; it is not the expression of personality, but an escape from personality."[3]

This idea of "impersonal" poetry seems almost the polar opposite of how poetry is viewed today. However, in the context of a supposed "battle of the sexes" and a "crisis of masculinity," it makes perfect sense: for Eliot, the work of poetry was to maintain literary tradition in the face of a perceived breakdown of that tradition. And of course, while Eliot does not state it overtly, that tradition is white, western, and, of course, male. The threat facing that tradition, among other things, is the one posed by the increasing imposition of female concerns on all facets of culture, including the artistic ones. So the poet must bolster a crumbling tradition through self-abnegation, embracing the objectivity of impersonality rather than the subjectivity of emotion.

And if the artist must be objective, then he must also be male, for as Susan Bordo has demonstrated, philosophical and cultural tradition had since Descartes established that women were incapable of objectivity, being too mired in concerns of the body to engage in the pure pursuits of the mind. Or as Simone de Beauvoir so aptly put it, "[Man] thinks of his body as a direct and normal connection with the world, which he believes he apprehends objectively, whereas he regards the body of woman as a hindrance, a prison, weighed down by everything peculiar to it" (1989, 8). In this formulation, according to Susan Bordo, men can aspire to pure scientific and intellectual objectivity—pure mind, to use Descartes's designation—while women, being more weighed down by physical limitations, become not just associated with, but equated with, the body. Enlightenment rationality, Bordo continues, can be productively read as "an aggressive, intellectual 'flight from the feminine' into the modern scientific universe of purity, clarity, and objectivity" (1987, 5). What was deemed feminine was seen as the antithesis of pure thought and objectivity, and what was seen as purely objective and rational pursuits were seen as by definition the antithesis of the feminine. Therefore, women were considered unable by their very nature to engage in intellectual pursuits.[4]

Furthermore, until the nineteenth century when the efforts of female activists began to stage a challenge to received gender roles, the idea was widespread that women could not—or at least should not—write, despite the fact that so many of them did, and quite successfully, too. As so many feminist theorists have pointed out,[5] at its heart, the author was defined as male, the subject of his writing unapologetically yet unadmittedly masculine: "What not so long ago was called the 'human' experience, whether analyzed by history, literature, psychology or whatever, was actually the 'male' experience, one that ignored women and took men for the norm" (Rosen 1993, xi).[6] In this sense, then, Eliot's highly influential treatise on modernist literary endeavor served as an uncritical continuation of the masculinist view that only men can be true poets, a view made more insidious for never overtly making that assertion, but surreptitiously yet unmistakably implying it nonetheless. Traces of Descartes's ideas about objectivity can be found in Eliot's formulation of artistic impersonality. In addition, Greg Forter has argued that Eliot's "aesthetic of (masculine) self-abrogation was also a formal assertion of whiteness" (2011, 7), and Jerry Phillips has traced the origins of the New Criticism to the racist and classist attitudes of the postbellum South, arguing: "This vision of the poem as a blending of 'extremes,' an achieved organic unity, finds its ideological corollary in the 'feudal society' of the old South, where social hierarchy and social order (allegedly) went hand in hand" (1997, 332).

The influence of "Tradition and the Individual Talent" seems even more pervasive when one recognizes the role it and essays like it played in spawning the New Criticism, an analytical mode popular from the 1920s through the 1950s that took as its sole focus a text's internal unity, rather than the social, political, and personal factors that went into its creation and reception. This emphasis on internal unity precluded a focus on what a particular text might have to say about the culture that spawned it. As Marianne DeKoven argues: "The triumph of New-Critical Modernism has made it appear blunt, banal, even gauche to discuss modernist writing as a critique of twentieth-century culture— to approach it, in fact, as anything other than the altar of linguistic and intellectual complexity in search of transcendent formal unity" (1991, 12). These ideas gave rise to William K. Wimsatt and Monroe Beardsley's 1946 essay "The Intentional Fallacy," which decried any consideration of the author's intention in the service of literary analysis.[7] The text, to Wimsatt and Beardsley, was an inviolable artifact not meant to be sullied by analytical association with the mode of its production. So not only did the texts of modernism eschew connection with the feminine or resort to overt misogyny or both, but the primary mode of modernist literary criticism defined this literature as having nothing to do with the mundane and defiled external world, thereby mandating that scholars not raise issues of race, class, and especially gender when discussing them. New Criticism, then, was derived from a social order in which gender, race, and class were strictly hierarchized binaries; it was a form of literary study that did not take political, cultural, or economic contexts into account.[8]

However, T. S. Eliot was not the only major modernist figure who strove for impersonality in his work. Virginia Woolf worked her entire career to hone what she called her "philosophy of anonymity" (1983, 186), and she was famously dubious of books by men that were marked with a "desire for self-assertion." Thus emerges her celebrated image in *A Room of One's Own* of the large letter "I" looming over the pages of the male-authored books she struggles to read (1995, 103, 104). These books' arguments are damaged, she posits: "They had been written in the red light of emotion and not in the white light of truth" (41). Woolf makes the case for impersonality in reference to books by male authors, while making a more explicit case that a women writer could, with further development and a room of her own, possibly write as well as a man. In other words, Woolf calls upon impersonality, not to make an implicit case for a masculine literary tradition but to make an *explicit* case for the development of a feminine one. For Woolf, a great work of literature by a woman would not be markedly different in strategy or structure from that by a man. Woolf does not advocate a reconsideration of literary traditions or a challenge to current definitions of greatness in order to accommodate female writers. Rather, she argues that, if given the same monetary support and education as a man, a woman writer could emerge worthy of fitting into that same literary tradition. She could emerge as Shakespeare's sister.

Thus Woolf and Eliot make almost opposite arguments, one advocating a putatively masculine view of literary endeavor and the other an admittedly feminine one. What I want to point out, however, is the fact that they both bolster their arguments with similar appeals to the impersonal—the removal of any acknowledgment within the work of authorial presence or perspective: the rejection of self-consciousness. Indeed, for Woolf, the fact that the male writers she evokes are "sex-conscious" as they write is the problem that diminishes their writing. Here Woolf equates sex consciousness with self-consciousness, recognizing that sex is a large part of self: "Virility has now become self-conscious—men, that is to say, are now writing only with the male side of their brains" (1995, 105). As Peter Schwenger puts it, "Becoming self-conscious of their sex, male writers are now laboring under a disadvantage that was formerly women's alone" (1984, 10). Female writers had (and still have) to grapple with the idea of what it means to be both a writer and a woman; the argument of *A Room of One's Own* is that, for the first time, male writers are becoming aware of their gender as well and the resulting self-consciousness causes stultifying, underdeveloped prose and the imposition of the overshadowing "I."

Thus, through a very different route, Woolf comes to a conclusion similar to Eliot's: self-consciousness in literature is anathema. And it is true that, for all its distancing, fragmented, and otherwise complex narrative experiments, modernist literature is remarkably devoid of overt self-conscious authorial intrusion—remarkable both because of the myriad modernist experiments with consciousness itself and because of the great proliferation of literary self-consciousness in the latter part of the twentieth century. There are, however, some instances of autofictional texts from this period that I want to address. Perhaps the most cited example of self-referentiality is Molly Bloom's exhortation to Joyce: "O Jamesy let me up out of this pooh" (*Ulysses* 1986, 633), and even here, "Joyce" himself does not make an appearance in the novel, nor does he let Molly up. Rather, Molly registers a vague awareness of her creator and of herself as a fictional character—a significant fact, since such charactorial awareness does not become commonplace in literature until much later in the century. In this brief passage, we can see the seeds of the trope of self-consciousness that will characterize postmodern fiction.

Another potential example of autofiction from the modernist period, depending on how one would classify it, is Gertrude Stein's *The Autobiography of Alice B. Toklas*, a memoir-esque depiction of Stein and Toklas's life together in Paris. This work could be viewed as both memoir and novel, for although the events depicted did ostensibly take place, the conceit is that Toklas herself wrote the narrative, until the end when we are told that Gertrude Stein is actually the author. Thus, Stein has written a narrative in which she herself appears as a character, but which is supposedly a referential narrative, and so not a novel. It is less important to me whether the narrative is actually referential or not and whether to classify it as a novel or a memoir; what is important to my argument is the fact that Stein, long before the autofictional trend was to emerge with any force, has constructed the kind of written persona for herself that requires the scare quotes so common in discussions of contemporary autofiction: "Gertrude Stein." In much of her other work, Stein seemingly adheres to the principles of impersonality, but as is so often the case with Stein, she is ahead of her time with this singular foray into autofiction. Benjamin Widiss puts it far better that I when he says: "Stein frustrates our accustomed temporal-formal account of literary history because she bids explicitly for celebrity in the *Autobiography*, even while she retains the trappings of impersonality as a playful mantle" (2011, 54).

Another example of modernist autofiction that is difficult to classify as either fiction or memoir is the work of Henry Miller.[9] Works like *Tropic of Cancer*, *Tropic of Capricorn*, and *Black Spring* are classified and published as novels, but their protagonist is referred to as "Miller." However, while "Miller" often appears eponymously in his work, his characters, seemingly based on real people, are often given pseudonyms, making it difficult once again to characterize the works as fiction or nonfiction. For the most part, Miller's work does not overtly toy with ideas about the nature of fiction and nonfiction or the possibilities of fiction to depict the truth. And, once again, determining whether to classify the works as fiction or nonfiction is somewhat beside the point. Rather, it is interesting to note that the characterized version of "Miller," whether accurate or not, is as clear a portrait as one could desire of the so-called modernist masculinity crisis. Indeed, to a contemporary feminist reader, Miller's works, which were once considered trenchant cultural criticism, are now difficult to read as anything but hyperbolic and somewhat panicked assertions of masculine power, expressed mostly through the sexual degradation of women. In this sense, then, Miller emphatically rejects the high modernist notion of impersonality by placing a written version of himself in his novels. However, the novels demonstrate without doubt the argument that the period was marked by a sense that male power was under siege and required constant reassertion.

Miller and Stein notwithstanding, modernist literature is almost completely devoid of autofictional authorial intrusion. And yet from the late 1960s to the present day, there has been a veritable explosion of this particular trope, demonstrating that one of the primary differences between "modernist" and "postmodern" literature is the self-consciousness that proliferates in postmodernism, of which autofiction represents but a small fraction. The examples of Stein and Miller demonstrate that, despite the stricture on authorial intrusion in modernist literature, its highly experimental nature lent itself to the eventual emergence of the metafictional experiments that typify postmodernist claims to authorial power. Whereas Miller's work links authorial intrusion to masculine sexual prowess, a novel like Vladimir Nabokov's *Bend Sinister* (1947) employs a more subtle brand of intrusion as a means by which to broadcast a generalized authorial presence and power. While "Henry Miller" is the central protagonist in Miller's work, there is no similar character named "Vladimir Nabokov." Rather, at the end of *Bend Sinister*, an unnamed presence emerges who holds the preceding story in his sheaf of written pages.

Nabokov's oeuvre is rife with charactorial doubles; often, the double is an author-figure of sorts, as in *Bend Sinister* when protagonist Adam Krug senses a mysterious watching presence, even catching a glimpse of that presence in a series of reflections in water which "gives a vivid, though somewhat esoteric, sign of the author's continued presence in the fiction" (Foster 1995, 27). As Krug's life becomes increasingly tragic, the author's presence is increasingly felt. Near the end of the novel, as Krug falls asleep in his prison cell, the author emerges fully into the narrative to rescue his creation from full awareness of his horrible situation: "It was at that moment, just after Krug had fallen through the bottom of a confused dream and sat up on the straw with a gasp—and just before his reality, his remembered hideous misfortune could pounce upon him—it was then that I felt a pang of pity for Adam and slid towards him along an inclined beam of pale light—causing instantaneous madness, but at least saving him from the senseless agony of his logical fate" (Nabokov 1947, 233). The author-figure shields Krug from awareness of the destiny ordained for him by that same author-figure, but the act of rescue—Krug coming into direct contact with his creator—drives Krug insane. After Krug is shot in the head, the novel ends with a scene in the author-character's study as he, surrounded by the jumbled pages of this very story, releases a moth trapped in his window, representing, perhaps, the soul of Adam Krug. This act of authorial intrusion was described by Nabokov himself as "a device never yet attempted in literature" (1989, 50). And while this is, of course, an overstatement of the originality of the strategy, Nabokov's assertion serves to bolster my point that authorial intrusion was relatively rare until suddenly it was not.

And it is this suddenness that I explore in this book, for as the second part of the twentieth century progresses, authorial intrusion becomes more and more prevalent as a literary trope. Following *Bend Sinister*, for example, the author-character is deployed in various forms in several of Nabokov's novels: doubling avatars who could be read as stand-ins for Nabokov himself appear in works as disparate as *Lolita* (1955), *Pnin* (1957), *Pale Fire* (1962), and *Look at the Harlequins* (1974). Yet at this early stage in the development of contemporary autofiction, there is yet no specific identification of these author-characters as "Nabokov." Furthermore, the idea that the author is a figure separate from the living man who shares his name is the crux of Jorge Luis Borges's 1960 story "Borges and I." Brian McHale chronicles how the narrative experiments of high modernism led somewhat organically to the instances of authorial intrusion found in works like *Bend Sinister* and subsequently to the more overt autofiction that proliferated in the latter half of the twentieth century: "The modernists sought to remove the traces of their presence from the surface of the writing, and to this end exploited or developed various forms of ostensibly 'narratorless' texts . . . . Paradoxically, the more they sought to efface themselves, the more they made their presence conspicuous" (1987, 199). In other words, it is a relatively small step from the conspicuous narratorless style of modernism to the similarly conspicuous postmodern strategy of calling overt attention to the presence of the narrator, even to the extent of causing him to materialize within the world of the narrative. It is also important to note that while it followed logically from the experiments of modernism, the burgeoning autofictional trend was also undoubtedly shaped by myriad social and cultural forces, feminism being not the least of these.

In that sense, the argument I want to make in this chapter is that both the resistance to self-consciousness in the modernist period and the embrace of self-consciousness in the postmodern are catalyzed in no small part by similar concerns about what I have been calling a "crisis in masculinity"—a crisis which has purportedly been going on, in various forms, throughout the twentieth century and beyond.[10] In the postwar period, as men returned home from war and women were expected to relinquish any gains they had made in the employment arena, there emerged a period of relative calm in gender relations. For middle-class white women, the expectations were that they would return to traditional household roles in order to bestow upon the returning white men the reigning authority appropriate to national heroes.[11] Various government housing, employment, and educational programs afforded many white men the opportunities to achieve middle-class economic status, some for the first time. Eventually, however, as Michael Kimmel puts it, "the 'masculine mystique'—that impossible synthesis of sober responsible breadwinner, imperviously stoic master of his fate, and swashbuckling hero—was finally exposed as a fraud" (2013, 262). This particular crisis of masculinity in the latter part of the twentieth century arose, according to David Savran, in response to what has been called the "women's liberation movement" or, more recently, "second-wave feminism":

[A] new masculinity became hegemonic in the 1970s because it represents an attempt by white men to respond to and regroup in the face of particular social and economic challenges: the reemergence of the feminist movement; the limited success of the civil rights movement in redressing gross historical inequities through affirmative action legislation; the rise of the lesbian and gay rights movements; the failure of America's most disastrous imperialistic adventure, the Vietnam War; and, perhaps most important, the end of the post–World War II economic boom and the resultant and steady decline in the income of white working- and lower-middle-class men. (1998, 5)

To Savran, this new masculinity was imbued with masochism and the threat of feminization. "Not surprisingly, this feminization was perceived by many as being the sign of a male identity crisis" (1998, 48). In many ways, Savran and Kimmel's arguments about postwar men are echoes of the argument made about men during the prewar and interwar periods. However, these ideas reverberated differently in the postmodern, versus the modernist, literature.

It is not my intention to reexamine the history of this period, especially as it has been done previously and so well by others. Rather, I wish to discuss the ways in which the second-wave women's movement and the attendant masculine literary response contributed to the rise of a renewed focus on the self-consciousness of metafiction and, in particular, the spate of autofictional novels by men in the postmodern period. Just as the modernist crisis of masculinity led to a reification of the self-abnegating attempts at universality and objectivity of high modernist literature, the postmodern crisis of masculinity was a contributing factor in the widespread manifestation of self-consciousness and metafiction in postmodern literature. In other words, the reaction at the end of the nineteenth century regarding intrusive narration was the reverse of the reaction at the end of the twentieth century. In chapter 2, I will make the point that this shift toward literary self-consciousness also had roots in the burgeoning idea that the author himself was a somewhat diminished figure, either due to the culture of late capitalism deemphasizing the influence of the individual (Jameson), the rise of the power of the reader to imbue a text with meaning (Barthes), or the reconceptualization of self-actualized identity as a mere subject constituted by the vicissitudes of conflicting discursive power structures (Foucault). It is my contention here, however, that all of these theoretical innovations were presaged and made possible by the revolutionary ideas attendant upon the women's movement (second-wave feminism) and the philosophical ideas emerging from it. In other words, an examination of the history of the rise of the women's liberation movement and the truly profound effect its ideas had on the culture at large serves to demonstrate that, in concert with the literary traditions of high modernism, feminism fomented the rise of postmodernism as much, or possibly more than, the poststructuralist theory that accompanied it.

I will focus on one particular element of that argument in my discussion of feminist literary theory. I take on this facet of feminist history partly because its origins are relatively straightforward and partly because at the same time that feminist literary theory began to emerge in force, the self-conscious autofiction that I chronicle here also began to proliferate in earnest. I have commented on the deeply entrenched modernist tradition of eschewing authorial and narratorial self-consciousness and pointed out that, in the latter part of the twentieth century, that embargo seemed to have been lifted, as self-consciousness in various forms surfaced as a defining characteristic of postmodern literature. Now I will demonstrate the ways in which the increased awareness of what Woolf would call "sex-consciousness"—particularly among male writers—contributed to the *self*-consciousness that developed in the literature of the late twentieth century and the beginning of the twenty-first.

It is instructive to trace this connection between masculine "sex-consciousness" and literary self-consciousness to the 1970 publication of Kate Millett's *Sexual Politics* because this book is widely regarded as the first example of feminist literary criticism. Indeed, at the time of its publication, some saw the book as the first coherent articulation of a more general academically generated basis for the women's movement of the 1960s and 1970s,[12] as this rather dismissive remark from the *Time* magazine review of the book demonstrates: "Until this year, however, with the publication of a remarkable book called *Sexual Politics*, the movement had no coherent theory to buttress its intuitive passions, no ideologue to provide chapter and verse for its assault on patriarchy" (1990, 16).[13] While this comment overstates things, to say the least, *Sexual Politics* did bring to the fore some important ideas about the role culture (rather than biology) plays in the determination of gender role definitions. Indeed, Millett draws a clear distinction between biological sex characteristics and culturally determined gender ones, drawing upon psychological theory that was only just emerging at that time. She argues that sex is political and that politics consists of "power-structured relationships, arrangements whereby one group of persons is controlled by another" (23). Millett also describes patriarchy as an ideological power structure rather than a natural, biological, or religious given. In 1970 these ideas were not widely known, much less widely accepted, and *Sexual Politics* can take much of the credit, if not for coining them, then for introducing them to a large audience.

Furthermore, *Sexual Politics* marks the first time a broadly read publication turned its attention to the sexist attitudes that laced British and American literature. Until this point, much conversation about literature by women involved a discussion of the femininity (or lack thereof) of female writers and how that femininity affected (or diminished) the writing. Male writers, on the other hand, were heretofore not studied as *male* but only as writers. Female writers were thought of as writing about female concerns from a feminine point of view, while male writers supposedly wrote about the "universal" human condition from an objective point of view. As a bold and highly necessary corrective, *Sexual Politics* turned its attention to works by men, highlighting the effect masculinity had on their male authors.[14] In so doing, according to Loren Daniel Glass, Millett's book "marks the beginning of a process whereby feminist literary criticism effectively dislodged masculinity from its privileged access to high literary cachet" (2004, 22). I would go even further than this to say that, by arguing that masculinity was a societal construct rather than a biological imperative, *Sexual Politics* successfully challenged the heretofore popular literary view put forward by the authors Millett analyzes, that authorship is an inherently masculine enterprise. The work of D. H. Lawrence, Henry Miller, and Norman Mailer is notable not just for its explicit sexual content but also for its ardent advocacy of male supremacy as being "naturally" ordained.[15]

Millett argues that each of these authors reacted in their writing to the ostensible "crisis of manhood" by portraying heroic male characters convincing (or coercing) women to submit to their "proper" and lesser role. Through detailed (and at times hilarious) analysis, not only does

Sexual Politics obliterate the argument that the objectification and degradation of women derives from nature, but it also shatters the image of
the male author as an objective observer of society. This insight was one
element of the supposed masculinity crisis, for *Sexual Politics* was on the
forefront of making masculinity visible as a construct and, as Sally Robinson has argued, "when dominant masculinity becomes visible, it becomes visible as *wounded*" (2000, 12). Millett posits that some of the most
celebrated male writers were not gods, but rather wounded human be-
ings imbued with patriarchal blind spots that caused them to attempt in
a somewhat panicked manner to prop up the masculine privilege they
perceived to be waning. She strips these emperors of their clothes, ex-
posing them as mortal men with highly masculine perspectives.

Sexual Politics evoked self-consciousness about masculinity and masculine privilege, an idea rather comically demonstrated by the reaction
of Christopher Lehmann-Haupt when he reviewed the book for the *New
York Times*. After praising it lavishly and even devoting an unusual two
days' worth of column space to his review, he admits to some misgiv-
ings, not so much about the book but about his own reaction to it. He
posits that "a male reader—especially one on such easy terms with conventional marriage and the division of labor endemic to our system as
this reviewer is (he earns the bread; she bakes it) . . . must be perplexed
to find himself applauding Millett's book" (1970a). Lehmann-Haupt seems
incredulous that someone reaping so many benefits from the patriarchal
system could find an argument against patriarchy as valid as he does.[16]
In this review, he unmasks his own masculine privilege, evincing an
awareness made possible by the analysis in *Sexual Politics*. Furthermore,
he inserts himself into his review more than once, discussing his personal life, his marriage, and even a recent fishing trip, somehow making
his personal response to the book relevant to the review of its merits.

This kind of authorial intrusion was essentially invited by *Sexual Politics*, which has rightly been criticized for engaging in the "intentional
fallacy" and equating the author's attitudes with those espoused by his
work and/or characters. Millett rather irresponsibly engages in a bit of
pop-psych Freudian analysis of the authors based on their novels. For example, the scene in which Mellors engages in anal sex with Lady Chatterley serves, according to Millett, to purge Lawrence's "own sodomous
urges," and she speculates that the degradation of women depicted in the

work of Henry Miller could be read as a reaction to his numerous tumultuous relationships (Millett 1990, 241, 304). To be fair, especially in the case of Miller and Norman Mailer, the novels in question often seem themselves to perform this equation between author and character. As Millett points out: "The major flaw in [Miller's] oeuvre—too close an identification with the persona, 'Henry Miller'—always operates insidiously against the likelihood of persuading us that Miller the man is any wiser than Miller the character" (1990, 295). Because of her equation of author to character, some of Millett's critical analysis seems facile to a contemporary reader, but it is instrumental to my argument about autofiction to point out that what Millett does in *Sexual Politics* is to reject the New Critical tenets of viewing the text as a sacrosanct and unified whole. Instead, she considers the texts from a cultural and author-centered perspective. Rather than allowing the author to absent himself from the text in the high modernist tradition, Millett—for better or worse—shoves him right back into his text, arguing that it is impossible to separate him from it. For my purposes, this approach is interesting in terms of a study of autofiction, emphatically NOT because the author-character is equivalent to his author but because autofiction performs a similar feat of calling attention to the presence of the author-figure through the use of an eponymous author-character. In other words, while I want in my analyses to maintain the ironic distance between the author and the author-character, autofiction by its very nature brings issues of authorship to the fore.

Similar authorial intrusion can be seen in Lehmann-Haupt's review. By including personal information in his review, Lehmann-Haupt suggests that his own perspective as someone "happily married and participating merrily in the system under Millett's attack" is somehow relevant to his review of the book and its arguments (1970b). This kind of personal revelation is, for lack of a better term, kind of weird in a review of an academic book. However, in this case, Lehmann-Haupt provides this information as an admission that he may be unable to review the book objectively. He points out the ways in which his review is colored by his own personal situation. (His admission does not preclude him from actually reviewing the book, of course; rather, he spends *two* days doing so.) That a book review might be affected by personal bias is, of course, nothing new, particularly in analyses of books by and about women, which have always suffered from the sexist attitudes of reviewers.[17]

What is striking here, however, is that Lehmann-Haupt is suddenly *aware* of his biases, confesses them, and even goes so far as to suggest that they might affect his perception of the book (he says he suspects the "guilt of the oppressor was tainting judgment" (1970b)). *Sexual Politics* has made Lehmann-Haupt self-conscious—possibly for the first time—about his own masculinity as a cultural construction. I say "possibly for the first time," because he admits to finding it "one of the most troubling books I have ever read" (1970a). Furthermore, in decidedly antimodernist fashion, he inserts himself into his own analysis in an almost autofictional manner. Lehmann-Haupt's emergent masculinity crisis seems to unfold on the pages of the review as he feels compelled to include his personal reaction to a challenge to the "naturalness" of his masculine privilege.

I do not wish to exaggerate my case by overdetermining a single review of a single academic text. There were, of course, many responses to the women's movement, both literary and otherwise, and it is not my purpose here to limn them all. But this particular example demonstrates in microcosm my larger argument that the advent of feminist literary theory, spurred by the women's liberation movement, was an instrumental catalyst in bringing about a shift in literature from the modernist to the postmodern, particularly the shift from a disavowal of self-conscious authorial intrusion to a seemingly wholehearted embrace of that trope.

Self-consciousness, self-reflexivity, and metafiction are terms often used to describe a particular characteristic common to postmodern fiction.[18] Robert Alter has defined the "self-conscious novel" to be a novel which "systematically flaunts its own condition of artifice" in order "to convey to us a sense of the fictional world as an authorial construct" (1975, x, xi). Linda Hutcheon defines "metafiction" in a similar manner, calling it "fiction about fiction—that is, fiction that includes within itself a commentary on its own narrative and/or linguistic identity" (1980, 1). And while Alter and others point out that such self-consciousness has been characteristic of some works of fiction since the development of the novel (indeed, what many take to be the very first work of novelistic fiction, *Don Quixote*, is highly self-conscious), it is unmistakable that self-conscious or metafictional practices have veritably exploded in the so-called postmodern era. Furthermore, many scholars have noticed that the self-consciousness of postmodern literature has often been an almost exclusively white male endeavor.[19] What few have pointed out thus far, however, is the extent to which the women's movement and the subsequent challenge to male privilege at all levels of social organization were a key stimulus of that self-consciousness.

In regard to many male writers of the 1970s and beyond, an increased awareness of the socially constructed nature of gender expectations and, in particular, of masculinity, led to an increase in the kinds of self-conscious narrative often referred to as "metafiction." One specific result of this burgeoning self-consciousness in literature is the form of autofiction that this book addresses. My argument here is that, in these autofictions, the author makes an appearance as a character specifically to stake a claim for the kind of masculine authorial authority that had heretofore never been seriously challenged. In other words, the literary response I am most interested in is not the strident assertion of male power and supremacy advocated by the biological essentialists at the time, but rather the self-conscious *insertion* into fiction of a male authorial figure who tries, often unsuccessfully, to gain and keep control of his narrative. These authorial intrusive figures are often not depicted as powerful, even while they make overt claims to power. Yet the powerlessness of the inter-diegetic author-*character* serves to reinforce the creative power of the extra-diegetic *author*—the author who exists outside the text, even as the connection between the two remains tenuous.

Thus it is my contention that the combination of increased self-awareness of masculine privilege and the resulting "crisis in masculinity" contributed to the trope of the disempowered male authorial figure who is an increasingly common character in postmodern literature. This character embodies the ambiguity of the late twentieth-century white-male condition of having a sense of entitlement to power coupled with a sense of that power waning. This contradictory condition is illustrated by the intrusive author-character, who is simultaneously both empowered— he created the narrative we read, after all— and disempowered—he cannot control his narrative from without and so attempts, usually unsuccessfully, to do so from within. As Andreas Huyssen says in relation to the modernist tradition of impersonality, "The male, after all, can easily deny his own subjectivity for the benefit of a higher aesthetic goal, *as long as he can take it for granted on an experiential level in everyday life*" (Huyssen 1986, 46, emphasis mine). In this more contemporary period, due in large part to second-wave feminism and feminist and poststructuralist theory, that privilege of taking his own subjectivity for granted is now denied the male author. But as Sally Robinson has pointed out, "there is much symbolic power to be reaped from occupying the social and discursive position of subject-in-crisis" (2000, 9). The result is that, in the face of diminishing authorial authority, this manifestation of the white male author is no longer willing to deny his own subjectivity in his writing; instead, he makes it manifest by inserting a characterized version of himself into his narrative in an attempt to reap the symbolic power—whether real or imagined—available to the subject-in-crisis.

Huyssen argues that, during the modernist period, white male writers were willing to suppress their authorial subjectivity in their writing because this subjectivity (based on gender, race, and often class privilege) was rarely under threat in the world outside the text. Indeed, as Aaron Jaffe has argued, male modernist writers developed complex "textual signatures" or what he calls "authorial imprimaturs" designed to assert the superiority of their work in the literary marketplace and ensure their place in the emergent academic canon (2005, 3). This canon, being defined against popular literature and culture, was therefore, according to Huyssen, defined as inherently male. I would perhaps reframe Huyssen and Jaffe's arguments to say that while male modernist writers thought it unseemly to assert their subjectivities in their writing, they were putting promotional systems into play that would render such assertions unnecessary, systems that would by definition exclude women and writers of color. By contrast, with the advent of feminist theory's assertion that gender privilege is a construct, not a natural right, white male writers began in their texts to make increasingly overt claims to that privilege.

Another spur to these overt claims to privilege was the poststructuralist notion of the fragmentation of subjectivity rather than the coherent wholeness of identity. This concept was, of course, nothing new for women and minority writers. The extent to which postmodernity has been characterized by a newly recognized sense of the fragmented self or subjectivity simply underlines the extent to which literary endeavor has traditionally been defined by the experiences and philosophies of white male writers and critics. As bell hooks has stated: "The overall impact of postmodernism is that many other groups now share with black folks a sense of deep alienation, despair, uncertainty, loss of a sense of grounding even if it is not informed by shared circumstance" (1990, 27).

For my purposes, one important "other group" is white male writers. Many scholars have pointed out the ways in which this exploration of fragmented subjectivity has served white male writers as a means to maintain their place as the primary arbiters of literary tradition. Most notably, Phillip Brian Harper echoes bell hooks in his argument about the ways in which mainstream white male writers' embrace of postmodern decentered fragmentation appropriates a sensibility long felt by minority populations, going so far as to argue "that marginalized groups' experience of decenteredness is itself a largely unacknowledged factor in the 'general' postmodern condition" (1994, 4). Harper argues that the decenteredness that came to be a hallmark of postmodernist literature can be found in a variety of literature of an earlier period written by minority writers, but it was only when white male writers embraced it that it became part of the literary mainstream termed "postmodernism."

Harper makes an excellent point regarding postmodern decenteredness, while my different but related argument concerns postmodern self-consciousness, which is *not* particularly evident in minority literature at any point during the twentieth century or even now. Rather, I assert that the self-consciousness evident in much postmodern fiction by white men can be traced to theories derived from the late twentieth-century women's movement. So Harper argues that postmodern decenteredness has its roots in the notions of decenteredness expressed far earlier in literature by minority writers; in a similar but not identical fashion, postmodern self-consciousness also has its roots in minority literary theories, particularly feminist ones, but not necessarily in the literature by female writers.[20]

Autofictions by women and minority writers are few, as though the self-conscious insertion of an authorial character into a novel is somehow the purview of white male writers only, as perhaps only they feel the challenge to their traditional patriarchal privilege and newly recognize the limited perspective their cultural position provides them. Again, to reiterate what Harper has argued, these white male writers feel decentered, perhaps for the first time, and thus decenteredness becomes a major theme in the postmodern literature that results. But whereas Peter Schwenger argues that "a new self-consciousness may have given rise to a male 'anxiety of authorship'" (1984, 14), I argue the converse: a male "anxiety of authorship" has given rise to the new self-consciousness manifested in postmodern fiction. As Sally Robinson so aptly points out, when white men are portrayed as "wounded," cultural imperatives emerge to salve those wounds through ironic reversal: "Announcements of a crisis in white masculinity, and a widely evidenced interest in wounded white men, themselves perform the cultural work of *re*centering white masculinity by *de*centering it" (2000, 12). It is easy to demonstrate how an autofictional approach could serve to recenter white masculinity. If a writer "enters" his novel as a character, claiming that he has lost or is losing control over that narrative, not only does he make himself (or at least, a characterized version of himself) the thematic center (protagonist) of the novel, but he also foregrounds his creative powers by reasserting his authorial power within the pages of that novel. Autofiction thus recenters the decentered figure of the wounded white male author figure.

For example, in John Barth's novella *Dunyazadiad,* the first in his 1972 trilogy *Chimera,* an unnamed author figure magically appears to Scheherazade, the famous storyteller of *The Thousand and One Nights,* and her sister Dunyazade on the eve of the former's marriage to King Shahryar whom they fear will surely kill her after their wedding night, as he has one thousand women before. The nameless writer claims to be from Maryland and gives just enough personal detail to make clear that he is indeed a characterized version of "Barth" himself. Dunyazade, the narrator of the story, takes this strange writer for a powerful Genie, and so he certainly must be, for it is this author-character who suggests to Scheherazade that she tell stories to the murderous King Shahryar to postpone her own death. And then it is this author-character who, after consulting his copy of *The Thousand and One Nights,* appears to the sisters each day to recite for them the story Scheherazade must tell that night. In this story, then, Scheherazade, the world's most famous storyteller, was actually enabled in that feat by the masculine storytelling power of the "Barth" character.

When the sisters first meet the "Genie," he explains that his life, like their king's, is in turmoil. However, his definition of turmoil is somewhat different from theirs: their king, after being cuckolded, has vowed never to sleep with the same woman twice and to kill each woman he has slept with, while Barth is also sleeping with a lot of women (what he calls "a brace of mistresses") but, unlike King Shahryar, the writer kindly does not harbor "a grudge against womankind" on their behalf (1972, 9). The writer-character's potentially waning masculine power is portrayed quite sensitively here, as the writer worries that he is aging quickly and is described as "bald as a roc's egg" (8).[21] He also laments that his writing has not been going as well as it ought, and he is unsure "whether he had abandoned fiction or fiction him" since "only critics, other writers and unwilling students" will read his "artful fiction" (9). Thus the writer-character feels that, for whatever reason, the culture he lives in finds him increasingly irrelevant and he hopes to find relevance—not just for his own work but for literature writ large—by going back to literature's origins.

In this autofictional tale, a white male author of waning significance attempts to reassert his importance by inserting himself not only into his fiction but into one of the most widely celebrated fictional texts of all time. In exchange for his help, Scheherazade offers her body to the writer, but he declines, saying he is too much in love with the mistress he has chosen from among the bevy he has been enjoying. Thus he seems magnanimous, agreeing to help Scheherazade merely for the pleasure of doing so, but as the story unfolds, it becomes clear that there is a much more important reward in store for the author-figure than yet another female trophy. Significantly, the autofictional author-character thus devised becomes the savior, not only of this tale by rescuing Scheherazade but of storytelling itself by positing himself as the origin of her famous tales (which are, of course, traditional folk tales with no traceable authorship) and, therefore, placing himself at the center of a centuries-old storytelling tradition.

The sex war at the center of *Dunyzadiad* begins to unfold as the writer explains to Scheherazade the true nature of storytelling: "The teller's role, he felt, regardless of his actual gender, was essentially masculine, the listener's or reader's feminine" (1972, 25–26). Thus he explains, although equality in sexual relations is something lovers should strive for "however short of it their histories and temperaments made them fall" (54), true equality in love or storytelling is unlikely. Subsequently, once the writer dictates Scheherazade's stories to her so that she can tell them, the proper gender roles are restored: the masculinity of storytelling is reaffirmed. It is no surprise then, that directly upon the 1,001st day of the storytelling, the unnamed writer reveals that once he began telling stories to Scheherazade, his own writer's block vanished, allowing him to complete two of the three novellas that will make up the trilogy that is

Chimera itself. The reader understands that, once the writer has written the story we are now reading—the *Dunyazadiad*—his trilogy will be complete, his status as writer restored, his masculinity reasserted. And of course, the significance of all this restoration of power and authority is amplified by the covert but unmistakable connection between the Genie character and John Barth himself. The autofictional nature of the novel forces the reader to imagine the idea, if only to immediately discard it, that the Genie *is* the extratextual Barth, so that the Genie's struggles are Barth's himself. This differentiates novels like *Chimera* from more mimetic works by authors such as John Updike, for although Updike's work deals with similar thematic issues, it does so in a purely fictional setting, with no overt metafictional gestures outside itself to the extratextual world. Even though some Updike novels may contain characters that resemble him, these characters are not overtly connected to him and, therefore, he is not directly implicated in their exploits. In the case of *Chimera*, the author-character is meant to be read as Barth the author, while at the same time, with a winking postmodern irony, he is also meant to be read as a fictional character. Barth slyly toys with readers, tempting us to equate character with author, only to pull the figurative (magic) carpet out from under such an interpretation. In this sense, then, autofiction provides one of Benjamin Widiss's "obscure invitations": "invitations to the reader not just to seek out the author from whom they spring, but to imagine him or her in a particular fashion and to attend to that imagination as a constitutive element of the reading process" (2011, 3).

Autofictions like *Chimera*, in which the particularized, characterized figure of the author serves to reify masculine authorial privilege, afford the opportunity to explore more fully one of Kaja Silverman's side points regarding the portrayal of masculine authorial authority. Silverman argues that authors' "autobiographical allusions or metacritical pronouncements which encourage us to look for an authorial imperative in their writings or films" are "antipathetic not only to normative masculinity, but to one of its primary buttresses, traditional notions of authorship" (1992, 11). The example cited above actually suggests the opposite: autofictions or "autobiographical allusions" are most definitely not antipathetic to traditional notions of authorship or to normative masculinity, but rather serve to reify it, no matter how much they seem on the surface to challenge it.

Silverman's larger argument about authorship is that the traditional disembodied authorial authority—the omniscient narrator who does not make an overt appearance in the fiction—is an important source of traditional masculine authority. And I would agree that this is so. However, with the advent of the feminist movements that fomented a cultural consciousness of the nature of masculinity as well as femininity, such disembodied authorial authority becomes less and less possible. Rather, authors were increasingly called upon to reveal their positionality. As Sally Robinson puts it, the "invisibility" that white men had been able to take advantage of for so long was now less tenable: white men were increasingly being seen as such, rather than as the universal and objective societal "norm." For Robinson, the result of this is that images of white men become visible, but visible as wounded, so that it is the wound not the whiteness or the maleness that becomes the focus: "Representations of wounded white men most often work to *personalize* the crisis of white masculinity and, thus, to erase its social and political causes and effects" (2000, 8). Robyn Wiegman puts it a slightly different way in her discussion of white supremacists when she argues that, since the Civil War, such groups, by claiming to have been "injured" by a loss of white social dominance, have thereby attempted to claim a "minoritized" status (1999, 117). The image of white dominance has shifted, then, from a universal and invisible power valence to a visible and particularized one (1999, 118). These white male writers are approaching (but not quite reaching) Patricia Hill Collins's concept of what she calls a "black feminist perspective" in which "each group speaks from its own standpoint and shares its own partial, situated knowledge. But because each group perceives its own truth as partial, its knowledge is unfinished" (1990, 270). I say that these writers do not quite reach Collins's black feminist epistemological perspective, because its ultimate goal is for each group to recognize its own perspective as unique and partial in order not to suppress other groups' equally unique and partial perspectives. The project of many of the autofictional novels I discuss here, however, is not to admit the validity of other groups' perspectives but rather to reify the white male perspective as the central one.

Of relevance to me is that the result of this entrance into visibility and particularity of white male writers is that as autofictional texts proliferate, they evince a similar result: the personalized figure of the author-character becomes the focus, rather than the social and political causes and effects of that now-visible whiteness and maleness.[22] As the individual author-characters become the focus of the text, they are particularized to the extent that they ostensibly (if fictionally) represent "real people" and are therefore not required to serve as generalized representatives of "maleness" or "whiteness," the way that so many female and minority characters—and people—are expected to do.[23] In this sense, while it does mark a shift away from the omniscience of disembodied authorship toward an increased awareness of the normative power of the dominant gender and race, autofiction also often acts in the service of recuperating masculine authorial privilege by exploiting the spectacle of the author-character. This is to say, while the author-character is often depicted as wounded or disempowered, these depictions gesture toward the actual author outside of the text who thereby retains his power. Autofiction thus demonstrates that, even if the author-character is disempowered, the actual author is still posited as the godlike creator of his own image.

Perhaps the most famous example of this godlike yet writerlike influence of the intrusive character is also one of the earliest: British novelist John Fowles's 1969 novel *The French Lieutenant's Woman*. This early example of postmodern authorial intrusion is an instructive precursor of the autofictions to come. Throughout most of the novel, the narrator is intrusive in the abstract: in a highly conversational style, he instructs the reader in the history and social mores of the Victorian period. Yet when it comes to the characters about whom he narrates, his knowledge is admittedly not as deep. In chapter 13, the narrator informs us that although until this point he has been employing the narrative convention that "the novelist stands next to God," he is unable to predict with complete authority what his characters will think or do. They have free will. Critics have pointed out that it is at this moment that our heretofore seemingly omniscient narrator ceases to be omniscient, as he admits that "knowing it all" is merely something authors *pretend* to be able to do (2004, 95). What is to my mind equally striking but far less often noticed, however, is that the moment that the narrator disavows omniscience is the same moment he emerges as a masculine figure. He ceases to pretend to be a sexless, all-knowing presence and admits to being a man. This instance of authorial intrusion, arguably the first in an ever-growing list of postmodern autofictions, is also an important example of the explicit gendering of the author as male, marking a clear departure from the implicit yet never overtly stated maleness of modernist authors.

It is no coincidence, then, that this novel involves in-depth depiction of the Victorian era, "An age where woman was sacred; and where you could buy a thirteen-year-old girl for a few pounds—a few shillings, if you wanted her for only an hour or two" (2004, 266). In important ways, *The French Lieutenant's Woman* combines Victorian and postmodern sensibilities. It depicts an era when women's movements and prospects were highly regulated, and women were not valued members of society, yet it depicts that era using the emergent literary traditions of an era in which ideas about women's roles and abilities were undergoing rapid, almost revolutionary transformation. For this reason, it makes sense that the narrator is a man who admits to having a man's limited perspective, saying, "Modern women like Sarah [the French lieutenant's woman] exist, and I have never understood them" (2004, 95). The narrator cannot understand a woman like Sarah who prefers to be shunned by society rather than join it, who runs from a man who wants to marry her in order to live a life independent and alone. An anachronistically "liberated" woman acts as the stumbling block for the author-character's omniscience, for he simply cannot figure out what she wants or predict what she will do. In order to admit this lack of knowledge to his readers, the narrator descends from the clouds of omniscience and takes on the form of a mere mortal man.

And, in the much-cited chapter 5, the author-character does this literally, taking on physical form and entering the train on which Sarah's lover, Charles, is a passenger. At first he merely stares at Charles, making him uncomfortable, but in a later chapter, the writer-character, known critically as the "impresario," watches as one potential ending for the novel unfolds, then turns back his watch fifteen minutes to allow an alternate and very different ending to occur. As will be the case in much autofiction, this scene simultaneously highlights the considerable creative power of that author to control his characters, construct the narrative, and even turn back time, while at the same time it makes visible the masculine authorial figure behind the didactic narrative voice, demonstrating that this creative power is, in fact, just a powerful man, not an omniscient god.

Or, in the case of Kurt Vonnegut's *Breakfast of Champions*, he is not even a very powerful man. Vonnegut's 1973 novel contains some material Vonnegut originally planned to include in his 1969 masterpiece, *Slaughterhouse-Five*, but which he excised and transformed into a discrete novel in its own right. In it, the writer of the novel enters as a character, unnamed, but unmistakable as "Vonnegut," as he claims to have invented the characters in the novel, including Kilgore Trout, a figure who had appeared in two earlier Vonnegut novels and continued to appear in his works throughout Vonnegut's career.

Like *The French Lieutenant's Woman*, *Breakfast of Champions* is different from most examples of autofiction in that the author-character is depicted as more author than character. In other words, in both novels, the unnamed author-character admits that the work he appears in is a fiction of his own making. Monika Fludernik refers to this emergence of the author-narrator into the fictional diegesis as "ontological metalepsis." Metalepsis is a term coined by Genette to indicate "any intrusion by the extradiegetic narrator or narratee into the diegetic universe (or by the diegetic characters into a metadiegetic universe, etc.) or the inverse" (1983, 234–35). Fludernik expands upon Genette's definition by differentiating between different types of metalepsis. Ontological metalepsis, for instance, "consists in the literal move of the narrator to a lower narrative level of embedded story world" (2003, 384). This metaleptic move is not typical of most autofiction. Usually, autofiction resembles either a memoir, where the author-character uses first-person narration to tell a supposedly true story (understood by readers to be fictional), or it resembles a novel in which someone with the author's name is rendered as a character in the third person. In these two novels, however, the narrator continually proclaims his authorial status, reminding us that the narrative we read is of his making, thus highlighting the existential crossing of boundaries that occurs when the narrator actually enters his fiction. In Fowles's novel, the author-character is described in third person by the all-knowing narrator, thus creating a distance of sorts between the figure telling the story and the figure supposedly constructing it.[24] In *Breakfast of Champions*, on the other hand, the author-character confesses his authorship using the first person, thereby creating a much more intimate relationship with the reader.

This intimacy is encouraged as we learn more about this author-character and the struggles he has been facing. While much of the narration in *Breakfast of Champions* resembles the distant, ironic, almost snarky commentary in many Vonnegut novels, this novel also has an intensely personal aspect not usually found in Vonnegut's work. So, amid pithy and satirically charged statements such as calling Christopher Columbus a "sea pirate" and the "Star Spangled Banner" "gibberish sprinkled with question marks" (1973, 10, 8), there are startling admissions that the author-character has been taking medication for depression, is concerned he might be schizophrenic, and that he has considered suicide. This book, he tells us, represents his attempt to "clear my head of all the junk in there" in an effort to preserve his sanity (5). At the beginning of the novel, however, things do not look good, as the author claims: "I have no culture, no humane harmony in my brains. I can't live without a culture anymore" (5). This admission is partly a comment upon the author's mental state and partly a criticism of late 1960s American culture. This "clearing of the head" is, he argues, "something most white Americans and nonwhite Americans who imitate white Americans should do. The things other people have put into *my* head, at any rate, do not fit together nicely, are often useless and ugly" (5). In a rather striking move, considering that this novel was published in 1973, the author evinces an awareness of his status as a white man, as well as an awareness that this status has resulted in his head being full of useless and ugly things that have affected his perspective and which should be cleared out.[25] Thus, in this novel, the presence of the author-character has transformed the typical detached and subtly ironic Vonnegut narrator into a highly personal and troubled figure indeed. It makes sense that there are hints of this narratorial character in *Slaughterhouse-Five*, since the two novels were once meant to be a single text; however, it is in *Breakfast of Champions* that the intrusive authorial narrator becomes a full-fledged autofictional character.

What I mean to say is that in *Breakfast of Champions*, "Vonnegut" the author metaleptically steps into his novel at the end to converse with his characters, all the while commenting narratorially on his limited ability to control their actions and fates. "Vonnegut" tells us that he invented Kilgore Trout, and "I made him snaggle-toothed. I gave him hair, but I turned it white," and "I had given him a life not worth living, but I had also given him an iron will to live" (1973, 32, 72). "Vonnegut's" mission in this novel, he says, is to make his existence known to Kilgore Trout, to tell his most famous creation that he *is* a creation and that "Vonnegut" is his creator. Then he will set Trout free. He tells Trout: "I am approaching my fiftieth birthday, Mr. Trout. . . . I am cleansing and renewing myself for the very different sorts of years to come. Under similar spiritual conditions, Count Tolstoi freed his serfs. Thomas Jefferson freed his slaves. I am going to set at liberty all the literary characters who have served me so loyally during my writing career. You are the only one I am telling" (301).

At first blush, this seems a quite blatant assertion of authorial power: characters equated to slaves or serfs over whom "Vonnegut" has the power of life and death, freedom and servitude. And throughout the novel "Vonnegut" repeatedly demonstrates that power, pointing it out to the reader as he makes phones ring, causes characters to say things, and claims that he "was on a par with the Creator of the Universe" (1973, 205). On the other hand, much like Fowles's impresario, "Vonnegut" informs us that this control is not absolute. Although he created his characters, "I could only guide their movements approximately. . . . It wasn't as though I was connected to them by steel wires. It was more as though I was connected to them by stale rubberbands" (207). These characters, like those in *The French Lieutenant's Woman*, have been endowed by their creator with free will. When he finally meets Kilgore Trout, a moment "Vonnegut" had been anticipating highly, the meeting does not go well, largely because "Vonnegut" did not realize that one of his characters, a large dog, was bearing down on him, ready to bite. Injured, "Vonnegut" tries to turn on his car's lights so Trout can see his face and instead turns on the windshield wipers. These mishaps serve to highlight the vast difference between "Vonnegut" and the "Creator of the Universe." His authorial power is severely limited, and even his entrance into the novel does not allow him to assert control more fully.

Furthermore, as he has already told us, "Vonnegut" is in crisis, worried he is losing his mind, as he tells himself: "This is a very bad book you're writing . . . . You're afraid you'll kill yourself the way your mother did" (1973, 198). This novel, meant to clear his head of all the errant images that have been troubling him, is not having the desired effect on its author: it is not restoring his sense of sanity. What finally does bring "Vonnegut" to a form of psychic healing (to allow him, in his words, to be "reborn") is the exchange he overhears between an arrogant artist character named Rabo Karabekian and citizens of the town that has just paid an exorbitant price for one of his paintings. During the course of the argument, Karabekian intones: "Our awareness is all that is alive and maybe sacred in any of us. Everything else about us is dead machinery" (226). And it is this statement that brings "Vonnegut" to the epiphany he has needed. "Vonnegut" says: "I did not expect Rabo Karabekian to rescue me. I had created him, and he was in my opinion a vain and weak and trashy man, no artist at all. But it is Rabo Karabekian who made me the serene Earthling which I am today" (225). It is his characters, saying unexpected things, which brings "Vonnegut" out of crisis: *Breakfast of Champions* portrays "Vonnegut" as a minimally powerful author-character. Conversely, the authorial prowess of Vonnegut sans scare quotes, Vonnegut the *actual* extradiegetical author of *Breakfast of Champions*, is highlighted and even celebrated. Through his writing, Vonnegut has cured "Vonnegut" of depression. In this sense, *Breakfast of Champions* demonstrates one of the central paradoxes of autofiction: it depicts a white male author in crisis whose waning creative power is not even sufficient to control his own narrative, while drawing attention, through the autofictional author-character, to the still-powerful and highly creative *actual* author who created the weaker character who shares his name. *Breakfast of Champions* restores and reasserts authorial authority by poignantly depicting the loss of that authority.[26]

A later example, but one which posits a similar reclamation of authorial prowess, is Richard Powers's 1995 autofiction *Galatea 2.2*. In it, novelist "Richard Powers" or "Rick" is granted a yearlong residency at the University of Illinois in Urbana, the place where ten years earlier he had earned his master's in literature. He returns to town alone, having just broken up with a longtime girlfriend, and finishes his fourth novel. After several abortive attempts to begin a fifth novel, "Rick" gets involved in a project developed by a group of cognitive scientists trying to build a computer construct that can mimic human consciousness well enough to fool someone into thinking it is human. The scientists want to build a consciousness that can pretend to be a graduate student of literature, so it becomes "Rick's" job to "teach" the computer about literature by reading and talking to it.

The novel consists of that story intertwined with flashbacks about "Rick's" recently ended relationship, and it eventually becomes clear that his writer's block stems from the break-up. His ex-girlfriend, C., had been the inspiration, and at key times the source, of material for his previous novels. It is unclear whether he can write a novel without her. As the story progresses, "Rick" turns his attention away from his writer's block and toward the computer construct, whom he has named "Helen" and whom he comes to consider a daughter of sorts. At times he believes that Helen may even exhibit actual consciousness, rather than a convincing simulation thereof. "Rick" also falls in love with "A.", a graduate student he has met only briefly but fantasizes about frequently, dreaming of a long-term relationship with her.

By the end of the book, both relationships are shattered: "A." spurns his advances, and Helen shuts down unexpectedly, either from an irreparable glitch or from despair at not being fully human. "Rick" is suddenly stripped of his female companions, but now imbued with their stories, he finds his writer's block lifted. The novel ends with him searching for a keyboard on which to begin, ostensibly, the novel we are reading. Just like the writer in "Dunyazadiad," "Rick" feeds off the stories of women in order to keep his own writing going. Becoming the Pygmalion that the title implies, "Rick" constructs Helen into the being he needs, not for her own sake, but for his own writerly use. Helen's "death" is the sacrifice necessary for her to serve as his muse. Unlike "Dunyazadiad," however, *Galatea 2.2* implicitly critiques "Rick's" actions, a fact made clear through the title of the novel and through moments of self-awareness that "Rick" experiences. For example, when he achieves success as a novelist by writing a book about C.'s ancestors, he realizes that, rather than giving C. a gift, he has usurped something that was hers: "The only thing she'd ever wanted was the thing I took away by doing for her" (Powers 1995, 278). The novel is replete with such self-criticism, as "Rick" looks back on his relationships—with C., Helen and even with A.—and sees where he was blind to what they really needed because he was too busy imposing his own needs upon them. Perhaps the self-awareness of the author-character in evidence here marks the evolution in thinking about gender relationships from the time of Barth's book, published in 1972, to Powers's from 1995.

A similar kind of charactorial self-criticism is a fundamental characteristic of the autofiction of Philip Roth. Indeed, perhaps no contemporary American writer has focused more intently on the potentials and pitfalls of authorship than Roth. Arguably, his entire career has been a chronicle of the various travails an author faces when his work is construed (or misconstrued, depending on one's opinion) as aligning too closely with his actual life. For my purposes, I am not interested in the question that has fascinated so many critics before me of how closely Roth's personal life hews to that of his characters and, subsequently, how much of his work is "fiction" and how much is "true." In other words, I do not care much about Roth's actual life. Rather, I want to focus on the instances of Roth's oeuvre which play overtly with that line between reality and fiction by depicting a character named "Philip Roth" in what are often clearly fictional situations. I want to focus on Roth's autofictions. And certainly no other American author has delved as deeply into autofiction, in that three of Roth's novels feature protagonists who share his name: *Deception, Operation Shylock,* and *The Plot against America.*[27] The first of these—*Deception* from 1990—is also the most subtle, for the protagonist is only referred to twice as "Philip." But, as will be seen, these references have serious repercussions and serve as the crux of the novel as well as, perhaps, the catalyst for the more overt autofictions Roth would write later.

Deception is framed as a series of conversations between a writer (later identified as "Philip") and various others, mostly women. The primary conversations take place between the writer and a lover, "Maria," who comes to see him in his studio, unbeknownst to the writer's wife. They discuss how the writer has taken her words and put them in the mouth of a character in one of his novels, a fact she does not appreciate, as she is often "recognized" in the novel by friends who have read it and could potentially be recognized by her own husband, were he ever to read the novel in question.[28] She chides "Philip" for taking down her words exactly as she says them and then transcribing them into his novel, particularly since he often rails against reviewers who criticize him for being a fiction writer who never actually makes anything up (1997, 200). "Philip" counters that he both did and did not create her character: "You also exist and also I made you up" (200). In this sense, "Philip" defends his right to mold events and people from his life into fiction in whatever way he sees fit, and he asserts his creative prerogative to make a character out of a real person.

It is significant to my argument that "Philip" defends this right from a *woman* who challenges it. Another female challenge to his authorial authority comes from his wife, who finds the notebook into which he has transcribed the conversations with Maria and wonders whether they are fictional or real.[29] There are several charges "Philip" must fend off here. First, to convince his wife he is not actually cheating on her, he claims that the notebooks represent his fantasies about having a love affair with a character of his own creation. His wife then points out that if he publishes these conversations, she will be humiliated because readers will not realize that the conversations are fictional. To this, "Philip" responds: "They generally don't, so what difference does that make? I write fiction and I'm told it's autobiography, I write autobiography and I'm told it's fiction, so since I'm so dim and they're so smart, let *them* decide what it is or it isn't" (1997, 183). Here "Philip" rather deftly shifts the conversation from being between him and his wife to one between him and his readers. As he did with Maria, he glosses over the potential damage his writing might do to the real women in his life, instead staunchly defending his right as an author to use the women as fodder for his writing.

Tellingly, a male friend, in another depicted conversation, accuses "Philip" of just that: "You are a treacherous bastard who cannot resist a narrative even from the wife of his refugee friend. The stronger the narrative impulse in her, the more captivated you are. . . . You like it best when these soulful women can't actually tell their own tales but struggle for access to their story. . . . Every woman a fuck, every fuck a Scheherazade" (1997, 87–88). Just as the writer in "Dunyazadiad," "Philip" appropriates the stories of women and turns them to his own ends. The difference, of course, between *Chimera* and *Deception* is the almost twenty years that separate their publication. The writer in *Chimera* exhibits no compunction in absorbing the sisters' stories and making them his own, while *Deception* resembles *Galatea 2.2* by recognizing this absorption for what it is: the appropriation of the stories of women. Within the novel, "Philip" tries to justify this appropriation to his friend, his lover, and his wife and the various means by which he does so comprise the deceptions at the heart of *Deception*.

And of course, because the protagonist is named "Philip," the connection is directly made between the character and the eponymous author: we are thus encouraged, in our prurient curiosity about the "real" Philip Roth, to wonder whether that "real" Roth struggles with these questions of authorial legitimacy and appropriation. The autofictional nature of this novel suggests that through the character of "Philip," Roth subjects himself to the same degrading treatment as his characters. "Philip" explains to his wife that his own name must appear in the published novel (rather than the name of his usual charactorial stand-in, Nathan Zuckerman) because drawing that connection to his existence outside the novel is an important part of the enterprise: "I portray myself as implicated because it is not enough just to be present. That's not the way I go about it. To compromise some 'character' doesn't get me where I want to be. What heats things up is compromising me. It kind of makes the indictment juicier, besmirching myself" (1997, 177–78). This somewhat erotic description of being "besmirched" by the connection of character to author is a highly evocative explanation of the voyeuristic appeal of autofiction, both to the reader and apparently to the writer engaged in it. It also demonstrates the ways in which much autofiction represents a gender-marked struggle to maintain masculine authorial authority.

Thus the proliferation of postmodern autofiction arises in some respects from the increasing self-consciousness brought about by the second-wave feminist movement. This link between postmodern self-consciousness and gender consciousness has rarely if ever been drawn, but autofiction serves as an ideal vehicle through which to chart this connection. Furthermore, the proliferation of the autofictional author-character highlights the perceived waning of masculine cultural supremacy, as it manifests itself in a perceived waning of authorial authority. As the next chapter will articulate, the authorial self-consciousness and waning authority that characterize autofiction can also be traced to the theoretical debates catalyzed by poststructuralist literary theory about the nature of language and the cultural valence of the author-figure.

2 | Rage against the Dying of the Author

Philip Roth, Arthur Phillips, Ruth Ozeki,
Salvador Plascencia, and Percival Everett

> *Moreover, not only the creator but the characters (and the narrator,*
> *if any) as well will participate (in the same degree as the reader)*
> *in the creation of the fiction. All of them will be part of the fiction,*
> *all of them will be responsible for it—the creator (as fictitious as*
> *his creation) being only the point of junction (the source and the*
> *recipient) of all the elements of the fiction.*
>
> —Raymond Federman, *Surfiction*

An important stated tenet of New Criticism—the primary mode of literary criticism developed during and directly after the modernist period—involved the all-powerful author removing him/herself from the work (impersonality), while literary critics were meant to focus on the text alone, not on any consideration of the author's purpose (to avoid succumbing to the "intentional fallacy"). I say that this was a *stated* tenet of the New Criticism because contemporary scholars of the modernist period point out that, while they were not embodied in their texts in an autofictional style, authors were consciously shaping their styles and extratextual personae in order to participate in the publishing marketplace (Jaffe 2005; Goldman 2011). Despite or perhaps because of this overt modernist construction of authorial personae, subsequent decades saw the rise of the poststructuralist theories of the late 1960s and early 1970s, which led in turn to new conceptualizations of literary celebrity and in which the view of the relationship between author and text was somewhat different.

While New Criticism merely attempted to remove the figure of the author from analytical consideration, the poststructuralists set out to destroy the very concept of the author as a uniquely gifted and unitary subject. As

Brian McHale so pithily put it, "The postmodernist slogan, successor to modernism's 'Exit Author,' is 'The Death of the Author'" (1987, 199). According to many poststructuralists, the author is irrelevant to literary criticism, not because he has voluntarily removed him/herself from the text in an act of modernist impersonality but because he/she never existed as a discrete and coherent subject in the first place. Whereas the New Criticism embodied a philosophy of how an author should write literature as well as how a critic should analyze it, the tenets of poststructuralism disassembled the very notion of the conscious creative power of an individual, reducing the author to an author-function and a text from a work of literature to a cultural artifact. However, autofiction can be read not only as a reaction to these ideas but also as a corrective to the hyperbolic and somewhat premature claim that the author is dead.

Chapter 1 made the point that the proliferation of self-conscious narratives in postmodern fiction could be traced in part to the rise of the second wave of the feminist movement. I demonstrated that white male postmodern writers reacted to their increased awareness of the issues of gender and race by making evident their own positionality, often through the use of an autofictional author-character. But awareness of issues of gender and race are not the only elements involved in the self-consciousness that characterizes postmodern fiction. Almost simultaneous with the feminist movement was the rise of the strains of poststructuralist literary theory, which posited that knowledge of the world was accessible only through language. Subsequently, the concept of a linguistically constituted subjectivity replaced that of a fixed and stable identity.

The effect these ideas had on the concept of authorship are well documented, so I will rehearse them only briefly here. In *The Rhetoric of Fiction*, Wayne Booth somewhat resuscitated the concept of the author's presence in his or her work, claiming that even in the face of modernist impersonality, there always exists the "implied author" because "readers will inevitably construct a picture of the official scribe who writes" (1961, 71). But this resurrection of the image of authorship was only partial: the author here is merely an implication, not a full-fledged human creator. The dismantling of the authorial concept continued when, in 1967, Roland Barthes's essay "The Death of the Author" was published in the American journal *Aspen*.[1] In it, Barthes famously argues that once a literary text is published, the author is no longer relevant to its interpretation: the author is "dead." Two years later, Michel Foucault, some say in response to Barthes's essay, delivered his lecture entitled "What Is an Author?" in which he took issue with some of Barthes's pronouncements, arguing that while the autonomously creative individual known as the author might not really exist, the *idea* of an author has always been instrumental in textual interpretation. In a somewhat distant echo of Booth, Foucault coined the term "author-function" to describe the ways in which the concept of authorship is used to delimit how a text should be read and what it can mean. But whereas the implied author is a manifestation that readers constructed within the text, the author-function represents the extratextual, cultural representation of the authorial image.

What Foucault did not do, however, was assert the primacy of the author as an actual human figure authorized to influence the interpretation of his/her written work. Thus both Barthes and Foucault argued effectively to negate the actual person of the author as a source of meaning for a literary text. As Claire Boyle puts it, "A central tenet of poststructuralist thought is precisely to deny the possibility of establishing via the text any connection with its flesh-and-blood originator beyond the text" (2007, 23). This idea, emerging as it does some years into the widespread practice of the New Critical tenet of literary impersonality, had and continues to have a far-reaching impact on postmodern literature. For while the New Critics made the *text* the analytical focal point, Barthes's piece overtly embraces the role of the *reader* in determining a text's meaning, going so far as to say that the death of the author heralds the "birth of the reader" (1977, 148). In a similar vein, Foucault's idea of the "author-function" is also a reader-made construction; decisions about which of an author's writings (consciously crafted artistic works as opposed to shopping lists) are to be included in an author's oeuvre are made by a discourse community of readers of that author's and other authors' work. And of course this putative "birth of the reader" soon gave rise to the theoretical subgenre known as "Reader Response Theory," in which a text is analyzed in terms of how it affects its readership, either singularly or in the aggregate. While very different in focus—New Criticism directed attention to the text and poststructuralism directed attention toward the reader—both critical modes deemphasized and even negated the importance of the author to the text. Taken together, these movements away from consideration of authorial intention and creative prowess had a demonstrable effect on the emergent literature. One of these effects is the autofictional impulse, which proliferates at this contemporary moment in direct response to the perceived diminishment of authorial importance fomented by the rise of poststructuralist theory.

It is not my purpose in this chapter to relitigate the debate over the strengths and weaknesses of the death of the author trope; such arguments represent well-trod ground. Rather, I want to discuss the unmistakably pervasive influence that the death of the author notion had and continues to have on postmodern writers, whether they are versed in these literary theories or not. Indeed, as Judith Ryan has argued in her book *The Novel after Theory*, "It is possible for a text to 'know about' theory even when its author does not admit to knowing it or has had no verifiable access to specific theoretical texts. In some instances, the intellectual climate, from current ways of thinking to fashionable use of language, seeps into texts without their authors' awareness" (2012, 6). I would argue that we can read contemporary American autofiction as one manifestation of the kind of "theory novel" that Ryan discusses.

Furthermore, just as the "death of the author" has emerged in much postmodern fiction, it is undeniable that, whatever interpretative stance one takes, the trend of literary criticism for the past several decades has been characterized by a decided shift *away* from considering the author as a source of meaning.[2] This shift has been exacerbated in recent years by the advent of new media and the resulting proliferation of crowd-sourced websites, blogs, twitter journalism, and self-publishing. Advances in new media have democratized the notion of authorship to such an extent that now seemingly anyone and everyone can be an author. In the face of these putative assaults on the traditional view of the inimitable creative prowess of (usually white, usually male) authors, autofiction serves as an ideal conduit through which to examine contemporary views of authorship. The intrusive authorial characters in autofiction expose the fissures in the death of the author concept by simultaneously thematizing both the nature of the traditional author's power and the extent of his impotence.

I am, of course, not the first to notice such fissures: Benjamin Widiss has stated unequivocally that "Roland Barthes' tremendously influential account of complete authorial self-effacement as the sine qua non of modern textual production—while rhetorically prodigious, conceptually dazzling, and endlessly provocative—was (and remains) largely inaccurate" (2011, 5). My aim in this chapter is to take Widiss's claim in a new direction by demonstrating how the author-characters of autofiction often revolt against the idea of their "death" by overtly asserting authorial power within their works, often through the use of autofictional characters. Thus the death of the author concept—the sense that the author, beyond writing the work, has nothing of value to contribute to its subsequent interpretation—serves as a catalyst for the abundance of self-conscious fiction in the postmodern era because a fictitious, charactorial version of an author serves as a reassertion of authority in a cultural landscape that increasingly devalues authorship. Autofiction, then, employs a variety of methods to demonstrate the continuing power and relevance of authors and authorship. For example, author-characters may assert this power in insidious and malicious ways, working to harm their characters or deceive their readers, as in Martin Amis's *Money* or Paul Auster's *City of Glass*. Or author-characters may confront the threat to their power by those who would usurp their authorial authority, as in Philip Roth's *Operation Shylock* or John Barth's *Coming Soon!!!* In a manner related to the previous chapter, these poststructuralist autofictions often involve melodramas of beset male authorship (*pace* Nina Baym).

Furthermore, the autofictional nature of these narratives simultaneously suggests and denies that it is their extratextual authors (in addition to their fictional avatars) who are facing these challenges. These novels depict "Philip Roth" and "Paul Auster" with some of the same biographical details of Philip Roth and Paul Auster, thus inviting the equation of the character to author. These author-characters also engage in activities so outlandish as to be obviously fictional, thus severing or at least loosening the connection between character and author. The result is a series of texts that point directly to authorial presence and power both within and outside the text, demonstrating that the author is far from dead, but equally far from being the omniscient arbiter of meaning he had once been considered to be.

Because of the confusingly contradictory nature of its author-character, autofiction belongs to the group of contemporary texts that present what Benjamin Widiss calls an "obscure invitation" to the reader "not just to seek out the author from whom they spring, but to imagine him or her in a particular fashion and to attend to that imagination as a constitutive element of the reading process" (2011, 3). And autofiction certainly does make authorship a constitutive element of the reading process, for while it is important to maintain a distinction, for example, between Philip Roth the author and "Philip Roth" the character, the presence of the latter inevitably evokes the former, even if only to emphasize his absence. In other words, "Philip" the protagonist continuously recalls Roth the author, while emphasizing the fact that the two are distinctly different figures. This paradox is made especially evident when the "Philip" in the novel is embroiled in clearly fictional situations involving encounters with improbable people and adventures that could not have occurred outside the novel. Thus, much more starkly than memoirs or autobiographies, autofictions mandate both a connection to and distance from the extratextual author.

Thus a central contradiction of autofiction is that it employs author-characters to conspicuously assert the presence of the author as a creative force, while it forces us to recognize the difference between that intratextual character and the extratextual author. Furthermore, the more the intrusive author-character asserts his authority within the text, the more the waning of that power becomes evident outside the text, while the constant presence of the author-character serves as a continual reminder to the reader that, although his power may be diminished, the author is clearly not dead to his text. Autofiction lends support to Widiss's assertion that "far more often an apparent or incomplete authorial evacuation masks a deeper strategy of self-inscription—a studied self-occlusion that provokes in the reader not liberation or even indifference but rather a desire to find precisely that which initially eludes detection" (2011, 6). Autofiction, by this estimation, does not demonstrate the death of the author but inspires a readerly effort to find him. By way of contrast, Sally Robinson has argued that "threatened by 'theory,' 'politics,' and the rise of popular culture, the white male author is suffering a second kind of death" that, in Robinson's conceptualization, involves becoming more visible (2000, 88). Robinson posits that the perceived death of the author gives rise to literary images of wounded white male bodies. To my mind, the autofictional author-character becomes part of this "making visible," as characters proliferate who not only represent white male authors but who represent *the* white male author of the book in which they appear. To synthesize the ideas of Widiss and Robinson, then, autofictional author-characters become visible as wounded yet entrenched self-inscriptions. In other words, autofiction certainly reinscribes the author but reinscribes him as damaged goods.

To flesh out my argument, it will be helpful to briefly explain the tenets that undergird the concept of the death of the author, particularly because this idea represents an evolution on Barthes's—and other thinkers'—part away from a very different idea of authorship. In his article "The Writer on Holiday," Barthes suggests that the cultural image of the writer is an image of an all-powerful artistic figure—a "superman"—who maintains his creative mystique even while on vacation: "Unlike the other workers, who change their essence, and on the beach are no longer anything but holiday-makers, the writer keeps his writer's nature everywhere. By having holidays, he displays the sign of his being human; but the god remains" (1972, 30). Indeed, Barthes argues here that seeing the writer behave like a normal man only confirms that his writerly creations are evidence of his superhuman powers: "To endow the writer publicly with a good fleshly body, to reveal that he likes dry white wine and underdone steak, is to make even more miraculous for me, and of a more divine essence, the products of his art" (31). Clearly Barthes's concept of an author's worth evolved quite a bit over time. This image of the author as a creative deity is a far cry from the culturally irrelevant nonperson depicted in "The Death of the Author." But this image is what novels employing autofictional author-characters often gesture toward. As the aura surrounding the authorial persona diminished with the advent of poststructuralist ideas about the nature of language and subjectivity, literary authorial intrusion emerged as an attempt to resurrect that authorial mystique. Indeed, the autofictional novels I discuss often thematize death of the author concerns by depicting an author-character who realizes that his authorial authority is waning.

Seán Burke has argued that this godlike image of the author was derived in part from the existentialist philosophies of Jean-Paul Sartre. Sartre's idea that the human being ought to actively construct his/her own identity was reflected as well in his ideas about authorship: "Sartre extended the notion of a free subjectivity beyond philosophy to literature and politics, and provided his generation with the model of the engaged author, a politically committed writer whose work and whose activities maintained the ideals of personal and political freedom in all aspects of day-to-day existence" (1998, 11). In this conception, the author remains intimately connected to and influential within his work even after he has written it. This image of authorship hearkens back to the pre-twentieth-century tradition of biographical criticism that focused primarily on drawing direct lines of connection between the life of the author and his work.

With the advent of poststructuralist theory, of which Barthes himself was on the forefront, ideas about the efficacy of language to convey the real world and the nature of subjectivity inflected ideas about authorship. If there were no such thing as a unified identity, but only linguistically determined subjectivities, then there could exist no center of creative power known as the "author." As Barthes says in "Death of the Author," "Linguistically, the author is never more than the instance writing, just as *I* is nothing other than the instance saying *I*: language knows a 'subject,' not a person" (1977, 145). Rather than an author, according to Barthes, there exists merely the "scriptor," the fleeting subjectivity who serves as a nexus of previously written elements of language that come together to form a text, and who only exists during the text's enunciation: "The modern scriptor is born simultaneously with the text, is in no way equipped with a being preceding or exceeding the writing" (145). Such a "text" (from which Foucault was to differentiate the idea of the literary "work" created by a godlike author) is therefore imbued with meaning only in the instance of reading (enunciation), rather than by an author in an inspired moment of creation: "There is no other time than that of the enunciation and every text is eternally written *here and now*" (145). Subsequently, each act of reading creates a different text, such that "The old notion of authorial originality is not justified, since every text is in fact nothing more than a web of language" (Ryan 2012, 23). Authorial prowess, then, is an illusion and a text's meaning and power (if they exist at all) are fleeting and arise purely from the readerly context in which a text is received.

Or, as Foucault would have it, a particular discourse's "status and its manner of reception are regulated by the culture in which it circulates" (1977, 123). And this is where the ideas of Barthes and Foucault differ markedly from the *sola scriptura* philosophy espoused by the New Critics. Whereas the latter had determined that considerations of textual production, publication, or distribution should have no bearing on literary criticism and that the text itself was where inherent and eternal meaning resided, this newer breed of literary philosopher maintained that meaning is not inherent in the text but rather determined by the historical and cultural discourses surrounding it (for Barthes, by the "reader," for Foucault, by the "discourse community"). As Seán Burke puts it: "Earlier movements against the author had taken the form of re-actions against biographical positivism. The author was simply to be re-moved or sidelined in order to focus in New Criticism on 'the words on the page,' in Russian Formalism on 'the literariness of literature,' but these exclusions remained essentially provisional and did not take the form of a prescriptive or eidetic statement about discourse" (1998, 14). In other words, whereas the New Critics viewed the author as simply irrel-evant to a text's meaning, these poststructuralist thinkers posited the author-figure as a constructed concept whose sole purpose was to *fix* a text's meaning: "To give a text an Author is to impose a limit on that text, to furnish it with a final signified, to close the writing" (Barthes 1977, 147). To Barthes and Foucault, then, a text's meaning is subject to change with the times, as is the cultural valence afforded to the figure of the au-thor, both as an individual and as an abstract concept.

According to this formulation, authors are nothing more than "author-functions," as Foucault so famously proclaimed. Originally delivered as a lecture in 1969, two years after the publication of "The Death of the Au-thor," Foucault's "What Is an Author?" makes the case that an author's name is less a signifier of a creative human being than "a means of classif-ication" of texts, serving not only to differentiate certain texts from one another but also to group them into culturally determined categories. As Barthes draws a distinction between the author and the "scriptor," Fou-cault posits one between the author and the actual "writer": the author is not the person who writes but rather the symbolic entity that serves to organize texts into their respective discourse categories. Foucault argues that this symbolic entity, this author-function, emerges from the inher-ent "scission" or separation of the actual writer of the text and its sup-posed author (1977, 129). He goes on to argue that the writer is of mark-edly less cultural importance than the author-function, as the latter serves as the rubric under which texts are evaluated and classified as literature.

So, unlike Barthes, Foucault argues that the author does have a func-tion in literary analysis but that author-function is not inextricably con-nected to the human person who wrote the text. Rather, the author-function is a cultural image that acts as an organizing principle for the texts written by a particular writer that are referred to by that writer's name. Foucault puts it this way: "We can conclude that, unlike a proper name, which moves from the interior of a discourse to the real person outside who produced it, the name of the author remains at the contours of texts—separating one from the other, defining their form, and characterizing their mode of existence" (1977, 123). The argument being espoused here is that a proper name works differently when applied to an actual person than it does when applied to the author-function, which is not a person but a symbolic entity. With a person, Foucault argues, the proper name connects a discursive act to the "real person outside who produced it," while the name of an author serves a sort of classificatory purpose, corralling particular texts under its umbrella and keeping others out (123).

However, in order for the author-function to function, it must also evoke the proper name of the writer who is, presumably, a "real person outside." There can be no "author-function" without an onomastic connection to an actual writer's (or scriptor's) proper name. Subsequently, the differentiation between the scriptor and the author, or the writer and the author-function, is not as definitive and easily achieved as Barthes or Foucault imply. What a study of autofiction makes clear is the fact that this uneasy yet important *distinction* between the scriptor/author or the writer/author-function rests upon an equally important *equation* of the former's name to the latter's. By including eponymous author-characters, autofiction explores, exploits, and sometimes explodes the distinction between writer and author, because the author-character simultaneously evokes the proper-name designation of the actual person and the symbolic designation of the author. The result is a novel that makes constant metafictional reference to the extratextual existence of its author, who is portrayed within the text as a character, possibly giving the lie to the idea that the author is dead or irrelevant to the text. Perhaps the most potent example that makes this point is Barthes's own autofiction, *Roland Barthes by Roland Barthes*. This work, part autobiography, part novel, includes facts and photos from "R.B.'s" life, but also demonstrates Barthes's pronouncement in "Introduction to the Structural Analysis of Narratives" that "the one who speaks (in the narrative) is not the one who writes (in real life) and the one who writes is not the one who is" (1975, 261).[3]

Barthes's autofictional book of literary criticism arguably serves as an early example of the contemporary trend of literary autocriticism, which combines theoretical and/or literary analysis with a discussion of the writer's personal relationship with that theory or literature. Nicholson Baker's *U and I: A True Story* (1991) chronicles Baker's relationship with the work and eventually the person of John Updike. Throughout, Baker quotes Updike from memory (often erroneously) in an effort to demonstrate how a writer's (in this case, Baker's) work can be affected by feelings of love for and intimidation by a literary giant like Updike. Inspired in similar ways, J. C. Hallman contributes to this genre with his 2015 book *B & Me: A True Story of Literary Arousal*, in which he discusses his own obsession with Nicholson Baker's work. Chris Kraus's memoir *I Love Dick* (2006) provides cultural and artistic analysis under the guise of love letters written to sociologist Dick Hebdige. Thomas Beller's *J. D. Salinger: The Escape Artist* (2014) chronicles his personal and our general obsession with that reclusive writer, and Maureen Corrigan's *So We Read On* (2014) traces her personal connection with *The Great Gatsby* by linking it to a historical account of how the novel earned its place in American letters. These and countless other examples help demonstrate the pervasive cultural saturation of autofictional authorial intrusion. Indeed, the metafictional intricacies here become almost too precious as these writers write about reading the work of other writers. In the aggregate, however, what emerges from these contemporary paeans to (male) authorial greatness is a reification of the "author" as an actual human person endowed with godlike power to inspire.

By contrast, Seán Burke has argued that Barthes and Foucault's encomiums about the irrelevance of the author were not particularly necessary in the mid-twentieth-century critical context in which they emerged, since many elements of New Criticism had already done away with biographical positivism in literary analysis. As Burke puts it: "For a tradition suffused with notions such as the intentional fallacy, the unreliable narrator, the implied author, Barthes's essay might well seem aimed at a target that had long since retreated out of range. . . . there is no question that injunctions such as the intentional fallacy, and the edict that criticism should limit itself to the 'words on the page' sufficed to thoroughly distance their activities from any form of theocentric *auteurism*" (Burke 1998, 25). In other words, in terms of analytical consideration, the author was already dead and had been for years when Barthes made his famous pronouncement. Burke goes on to discuss how Barthes, Foucault, and especially Derrida employ the idea of the death of the author to assert both the primacy of literary criticism over literature and the primacy of the critic over the author. According to Burke, these philosophers presided not over the dethroning of the author but rather over the coronation of the literary theorist and scholar (and certainly the above list of autofictional literary criticism gives credence to this perspective).[4] Not only is this theoretical presumption part of what authors like John Barth and Philip Roth are reacting against, but as Burke points out, the death-of-the-author assertions of these French philosophers achieved a very different valence as they crossed the ocean to the United States. Once removed from the "specific historical and ethnological circumstances in which Barthes, Foucault, and Derrida promulgated extreme anti-subjectivism," the death-of-the-author argument "retained its characteristic hyperbole without recapturing the sense of epochal necessity which motivated its initial formulations" (1998, 180). Therefore, American scholars and writers absorbed these anti-authorial, anti-subjectivist ideas untethered from their original philosophical context, causing them to be construed by some American literary authors as an attack on their authorial authority. American autofiction is, in many respects, indicative of precisely that idea.

And this is one reason that, at the same time that Barthes and Foucault were making pronouncements about the death of the author and the rise of the author-function on one side of the Atlantic, many American writers were making a case for authorial intrusion on the other side. In 1967, the same year in which Barthes published his most famous essay, John Barth also published his in the *Atlantic*: "The Literature of Exhaustion." In it, Barth argues that the rise of the "intermedia arts" (art that includes music and performance in spontaneous artistic "happenings") has contributed to the obsolescence of the idea of the artist as a unique man of genius. Barth laments the loss of "the most traditional notion of the artist: the Aristotelian conscious agent who achieves with technique and cunning the artistic effect; in other words, one endowed with uncommon talent, who has moreover developed and disciplined that endowment into virtuosity" (1984, 65). In this clear rebuttal of the death-of-the-author idea, Barth argues that in earlier days the artist was considered to be a man of great and unusual prowess who worked very hard to hone his skill and become a master of his craft. This concept of the artist, Barth argues, is an undemocratic idea to be sure, but it has somewhat unfairly been "condemned as politically reactionary, authoritarian, even fascist" (65).

Barth disagrees with this characterization of the author as authoritarian and goes on to advocate for the image of the artist as singular creative genius, especially in fiction. This concept of the artistically potent individual author is more essential than ever, Barth says, because the traditional forms of literary fiction are "exhausted" and "the novel's time as a major art form is up," unless the efforts of the powerful authorial virtuoso can revive it by writing fiction that chronicles that very exhaustion (1984, 71). Barth himself claims to address the "used-upness" of fictional literary forms by crafting "novels which imitate the form of the Novel, by an author who imitates the role of Author" (64, 72). In so doing, Barth's work recalls the similarly metafictional origins of the novel, as seen in *Don Quixote* and later in *Tristram Shandy*. According to Barth, bringing the novel through this moment of literary and fictional exhaustion requires a return to those older traditions and to an older ideal of authorship. It requires, in his estimation, a resurrection of the concept of the author as an unusual talent and unusually brave soul: "The commonality, alas, will *always* lose their way and their soul; it is the chosen remnant, the virtuoso, the Thesean *hero*" who will "with the aid of very special gifts—as extraordinary as saint- or herohood and not likely to be found in The New York Correspondence School of Literature— go straight through the maze to the accomplishment of his work" (75– 76). Now, there is a great deal to unpack in that statement, for what Barth is arguing is that the kind of figure who can rescue the novel from the literary trash heap upon which we might find the sonnet or the epic poem is the strong (and decidedly masculine) figure of the author as solitary and godlike genius. He argues that the powerful author is necessary if we are going to shore up the exhausted fragments of modern literature and build some kind of newer and truer form. To Barth, then, the author is very much alive and is the true hero of contemporary literature because he must not only be strong enough to write it, but he must appear as a character within it. And while Barth makes this argument about postmodern literature in general, it is a particularly trenchant one in regard to the authorial intrusion of autofiction, for autofiction evokes the literal presence of an author-figure in the text who attempts through that presence to delimit and define the potential meaning of the text.

This image of the writer as "Thesean hero" is further amplified in Barth's seminal postmodern short story "Lost in the Funhouse" in which young Ambrose becomes lost in an amusement park funhouse and, depending upon how one reads the story, may never find his way out. In a similar fashion, the story's narrator becomes equally lost in the telling of the story, declaring, "We should be much farther along than we are; something has gone wrong; not much of this preliminary rambling seems relevant," and lamenting, "I'll never be an author" (1969, 75, 83). And yet while the boy and the narrator have difficulty navigating the funhouse in the park and the funhouse of narrative, respectively, the constant metafictional speculation on the progress of the story repeatedly gestures to the omnipotent guiding force of the powerful author outside the text, whose presence is felt even though he is absent from the story. Authorial intrusion, for Barth, becomes the means by which the author can have a hand in shaping the interpretation of his story.

It is this form of absent presence in metafiction generally and autofiction more specifically that I want to address. As literary and cultural criticism continued to maintain the writer's irrelevance to literary meaning, the number of novels featuring an intrusive, autofictional authorial presence increased. Regardless of the legitimacy of the perception, the perceived loss of authorial cultural capital and authority has resulted in an ever increasing spate of novels in which the author emerges as a character in order to exert authorial control, at least within the world of the novel. Often the author-character's putative writerly powers exceed the author's extratextual ones.

For example, the author-character in Ronald Sukenick's 1968 novel *Up* envies the strength and virility of his creation "Strop Banally," who is more successful than his creator: "But Banally's complete triumph is his creator's defeat, for Strop remains a symbol, an abstraction, unreal" (1999, 41). Strop Banally's strength comes from his fictionality, from his being an authorial creation, while the author-character struggles to thrive in an extratextual world not of his own making.

This sense that the fictional world is a better place for a writer-character than the real one might explain why some of the first autofictions that emerge in the United States during this time were semiautobiographical.

In fact, such works were at the time often referred to as "fictional memoirs," including Frederick Exley's trilogy, *A Fan's Notes: A Fictional Memoir* (1968), *Pages from a Cold Island* (1975), and *Last Notes from Home* (1988) and George Cain's *Blueschild Baby* (1970), one of the few autofictions by an African American author. In each of these, fictional elements mingle with autobiographical ones to the extent that, when the works were first published, their authors felt the need to explain or even apologize for the resulting confusion. For example, Exley insists in *A Fan's Notes* that, although it is subtitled *A Fictional Memoir*, it should be read as a work of fiction: "Though the events in this book bear similarity to those of that long malaise, my life, many of the characters and happenings are creations solely of the imagination. . . . for this reason, I ask to be judged as a writer of fantasy" ("A Note to the Reader" 1968). Not only does this admonition assert the fictionality of a semiautobiographical text, but it also overtly lays claim to the creative power of its author by calling attention to the book's status as "fantasy." This impulse toward, yet discomfort with, blurring the lines between fiction and nonfiction can be seen in many autofictions from this trend's incubational period, the late 1960s and 1970s. These early works can be connected to the rise of what came to be known as the New Journalism, as I will discuss in chapter 3.

Ultimately, much of the literary power that autofiction wields is conveyed through the onomastic connection between the extratextual author and the author-character within the text, who usually narrates in the first person. Although even the most elementary reader of novels knows not to equate an I-narrator with the author, such an equation becomes impossible to avoid when the I-narrator and the author share a name. The result is a reading experience in which we are constantly forced to adjust and readjust our relationship to the text, for some of the information provided about the author-character might match the actual biographical history of the author. For example, Philip Roth's *Deception* exploits his readers' prurient curiosity about celebrity authors' real lives and their tendency to equate characters with their creators.[5] By depicting a "Philip" whose life and experiences are tantalizingly similar to the actual Philip Roth, *Deception* seems to be divulging highly personal and titillating information about Roth himself. Autofictions such as these tease readers with the promise of details about the authors' lives, despite the fact that readers of fiction simultaneously know that promise to be a lie. Indeed much of the pleasure in reading autofiction comes from the fleeting idea that the fiction might be fact, even as readers usually understand the difference between the author and the author-character.[6]

And if the events in *Deception* seem believable, the events recounted in Roth's next novel, *Operation Shylock*, certainly do not; that novel depicts "Philip" traveling around Israel in pursuit of an impostor claiming to be the "real" Philip Roth. Even more improbably, the novel culminates with "Philip" agreeing to act as a spy for the Israeli Mossad. Novels like *Deception* and *Operation Shylock* are more stimulating as autofictions than they would be as traditional fictions, because the inclusion of actual authors' names and likenesses evokes the celebrity persona of the real-life Roth. As "Philip" himself says, the use of his own name in a novel "makes the indictment juicier" (1997, 178). What he means, of course, is that the salacious material becomes even more so when readers suspect— if only momentarily—that it might be factual rather than fictional.

The way in which certain forms of autofiction capitalize on authorial celebrity can be further illuminated through the conception of "celebrity-function" coined by P. David Marshall which, he argues, "is as important as Foucault's 'author-function' in its power to organize the legitimate and illegitimate domains of the personal and individual within the social" (1997, 57). Celebrity, then, is a sociocultural construction in the same vein as Foucault's conception of authorship. In this context, Marshall argues that a celebrity is an "intertextual sign," constructed by "the circulation of significant information about the celebrity in newspapers, magazines, interview programs, fanzines, rumors and so on" (58). The intersections between these different kinds of text that surround a figure are what constitute that figure as a celebrity. In this formulation, an autofiction with a celebrity writer-character at its center provides another text through which that celebrity is mediated. Fans of a particular celebrity might possibly confront an autofictional text in much the same way they might a tabloid: they know at the outset that much of the information conveyed may be untrue, but they enjoy reading it anyway. All of the different pieces of information serve to construct the celebrity-function, which takes on a meaning distinct from the actual person around whom the function has developed.

In this sense, Jonathan D'Amore's argument about autobiography applies here to autofiction: it is "more a reiteration or reframing of a public self rather than a revelation of a private one" (2012, 2). In his discussion, D'Amore claims that autobiographical authors such as Dave Eggers and Edgar Wideman know that they are not so much revealing their personal selves in their memoirs as working and reworking their public face. I would argue that novels evincing authorial intrusion are even more overtly doing this. Because autofictions are admittedly fictional, the authorial personae they shape are also admittedly fictional. But even so, these textual authorial personae draw an onomastic connection to the authorial personae that exist outside the text. As Joe Moran argues about celebrity autobiography, such texts "often provide a productive way of dealing with anxieties about the survival of authorship as a meaningful activity in an age when ideas and images are often corporately owned, and the dangers of being trapped in a persona which assumes simplistic connections between writer and work" (2000, 69).[7] As I have argued, autofiction also reflects these anxieties about the survival of authorship, but often does so satirically, thwarting such simplistic connections between writer and work by painting a picture of the author-character and/ or his situation that does not reflect the extratextual reality. Celebrity autofiction, then, represents one way an author can participate in the construction of his image, while it also evinces a postmodern awareness that the image is just that: a construction. Thus autofiction could be read as a response to what Celia Lury refers to as the undermining of the "cultural producer's protected position as originator" by "the commercial exploitation of the possibilities of replication offered by the technologies of culture" (2002, 51). Autofiction allows an author to take an active yet ironic role in constructing his authorial persona in the face of cultural and corporate forces that threaten to diminish that role.

For example, Mark Leyner's fiction satirizes readers' and spectators' fascination with celebrity voyeurism by positing his authorial alter ego as a literary celebrity of such proportions as to require a phalanx of staff and bodyguards he calls "Team Leyner." I am thinking in particular here of *Et Tu, Babe?* (1992), but Leyner's other novels also focus to varying extents on the hyperbolic and outlandish events in the life of this author-character. Although Leyner's protagonists are named "Mark Leyner" and are rendered in the first person, the plot lines are so extravagant as to make it impossible to sustain any real equation—other than onomastic— between the author and the author-character. Indeed, whereas *Deception* is intriguing because is relies upon the potential for a real connection between author and character, Leyner's work is intriguing because it pushes and then breaks the limits of that connection. While a reader would not believe that the "real" Leyner has had some of the experiences chronicled in these novels (like having his liver tattooed or inhaling a vial of "Lincoln's Morning Breath" stolen from the Smithsonian), the fact that this character shares Leyner's name produces a very different reading experience than if his name were as fictional as the rest of him. By repeatedly gesturing outside the text by evoking the author's name, regardless of—and perhaps because of—the infidelity to the "truth," the novel calls attention to the extratextual author as the creative agent at the heart of the narrative.[8] Indeed, *Et Tu, Babe?* depicts "Mark Leyner" as a strutting egomaniac with a huge international fan base so enamored of his work that they make death threats to critics who dare to give him a bad review. "Leyner" as author is so important that he is unmetaphorically considered the center of the universe, as evidenced by an "exhibit at the World Institute of Advanced Science that will reevalutate evolution from the Big Bang . . . to the present moment as one teleological process leading inevitably to the birth of Mark Leyner" (1992, 168).[9] Thus, while Roth uses autofiction to plumb the depths of literary celebrity, Leyner employs it to satirize the excesses of the culture of celebrity and celebrity worship.

However, as so often happens in autofiction, while "Leyner" asserts the power and popularity of his authorial celebrity, thus giving the lie to the death of the author, he simultaneously demonstrates the waning cultural power of authorship. This waning power is emphasized through the humor that arises from the unlikely, even ridiculous, notion that a literary author would achieve the levels of celebrity that "Leyner" does. So while "Leyner" the author is the center of his fictional universe, the joke is on authors like the actual Leyner who clearly are not. In this sense, *Et Tu, Babe?* represents the converse of what *Breakfast of Champions* has to say about authorship, for while "Vonnegut" is fairly ineffectual within the text but clearly a powerful creative force outside it, "Leyner" is hyperbolically powerful within the text in order to demonstrate the author's relative irrelevance in our celebrity-obsessed culture. The intrusive author-character in both novels, though, constantly brings the figure of the author to the foreground of consideration, rather than allowing that figure to be relegated to the role of "author-function."

Anxieties about the decreasing cultural valence of and lack of individual agency in authorship were a primary reason for the proliferation of autofictional texts in the late 1960s until the present day. At about the same time that these poststructuralist ideas were emerging, Harold Bloom added another nail in the coffin of the powerful authorial genius with the 1973 publication of his book *The Anxiety of Influence.* In it, Bloom makes the argument that writers of the present are not only influenced by the great writers of the past but are often also stymied by that influence, tempted to replicate the work that has come before and, as a result, doomed to produce work that is inferior and derivative. "Strong poets" must have "the persistence to wrestle with their strong precursors, even to the death" (1973, 5). This is very difficult to do, according to Bloom, for as writers attempt to produce great literature themselves, they are imbued with the anxiety that they will not live up to or emerge from the influence of the great writers who came before them. This "anxiety of influence" is highly Oedipal, of course, as new generations of writers must rise up and absorb, break free of or even murder their precursors in order "to clear imaginative space for themselves" (5).[10]

On one hand, Bloom's formulation of authorship reverberates with those of Barthes and Foucault, in the sense that the writer is rather powerless in the face of the vast tradition of literary accomplishment that preceded him (and it is always "him"). On the other hand, however, Bloom's idea that a writer must—albeit unconsciously—misread and appropriate previous literary production in order to move ahead with his own work imbues the writer with a great deal of individual creative agency. It is perhaps no wonder that writers who felt their authorial authority slipping away—writers, that is, of autofiction—would embrace Bloom's concept of the author as creative genius able to emerge victorious from the tendentious fray of literary endeavor in order to take his rightful place in the long succession of literary giants. Thus the influence of *The Anxiety of Influence* can be felt, both structurally and thematically, throughout the work of the primarily male autofictionists. It can be felt structurally in the terms I have already elaborated upon: the author-character emerges within the text in order to control it from within, to highlight the continued textual presence, rather than the death, of the author. The autofictional author-character is anxious to exert an influence over his text. The power of Bloom's model of poetic creation garners its power,

Asha Varadharajan argues, "from his desire to transcend society or social constraints altogether and from his belief that the strong poet transcends the physical and geographic traumas of exile" (2008, 468). The "strong poet," in Bloom's estimation, much like Barth's "Thesean hero," still has an important role to play in the continuation of literary traditions; autofiction represents an effort to prove this is so.

The echoes of Bloom's seminal text can be seen in the themes of autofiction in the sense that a surprising number of autofictions focus on characters who feel their authorial power is being Oedipally challenged or usurped, often by a father or father figure. For example, in Ben Marcus's *Notable American Women*, "Ben" struggles to find his voice amid an authoritative family structure ruled by his mother, who has relegated his father to a pit in the backyard. The novel's narrative voice alternates between that of "Ben" and that of his father, who reviles "Ben" and undermines the veracity of everything he says. The father articulates their clearly Oedipal struggle by noting that, as the son, "[Ben] will have the final cut of this so-called introduction to his family history, and I'll not know the outcome unless he decides to share with me how he has savaged and defathered me for his own glory" (2002, 3). But Ben's father continues to grasp for the credit for "Ben's" work: "Indeed, a father is in no small way the first author of anything the son endeavors to write—is he not? . . . When so viewed, a father can rightly see his own name, Michael Marcus, just above his son's writing, instead of the name of his son" (5). In this sense, the father threatens to claim the creative power of the son as his own, and "Ben's" appearance in the novel as a character symbolizes an effort to retain that power despite his anxiety of influence.[11]

Father issues also dominate Bret Easton Ellis's *Lunar Park* when "Bret's" alcoholic and emotionally abusive father comes back to haunt him as a ghost, trying *Hamlet*-style to direct "Bret's" actions. "Bret" also suffers from an anxiety of influence of sorts, fearing—somewhat legitimately—that his own drug and alcohol abuse will preclude him from connecting to his son. In other words, "Bret" worries that he will become like his father; what he doesn't understand is that his father's ghost appears to try to stop that from happening, to help him break the cycle of addiction. "Bret's" anxiety of influence arises when he admits he has a complicated relationship to his father's abuse: although (or perhaps because) he was traumatized by it, his father's abuse was instrumental in "Bret's" becoming a writer (2005, 6). "Bret" voices a very basic fear, then, that his highly successful yet controversial writing career is somehow due to his abusive father, so that as much as he wants to disavow any connection to him, "Bret" owes his father for the parts of himself that he values most.

In contrast, "Arthur" in Arthur Phillips's *The Tragedy of Arthur* faces a different sort of conflict with his father. Arthur Sr. has always been completely enamored of Shakespeare, a love that "Arthur" has never been able to share. Rather, the figure of Shakespeare becomes both a symbolic sibling to "Arthur," always vying for and winning his father's true affection, and a substitute father figure whom "Arthur" must try to destroy through his own writing. Thus "Arthur" somewhat quixotically attacks Shakespeare, expressing disdain and disbelief that our culture has so vaunted this playwright who was, according to him, not even the best of his own time. In this sense, "Arthur" plays out the ultimate Oedipal conflict, not just against his father, not just against another writer, but against the entirety of western culture which has arguably built itself around the work of Shakespeare. Tellingly, "Arthur" decries Harold Bloom's 1998 book *Shakespeare: The Invention of the Human*, which makes this very argument, bringing full circle the anxiety of influence.

This somewhat impractical competition with Shakespeare is perhaps most succinctly expressed in the paratextual material of the novel *The Tragedy of Arthur*, in which there appears the standard list of works "Also by Arthur Phillips." Because the novel ostensibly includes the text of a heretofore unknown Shakespeare play, another list of works appears alongside Phillips's: "Also by William Shakespeare." Phillips's four other novels are then juxtaposed with the considerably longer list of Shakespeare's plays and sonnets, providing a comic and intentionally phallic comparison in which Shakespeare's is inarguably larger. By inviting this comparison of the works of the two writers, Phillips is pointing out the sad hopelessness of "Arthur's" petulant competition with Shakespeare. In this way, the inherent irony of autofiction is demonstrated: Phillips makes it clear that the character of "Arthur" is meant to be somewhat risible and that, despite sharing a name, Phillips is not "Arthur."

In the world of the novel, "Arthur" has his opportunity, if not to challenge Shakespeare's talent, at least to sit in judgment of it in a very public way. For it is revealed that his father, the Shakespeare lover, has long been in possession of a folio of a lost Shakespeare play titled, coincidentally, *The Tragedy of Arthur*. The play, which chronicles the rise and fall of legendary Arthur, King of the Britons, is fastidiously checked by experts and finally—to "Arthur's" great dismay—deemed authentic. He remains unconvinced, suspecting that his father, a convicted forger, may have written it himself. The novel, then, takes the form of a memoir-esque "preface" to the text of the supposed Shakespeare play, which appears after the preface.[12] Because his father left the play to him in his will, "Arthur" has the authority to publish the text however he likes and, therefore, to append his story to what will certainly be the most important publication of the century. This means that, in order to get to the Shakespeare, readers and scholars worldwide will have to go through "Arthur's" preface, a fact not lost upon him. In a manner reminiscent of Nabokov's Kinbote, "Arthur" somewhat haughtily declares: "But if you are to understand this play, its history, and how it came to be here, a certain quantity of my autobiography is unavoidable. . . . I certainly am not the hero. But I do have the legal right to occupy this discovery space outside the play for as long as I wish" (2011, 2). And occupy it he does, as he rather lengthily relates his own story and, in the process, attempts in Bloomian fashion to destroy Shakespeare's. Throughout the preface, "Arthur" exhorts the reader to ignore the following play, warning that it is a forgery and that "*Arthur* is bad. The play is bad. It is bad. Don't read it" (238).

"Arthur's" twin sister recognizes his rivalry with Shakespeare and, therefore, his motives for asserting that this play is not genuine: "IF IT IS and you kick and scream that it's not? Then either people will believe you and you'll succeed in tearing down Shakespeare himself, denying him a readership, proving, I suppose, once and for all that you're his equal, if not absolutely his daddy" (2011, 217). Thus *The Tragedy of Arthur* depicts "Arthur's" attempt to assert his authorial authority in the face of the greatest possible challenge to any writer's authority: the author-function that we have made of William Shakespeare. But as will always be the case, Shakespeare has the last word, as the novel ends with the authenticated play *The Tragedy of Arthur*. And, once again, it is important to point out the difference between the intertextual world in which "Arthur" must share his stage with a newly discovered Shakespeare play, and the extratextual one in which Phillips exposes his namesake avatar to humiliation and a certain amount of well-deserved comeuppance. *The Tragedy of Arthur* aptly illuminates the ironic distance between author and author-character, and it is in this distance that the playful humor of autofiction is located.

Just as "Arthur" feels his own authorial authority threatened by the inescapable juggernaut that is Shakespeare, "Percival Everett" finds a similar challenge when he is tapped by a staffer of white-supremacist hero Senator Strom Thurmond to ghostwrite Thurmond's proposed book, *A History of the African-American People*. This novel, whose lengthy title is *A History of the African-American People [Proposed] by Strom Thurmond as Told to Percival Everett and James Kincaid [A Novel]*, is one of the few autofictions by an African American writer and consists of letters written between the various participants in this book project. "Percival Everett" (like his real-world namesake) is a black novelist and is understandably concerned and more than a little curious about why Strom Thurmond would want to write a history of "the African American people," why he would want "Everett's" help with the project, and what qualifies Thurmond to undertake it in the first place. Mostly out of curiosity, "Everett" agrees to work on this book. Thurmond's staffer then begins to send "Everett" example after example, supposedly researched by Thurmond himself, of historical figures making apologias for racist actions and legislation. The staffer exhorts "Everett" to "write up" these examples into some kind of coherent historical account, a project that is not only odious but seemingly impossible, although Simon & Schuster is supposedly quite interested in publishing the finished work. Eventually the project collapses under its own weight, and Strom Thurmond, Godot-like, never actually appears but rather remains a distant yet influential persona: an absent author-figure. Furthermore, Thurmond represents the "great white father" who threatens (with the help of a major publishing house) to shape a historical account of African Americans, the very people he spent his career trying to deny their civil and human rights. "Everett," while wary of the project, inserts himself into it in order to maintain a modicum of control over a story that should belong to him more than to Thurmond. All he can do, however, is watch mostly from the sidelines as the writing and publishing of the narrative remain largely under white control. His authorial intrusion into the project does not provide him any greater influence over it. Rather, it is made manifestly clear that it is Thurmond who has the institutional and financial imprimatur to tell this or any story.

It is not always a father figure who threatens to usurp the autofictional author-character's authority. For example, in Philip Roth's *Operation Shylock*, "Philip" discovers that a man resembling him is traveling through Israel claiming to be Philip Roth and trading on Roth's reputation as a Jewish celebrity in order to advocate a controversial scheme to relocate Jews of European descent back to Europe (1994, 44). The fact that this man is somewhat successful in garnering support using Roth's name demonstrates the slipperiness of authorial authority and supports the Foucauldian argument that such authority is attached not to the physical figure of the author but to his culturally constructed persona.

When "Philip" travels to Israel to confront this man, the impostor chides "Philip" for not using his writing ability and his authorial celebrity to do more to help the Jews, something for which Roth himself has been scolded many times (1994, 41). *Operation Shylock*, then, depicts a character who embodies all the accusations Roth has faced of betraying the Jews in his fiction, and the character of "Philip" has the opportunity to confront and ultimately defeat this accuser within the text and, therefore, all other accusers outside it. In true Oedipal fashion, "Philip" sleeps with his rival's girlfriend, who tells "Philip" that the false Philip is impotent and must rely on a penile implant. In this way, the character of "Philip" metaphorically castrates the man who would appropriate his authorial authority (while the extratextual Roth has a hand in that castration as well, choosing to portray the impostor as having erectile dysfunction). The autofictional entrance of the author-character into the novel emphasizes the sense of urgency felt by writers to exert whatever control possible on their authorial persona, or at least to portray that sense of urgency in their narratives.

John Barth's *Coming Soon!!!* is yet another example of Oedipal autofiction, but this one depicts both the metaphorical father as well as the son, and in this narrative, it is the father who emerges victorious. Much of this novel is presented from the point of view of Johns Hopkins "Hop" Johnson. Hop is an aspiring novelist who engages in a novel-writing competition with eminent novelist "John Barth." Hop writes what he calls "c-fiction": "where the traditional job-descriptions of 'author' and 'reader' (or, one might say, of Daedalus and Theseus) are up for grabs" (2001, 13). Originally Hop wants to collaborate with "John Barth," to combine their efforts to create one single "metanovel," consisting innovatively of one "e" version and one "p" (print) version. "Barth" demurs, suggesting instead that they hold a race to see who can finish his respective novel first. The two writers agree to these terms while urinating side by side in the men's room. As if this setting does not make clear enough the fact that this writing competition equates to a penis-length competition, "Barth" responds to Hop's declaration that he writes with a keyboard rather than a pen by saying "Too bad for you. . . . You've lost hold of a basic metaphor" (105). Once again, "Barth's" comment demonstrates that autofiction is a primarily masculine arena.

In *Coming Soon!!!* the generational challenge is clear: "Barth" represents the traditional print novelist who exerts authorial mastery to craft the story (he is, after all, the "Thesean hero"), while Hop is writing e-fiction (now typically referred to as "digital storytelling" or "hypertext") in which the reader, by clicking where he/she wants, is instrumental in providing a structure for the content written by Hop. So whereas "Barth" strives to maintain authorial authority, Hop consciously cedes much of that authority to the reader. By the end, Hop is unable to finish his novel and unable in any case to find a prospective publisher for the portion he has completed. In the Oedipal contest "Barth" (and, of course, Barth) emerge, having won a victory for the older narrative traditions of individual authorial authority. As Bloom suspected all along, the old masters always emerge victorious.

In addition to the generational conflict, *Coming Soon!!!* also represents the perceived increasing threat that new media pose to novelists. Published in 2001, *Coming Soon!!!* depicts as ominous the development of e-fiction or hypertextual, digital storytelling, in which readers have a role to play in constructing the text by choosing the order in which they will read its content. Traditional "p-fiction," as Hop terms it, "is destined to become . . . ever more a pleasure for special tastes, like poetry, archery, opera-going, equestrian dressage" (2001, 22). This new-fangled e-fictional trend (or at least Barth's concept of it) is even represented in the pages of *Coming Soon!!!* which often includes images of "buttons" that a reader can pretend to click as he/she moves through the novel. John Barth has tentatively explored this medium, albeit a print version thereof, in his 1997 short story "Click." In it, the reader is given the illusion of options on which to click but which, being print, are not "active."[13] Like a true postmodernist, Barth gives the illusion of reader choice but maintains tight control of the authorial reins. In *Coming Soon!!!* the potential threat to traditional print narrative posed by e-fiction is neutralized by the fact that Hop cannot finish his novel, which has become an unwieldy and incomprehensible monster on a 3.5-inch floppy disk. In reality, in the almost two decades since *Coming Soon!!!* was published, hypertext failed to revolutionize fiction writing and reading in the ways many anticipated, and the traditional novel is still a very popular genre.

However, even though it may not typically take the form of hypertext, the undeniable effects of digital "new media" are being felt by those dedicated to traditional print culture. Digital media provide new modes for written communication and new opportunities for increasing numbers of people to disseminate their written work to large audiences. In other words, through internet social media anyone can be a writer, and a single individual can even garner a huge following and substantial advertising revenue. Much attention has been paid to the effect that myriad social media have had on traditional media outlets such as newspapers and publishing houses. But there has also been a real effect on the cultural view of authorship, an effect John Barth was already articulating in "The Literature of Exhaustion" when he lamented that the "intermedia arts" threatened to eliminate the "most traditional notion of the artist" as a man endowed with "uncommon talent" and "virtuosity." Barth recognized the "aristocratic" nature of his view of authorship as being something for which only a few select men were fit. Barth's thoughts in 1967 anticipate the argument of media scholars like Paul Levinson, who in 1997 noted that these aristocratic notions of the artist tend to develop simultaneously with the advent of emergent technologies: "Indeed, new media since the printing press have in every case served to ultimately further the democratization it engendered, with the result that critics of the new media have usually been defenders of the elite, attempting to bar the new onslaught of the masses" (1997, 56). Loren Daniel Glass makes a similar point in *Authors, Inc.* when he argues that with the rise of popular fiction during the nineteenth century, "The national mass public came to consist of potential authors and cultural producers; readers became theoretically interchangeable with the famous authors whose texts they read" (2004, 11). In this sense, then, the development of new media could also be read as an Oedipal conflict of sorts, as this technological "son" threatens to overthrow, if not the cultural legitimacy, definitely the primacy of its parental print genres.

The infringement on print culture perpetrated by digital media has instigated a lament that the novel is dead and exacerbated the fears that the author is, too.[14] Kathleen Fitzpatrick has theorized that "the discourse of postmodernism is cultural criticism's expression of the anxiety of obsolescence" (2006, 46), meaning that cultural fears about the loss of the subject and the author, the decline of the novel amid the rise of new media, the death of the author, and the loss of Jean-François Lyotard's "master narrative" are all centered around the fear of obsolescence. But these fears of obsolescence may not reflect actual threats to cultural mores. About literary fiction, she argues: "By depicting the genre as an endangered species, critics and novelists alike have built a protected space around the novel—and, not incidentally, the novelist—in which the form and its practitioners are kept safe from the encroachments of the changing contemporary world" (26). I would argue that it is from this protective environment that the autofictional author-character emerges, symbolically entering his narrative turf and thus attempting to "protect" his authorial authority from within.

At times, the protection afforded by the author-character is evoked through his/her emerging in the novel as a minor character, described in the third person. These third-person author-characters are generally depicted as somewhat menacing, as though the enemies with whom they are engaged are the other characters in the novel. Such characters ("Martin Amis" in *Money,* "Paul Auster" in *City of Glass,* "Douglas Coupland" in *JPod,* and "Jerry Shteynfarb" in Gary Shteyngart's *Absurdistan*) tend to hover like bystanders around the central action in a vaguely threatening way, often seeming to harm protagonists under the guise of trying to help. "Paul Auster" expresses concern for protagonist Quinn, but is accused at the end of the novel of having treated him badly. "Martin Amis" sits gleefully by as the life and career of gluttonous protagonist John Self implodes, helping Self unravel the mystery of how it all happened, but not exerting any authorial power on his behalf. "Jerry Shteynfarb" undermines the protagonist and steals his girlfriend, while "Douglas Coupland" emerges repeatedly and coincidentally in protagonist Ethan's life until, at the end, Ethan and all the other characters end up working for him. In each case, these third-person minor author-characters exude either impotent powerlessness or malicious ill will.

A particularly striking example of third-person autofiction is Salvador Plascencia's *The People of Paper* (2005). In this novel, "Salvador" (usually referred to in the novel by the godlike moniker "Saturn") focuses his attention on the small town of El Monte, California. The characters he has created there somehow sense, resent, and ultimately resist his authorial presence. To thwart his omniscient gaze, the townspeople cover their homes with lead and remain indoors: "Saturn's power is of a piercing strength, able to penetrate asbestos and wood shingles, tar paper, plywood" (2005, 84). Federico de la Fe, the instigator of the resistance movement, tells his fellow characters: "We are part of Saturn's story. Saturn owns it. We are being listened to and watched, our lives sold as entertainment. But if we fight we might be able to gain control, to shield ourselves and live our lives for ourselves" (53). Thus *The People of Paper* foregrounds the inherent colonizing nature of the omniscient author-figure, a nature made overtly manifest when "Saturn" resolves to rout the insurrection of his characters in order to impress his ex-girlfriend, who left him for a white man (Plascencia is Latino): "A whole war for you. To prove that I too am a colonizer, I too am powerful in those ways. I can stand on my tippy toes, I can curl my tongue and talk that perfect untainted English, I can wipe out whole cultures, whole towns of imaginary flower people" (238). In this way, *The People of Paper* reiterates the connection I have been making between authorial authority and white male privilege, as "Saturn" attempts to assert that privilege, first by creating, then surveilling, then destroying a town full of people. The autofictional elements of the novel amplify that idea, as we are forced to make the connection between the striving yet troubled author-character and Plascencia himself.

Not only are autofictions by women and people of color shockingly rare (given how commonplace they are among white male writers), but when they do appear, such works often employ the third person to represent their author-characters, rather than the first-person narratives that are more typical with white male writers. It is as though the author-characters in such autofictions are reluctant or unable to assume the authority of the first person—authority that seems to come as easily as a birthright to authors steeped in white male privilege. Two female autofictions of interest here include Kathy Acker's 1988 *Empire of the Senseless*, in which the controlling computer construct "Kathy" is referred to only once, and Ruth Ozeki's 2013 *A Tale for the Time Being*, in which "Ruth" is one of two main protagonists.[15] Percival Everett's 2009 *I Am Not Sidney Poitier* is one of three autofictions written by Everett, and the minor character "Professor

Everett" is rendered here in the third person.[16] I grant that these are only a few examples and not nearly enough for a substantial analysis of the effects of nonwhite and female writers on autofiction. However, it is notable that the third-person author-characters in these works, particularly *I Am Not Sidney Poitier* and *A Tale for the Time Being*, are neither impotent nor malignant, but rather seek to help their protagonists (*The People of Paper* notwithstanding). Furthermore, "Professor Everett" and "Ruth Ozeki" help their protagonists through collaboration, not control.

For example, "Professor Everett" serves as mentor and friend to the protagonist in *I Am Not Sidney Poitier*, even crossing state lines to bail him out of jail. Rather than exert authorial authority, "Professor Everett" tells the protagonist: "I'm going to hip you to the truth. I'm a fraud, a fake, a sham, a charlatan, a deceiver, a pretender, a crook" (2009, 101). Japanese American Canadian writer Ruth Ozeki provides an even more experimental use of the author-character in *A Tale for the Time Being*. This novel alternates between the first-person diary of sixteen-year-old Nao (pronounced "now"), a Japanese American girl who has moved with her family to Tokyo after her father lost his job, and the third-person story of "Ruth Ozeki," who lives on a remote island off the coast of British Columbia and finds Nao's journal washed up on the shore as detritus from the 2011 tsunami that hit Japan. As "Ruth" reads the journal, she becomes more and more engaged in Nao's troubled life and wishes to help her but realizes that the account she is reading must be several years old at least. Yet "Ruth" finds that Nao's journal alters in response to her reading of it, and ultimately "Ruth" is able to have an effect on the lives of the people Nao describes in her journal. Although she and "Ruth" never meet, Nao often directly addresses her imagined reader and eventually begins to lose faith in a reader who could be her friend; in other words, Nao loses faith in the power of her own writing to save herself. As a result of this loss of faith, part of Nao's narrative disappears before "Ruth" can read it, leaving only blank pages behind. "Ruth" wonders if, just as she has conjured Nao by reading her narrative, Nao has in turn conjured her by writing it. "Ruth," a writer herself, determines that she must somehow find the missing words and thereby help Nao; it is important to note that she wants to *find* Nao's words, not write them herself. "Ruth" wants to read Nao's story, not create it, saying, "I don't like having that much agency over someone else's narrative" (2013, 377). By helping Nao, by finding her words, "Ruth" is able to finish her own story, so that, in a way, each writes the other into being.

Thus, unlike most of the autofictions I have been discussing, the author-characters in evidence here do not seem to be attempting and failing to exert authorial control, but rather attempting and succeeding in making connections to their protagonists and using what power they have to aid them in a sort of parental or collaborative role. To make this point, "Ruth" quotes Japanese writer Irokawa Budai as saying, "There is no God in the Japanese tradition, no monolithic ordering authority in narrative" (2013, 148). For "Ruth" and "Professor Everett," the protagonist is not the enemy (as in *Money*), or a figure of ridicule or pity (as in *City of Glass* and *Absurdistan*), but a ward or surrogate child. Perhaps for that reason, these author-characters do not evince any of the "anxiety of obsolescence" that Kathleen Fitzpatrick outlines. It could be surmised that one reason these authors do not feel obsolete or disempowered is because, being from underrepresented groups, they never were empowered in the first place. Fitzpatrick puts it this way: "anxiety of obsolescence both requires social privilege to be mobilized as a discourse and conceals the repressed anxiety that the threatened disappearance of that privilege engenders" (2006, 20). Writers like Everett and Ozeki do not have the social privilege to feel threatened by the loss of a cultural supremacy that takes the form of fear of obsolescence. Thus, in contrast to the famous "impresario" author-character in *The French Lieutenant's Woman* who, by turning back his watch, turns back time and forces his characters to play out three different endings of his own design, "Ruth" and "Professor Everett" work *with* their protagonists to achieve a mutually beneficial goal. For "Ruth" in particular, Nao has as much narrative agency as she, and they depend equally upon one another to bring their respective stories to a happy ending.

Autofiction emerges in connection with the anxieties about the nature and potential power of authorship that began to emerge in the advent of poststructuralist literary theory. Autofictional author-characters appear as a means to depict, combat, and sometimes overcome the perceived diminishing power of authorship, at times demonstrating its continued importance, at times that it is indeed on the wane. In this chapter I have attempted to trace this anxiety about waning authorial authority through the New Criticism, through the advent of poststructuralist literary theory to the increasing ubiquity of celebrity culture and the vicissitudes of emergent new media.

3 The New Journalism as the New Fiction

Tom Wolfe, Norman Mailer, Hunter S. Thompson,
Joan Didion, Mark Leyner, and Bret Easton Ellis

We were not writing autobiography or confession—we were at times
using those forms as ways of incorporating our experience into fiction
at the same level as any other data.

—Ronald Sukenick, "Thirteen Digressions"

Simultaneous with the rise of the poststructuralist theory that reconsidered the role of language and writing in meaning-making was the rise of what came to be known in the 1960s as the "New Journalism," among many other names.[1] For example, Tom Wolfe used the terms "new journalism," "literary journalism," and "participant journalism." *New Yorker* writer Dwight Macdonald (1965, 3) coined "parajournalism," which he meant pejoratively: "It is a bastard form having it both ways, exploiting the factual authority of journalism and the atmospheric license of fiction. Entertainment rather than information is the aim of its producers." David L. Eason claims that the self-consciously florid style of the New Journalism evokes a similarly self-conscious reaction in the reader, making this "metajournalism." Robert Sam Anson invented the term "gonzo journalism" to describe the work of Hunter S. Thompson. And both Wolfe and Thompson used "saturation reporting." All these designations were used to describe a form of reportage that embraced the writing techniques of fiction rather than the bare-bones, fact-heavy writing style of traditional journalism.[2]

As explained by Wolfe—one of the New Journalism's most famous practitioners and arguably its most vocal exponent—this new style of reporting involved the use of "techniques which had been thought of as confined to the novel or the short story, to create in one form both the kind of objective reality of journalism and the subjective reality that people have always gone to the novel for" (quoted in Dennis and Rivers 2011, 6). In essence, the New Journalism blurred the distinction between journalistic and literary writing, while attempting to maintain the boundary between factual reporting and fictional narrative. David Lodge, for example, points out that "the novel itself as a literary form evolved partly out of early journalism—broadsheets, pamphlets, criminals' 'confessions,' accounts of disasters, battles, and extraordinary happenings, which were circulated to an eagerly credulous readership as true stories, though they almost certainly contained an element of invention" (1992, 203). While this view of the history of the novel suggests that fiction and journalism have always been interconnected, journalistic conventions of the late nineteenth to the mid-twentieth century had insisted upon a clear demarcation between the two. By the 1960s, fiction had become accepted as the primary mode for evoking strong emotional identification in a reader, while journalism was considered to be a mode of more or less purely objective and accurate reportage. Thus the emergence of the New Journalism of the late 1960s marked a shift in journalistic focus toward producing factual reporting that engaged the reader in the way that a fictional narrative would.

In service of this goal, self-styled "New Journalists" turned away from the traditional role of the objective outsider recording observations. Rather, they became famous for throwing themselves headlong into their stories by immersing themselves in the world they were investigating. For example, Hunter S. Thompson actually became a member of the Hells Angels in order to report on them. Often (but not always) the complete submersion of the writer into his/her subject matter resulted in the inclusion of the writer's own persona within the resulting narrative. Some of these New Journalists began routinely breaking one of the cardinal rules of journalism by depicting themselves as integral parts of the story. For this reason, such works of metajournalism can be seen as a precursor to the current popularity of the memoir genre (which I discuss in chapter 5) and a precursor of autofiction as well.

Because the New Journalism began to emerge in the form of lengthy or serialized magazine profiles (rather than shorter newspaper articles), this form paved the way for the emergence of a longer journalistic/narrative genre that came to be known as the "nonfiction novel," defined by

David L. Eason as "the application of fictional techniques in the construction of a report of an actual situation" (1979, 1). The nonfiction novel has alternatively been called faction, hystory, or the documentary novel. Truman Capote created the term "faction" to describe his 1966 novel *In Cold Blood*, which he deemed to be of an entirely new literary genre. He also used the term "nonfiction novel" to describe that work, but he was not the first to have used that term. Robert Scholes coined "hystory," and his definition highlights the facet of New Journalism most related to autofiction: "The hystorian fights this tendency toward formula with his own personality. He asserts the importance of *his* impressions and *his* vision of the world" (1968).

In terms of New Journalism, these nonfiction novels sometimes took the form of book-length versions of serial magazine articles (like Norman Mailer's *Armies of the Night*), but were sometimes presented as longer works of fact-based narrative written in a literary style (like Truman Capote's *In Cold Blood*). The term "nonfiction novel" was not coined during the heyday of the New Journalism, as John Russell points out, but has had a long history of interconnectedness with the fictional novel.[3] I would agree with Russell that this long history indicates that "the place the nonfiction novel holds . . . bridges a clear distinction between fiction and literary journalism" (2000, 2). In other words—much like its New Journalistic cousins—the nonfiction novel straddles the line between fiction and nonfiction and reveals changing perceptions about the nature of both. And while there are as many methods of performing this mode of fiction-styled nonfiction as there are names for it, particular examples of New Journalism and the nonfiction novel can be seen as direct methodological and philosophical precursors to the kind of autofiction this book discusses.

In the late 1960s and early 1970s, both supporters and detractors of the New Journalism tended to boil its essential issues down to the question of the difference between fact and fiction. The primary focus for studies of this journalistic style involve a discussion of whether writing can ever convey the "truth" or whether all writing is by its very nature fictional. In this sense, the New Journalism was grappling with the very same questions as the poststructuralist theory discussed in chapter 2 (and, for that matter, the problems surrounding the art of faithful storytelling raised by the autofictions discussed in chapters 4 and 5). But whereas the poststructuralists were adherents of the theory that all writing was fictional, the New Journalists, as well as those autofictionists influenced by them, maintained a vital dedication to the idea that writing can, even must, convey the "Capital-T Truth." In other words, as stylistically innovative and philosophically sophisticated as they were, the New Journalists were nonetheless journalists.

Some New Journalistic nonfiction novels are quite predictive of the autofictional trend such as Tom Wolfe's chronicle of Ken Kesey's Merry Prankster movement, *The Electric Kool-Aid Acid Test* (1968), Norman Mailer's historico-journalistic trilogy depicting various social and political happenings (*The Armies of the Night* [1968], *Miami and the Siege of Chicago* [1968], and *Of a Fire on the Moon* [1971]), and Hunter S. Thompson's *Fear and Loathing in Las Vegas* (1972), which begins as an assignment to cover a vintage car race and evolves (devolves?) into a futile, drug-addled search for the so-called American Dream. Joan Didion's essays, compiled in books such as *Slouching toward Bethlehem* (1968) and *The White Album* (1979), take a slightly different tack, relating her personal perspective on contemporary culture. Works like these are of particular relevance to contemporary autofiction because they experiment with first- and third-person narration and feature the prominent intrusion of an author-character into the narrative. Because this highlighting—even centering—of the writer-observer in the written account is anathema to traditional journalism, it would be helpful for my argument to begin with a brief but comprehensive history of the rise of New Journalism, including a discussion of its main practitioners and its philosophical underpinnings. Such an examination brings to light the connections between the "participant-observer" in the New Journalism and the "author-character" in autofiction.

John Hollowell traces the origins of the New Journalism to the cultural upheaval that took place during the 1960s and "diverted the impulse for fiction into the special kind of journalism" (1977, 5). In Hollowell's estimation, happenings in the country were so vibrant and incendiary that traditional journalistic methods no longer sufficed for some journalists; more innovative methods of reportage were necessary to depict the perceived urgency of these events. Scholes argued that the excesses of style employed by the likes of Wolfe and Mailer "are in my view no more than indispensable equipment they must employ in doing justice to our times.

This is not to say that one must himself be hysterical to chronicle hysteria, but to suggest that hysteria cannot be assimilated and conveyed by one who is totally aloof" (1968, 37).

Even fiction writers struggled to make sense of this purportedly outrageous historical moment: for example, Philip Roth claims in his oft-cited article "Writing American Fiction," "The American writer in the middle of the twentieth century has his hands full in trying to understand, describe, and then make credible much of American reality. . . . The actuality is continually outdoing our talents, and the culture tosses up figures almost daily that are the envy of any novelist" (2001b, 120). And although it is, of course, ahistorical and somewhat narcissistic to assert that one lives in the most extreme period in history (in the past century alone, writers have made similar claims about the period after World War I, the post-Holocaust period, the days immediately following 9/11, and the current Trump administration), a survey of 1960s and 1970s analyses of the New Journalism indicates that this was indeed a widespread perception.[4] However, not all such analyses make this claim to historical uniqueness; below I will argue that we might just as accurately attribute the rise of the New Journalism not to unprecedented times but to emergent scientific and philosophical innovations.

Furthermore, not all analysts trace the beginning of the New Journalism to the 1960s. Everette E. Dennis and William L. Rivers go back further in history to link its inception to the complexities generated by reporting on the specifics of the New Deal, a time when the public statements of political officials were irreconcilable with the facts of a given situation. While it is unlikely that the 1930s marked the first time public figures lied to journalists, Dennis and Rivers's argument is that it was in this period that some journalists began to depart from the strict reporting of facts that had heretofore been the style. As Hollowell puts it: "The new journalism reflects a decreased deference toward public officials indicative of the decline in authority throughout society" (1977, 23). According to this interpretation, faced with evasive and mendacious public figures in the 1930s, some journalists "began to build the interpretative reporting structure that made its way back to city rooms everywhere" (Dennis and Rivers 2011, 2). To complicate its history even further, John C. Hartsock dates the first inceptions of new ideas about journalistic standards even earlier, to the end of the nineteenth century.

But however one dates the origins of New Journalism, it is clear that the main practitioners emerged in the 1960s. While they engaged with various types of subject matter using different styles, there was a kind of tacit agreement among these New Journalists that their goal was to employ what were usually considered literary (novelistic) techniques to present factual information in order to affect the reader more viscerally than traditional journalism was able to do.[5] According to Gay Talese, one of the New Journalism's most famous proponents, this form of journalism "seeks a larger truth than is possible through the mere compilation of verifiable facts, the use of direct quotations, and adherence to the rigid organizational style of the older form" (Talese 1970, vii).

In other words, the New Journalists eschewed the straightforward, often somewhat dry transmission of pure and unadorned factual information that had been the hallmark of traditional journalism since the early twentieth century. Rather, this new breed of journalists saw it as their mission "to reveal the story hidden beneath the surface facts" (Hollowell 1977, 23). To that end, New Journalists took up many of the stylistic strategies typically associated with fiction, such as including vivid descriptions of scenes and full conversations in dialogue, rather than short quotations from one witness at a time. Additionally and somewhat more controversially, New Journalists sometimes employed what came to be called "composite characters," or single characters crafted to represent an amalgam of real people. Frankly speaking, however, the only difference between a "composite character" and a full-fledged fictional character is a semantic one.[6]

New Journalists used these "literary" approaches in order to provide what they felt was a fuller picture of events, to immerse readers in the action the way that, heretofore, only fiction had been able to do. To that end, one of the most controversial elements of the New Journalism was the attempt to depict the subjects' internal frame of mind as the action was taking place, a feat that involved writing from that subject's point of view, rather than the objective journalistic one. Tom Wolfe in particular was noted for his rapid shifts of point of view from one subject to another and then back to that of the seemingly objective observer.

This shifting point of view between that of the journalist and of the person being portrayed or between various people being portrayed was often seen by traditional journalists as irresponsible and misleading, and understandably so, for it is highly debatable whether one could label as "nonfiction" the depiction of the inner workings of another person's mind. Traditional journalists protested that no writer could actually *know* what was going through the mind of someone about whom he/she was reporting. Writers like Wolfe and Truman Capote argued that their total immersion in the reportorial milieu and the in-depth research of every aspect of the story authorized them to surmise (and then depict in a vivid manner) the internal thought processes of their subjects. Both writers conducted exhaustive interviews with their subjects (most notably Ken Kesey for Wolfe's *Electric Kool-Aid Acid Test* and Dick Hickock and Perry Smith for Capote's *In Cold Blood*), and through these interviews they were able—they argued—to reconstruct the events being depicted and even reconstruct the state of the participants' minds. The resulting narratives include portrayals of events that are so vivid as to imply that their narrators were eyewitnesses. However, Wolfe was not actually present for the activities on the Merry Pranksters' *Furthur* bus in *Acid Test* (although he was there when Kesey was released from jail at the end), and Capote was certainly not present for the murders of the Clutter family in Holcomb, Kansas. Their highly descriptive and literary accounts of these events led many at the time to question whether the resulting narratives could actually be referred to as "journalism."

Another controversial yet common aspect of the New Journalism (and the one that leads most directly to the rise of autofiction) was that, in many cases, the point of view of the journalist him/herself became central to the telling of the story. This, of course, flies in the face of the traditional journalistic edict that the reporter must not become part of the story but rather must efface him/herself in order to report objectively. It was thought that if the reporter admitted his/her presence in the scene, the resulting report would be tainted with the subjective responses of the reporter, thus making the story less accurate. The adversarial stance the New Journalists took toward this tradition of objectivity was similar to the stance taken by the postmodern autofictionists toward the modernist imperative of impersonality. Furthermore, because the connection is unmistakable between journalistic objectivity and the modernist impersonality, it makes sense that New Journalism's challenges to the former emerged coterminously with postmodernism's metafictional challenges to the latter.

The New Journalistic rejection of the tenet of pure objectivity reflected a mind-set that, according to Ronald Weber, had been slowly emerging among a new generation of journalists. Weber articulates this new philosophy so well that a lengthy quotation is warranted:

> In the 1960s many reporters—often better trained than their predecessors, more professional in their attitudes, and consequently more self-conscious about themselves as professionals—grew notably restive with the detached, impersonal, seemingly objective point of view that dominated journalistic writing. They argued that in reality the reporter was never a totally neutral figure, that inevitably something of the personal crept into his work. Furthermore, to deny the shaping presence of the reporter because of theoretical demands of detachment and objectivity was to be fundamentally dishonest with the reader as well as oneself. Impersonal journalism implied that detachment was accuracy, that whatever was stripped of individual feeling and judgment was therefore to be trusted and relied upon. Professional newsmen increasingly offered evidence that this was not the case. (Weber 1980, 23)

The New Journalists realized that, try as one might, the perspective and biases of the observer—the journalist—could never be completely scrubbed from the resulting work. In order to achieve a more accurate representation of their subjects, then, the New Journalists overtly referred in their writing to their presence at the scene, to their role as observer of it, and sometimes even to the possible influence their observing might have had. By addressing and even emphasizing their own presence, they hoped to give as full a picture of the situation as possible in the belief that to obscure their own consciousness from the piece would be to negate the central force that organized and composed the piece in the first place. In other words, to deny or efface the presence of the writer would thereby omit one of the central facets of any work of journalism: the "who" of "who, what, when, where, and how." Thus traditional journalistic objectivity serves only to obscure bias, not to eradicate it. The quote from Weber demonstrates that the work of the New Journalists is indicative of the distrust of totalizing journalistic traditions that posited the reporter as a detached and completely objective observer; this distrust can be connected, of course, temporally and in spirit to the feminist and poststructuralist theories discussed in previous chapters.

New Journalism arose amid multiple cultural discussions about whether true objectivity was even possible, in reporting or anywhere else. And it was not just the objectivity of the detached journalistic point of view that was being challenged but the entire means by which a work of journalistic writing is composed and presented to the public. As Lester Markel, a seasoned reporter, explained in a March 11, 1961, article in the *Sunday Review* entitled "Interpretation of Interpretation," pure objectivity is impossible, even in the method for getting, writing, and publishing a story (and again, a long quotation makes the case very well):

> The reporter, the most objective reporter, collects fifty facts. Out of the fifty he selects twelve to include in his story (there is such a thing as space limitation). Thus he discards thirty-eight. This is Judgment Number One. Then the reporter or editor decides which of the facts shall be the first paragraph of the story, thus emphasizing one fact above the other eleven. This is Judgment Number Two. Then the editor decides whether the story shall be placed on Page One or Page Twelve; on Page One it will command many times the attention it would on Page Twelve. This is Judgment Number Three. This so-called factual presentation is thus subjected to three judgments, all of them most humanly and most ungodly made. (Markel, as quoted in Dennis and Rivers 2011, 3)

Here Markel articulates the journalist's conception of the poststructuralist worldview that emerges around this time: that there is no way to use language or writing to access an objective truth, if such a truth even exists. Markel argues that, through no fault of its own, journalism cannot generate godlike objectivity in the face of human decision-making. The molding and creating power of the journalistic writer (and publication editor) is in evidence throughout the story, whether the writer overtly admits it or not.

One example of a late century text that grapples with the difficulty of presenting the truth of historical events through the use of carefully curated "evidence" and the imperfect vehicle of language is Tim O'Brien's 1994 novel, *In the Lake of the Woods*. It relates the mystery of the disappearance of John Wade's wife, Kathy. This mystery is never definitively solved, despite the inclusion of several chapters entitled "Evidence" that list snippets from various disparate sources. Also included are authorial footnotes that provide "O'Brien's" perspective on the situation. The novel's initial implication is that all this evidence could provide a cumulative portrait of a marriage, definitive answers to Kathy's disappearance, and a clear sense of the My Lai Massacre, one of the central events of the novel. Quite early on, however, we realize that no concrete answers are available: "Even much of what might appear to be fact in this narrative—action, word, thought—must ultimately be viewed as a diligent but still imaginative reconstruction of events. I have tried, of course, to be faithful to the evidence. Yet evidence is not truth. It is only evident" (2006, 30). Here, as in Weber's point about journalism, the evidence is simply a series of judgments made by a writer about what to include (and exclude) in order to shape the narrative. If it even exists, the "truth" is not revealed, no matter how diligent the chronicler.

Arguably, Weber and Markel's ideas suggest at least a modicum of mainstream acceptance, not only of poststructuralist theories but also of the particular scientific principles that had emerged decades earlier and fueled those theories in the first place. For example, Werner Heisenberg's Uncertainty Principle determined in 1927 that the more accurately the *speed* of a particle was measured, the less able one would be to measure its *location* and vice versa. Thus the exact velocity *and* location of a particle could never be known, so the entire truth about a particle could never be known. By the late 1960s, this idea had seemingly seeped into the larger cultural consciousness, having an effect on the New Journalists, who recognize that pure objective knowledge is impossible. Similarly, the scientific concept of the "observer effect" indicates that the act of observing a particular phenomenon alters the outcome of the measurement of that phenomenon, necessitating that the presence of the observer be accounted for in scientific measurements, particularly those at a subatomic level. This effect has, of course, been witnessed on a broader human level as well. One iteration of the measured effect that observation has on human behavior is what was called the Hawthorne Effect. Coined in 1958, this term refers to an experiment done on workers at the Hawthorne Electrical plant, who seemed to work more efficiently while researchers were observing their output. Thus the awareness of being observed altered the workers' behavior. The influence of these various forms of observer effect is particularly potent in autofiction and in the work of some New Journalists, as these narratives overtly recognize the presence of the observer—or narrator—within the narrative, as Weber explains above. What I am driving at is that the effect of these various scientific, psychological, and philosophical theories can be seen in the New Journalism and the literary texts it spawned. As David L. Eason puts it: "Loss of faith in the objectivity assumption puts the question of a singular truth in doubt and proves an occasion for a redefinition of the role of the reporter in relation to the event he reports, the institutional framework of which he is a part, the form through which he communicates, and the audience which he addresses" (1979, 15–16). The New Journalists stepped in to try to perform that redefinition.

The combination of scientific theories about the limits of knowledge, poststructuralist concerns about the nature of language, and a desire to provide a more vital and intense reading and writing experience resulted in the central paradox of the New Journalism. On one hand, New Journalists felt that techniques usually reserved for fiction would provide a more direct connection with the reality and the spirit of the times, but this initiative burgeoned in concert with the realization that language is by its very nature unable to convey an absolute "truth," which had heretofore been the putative goal of journalism. Literary technique simultaneously represented a powerful tool that journalists were finally authorized to use and an instrument always already blunted by the inherent inadequacy of language and the ultimate unknowability of the world itself.

The effects of these issues on postmodern fiction have been well documented; they resulted in a turn toward the experimental and the metafictional in contemporary literature. As Robert Scholes (1975, 7) so famously declared, "It is because reality cannot be recorded that realism is dead. All writing, all composition, is construction. We do not imitate the world, we construct versions of it. There is no mimesis, only poiesis. No recording. Only construction." From this idea arose the sense that literary realism was no longer a viable mode of writing and that literature was in a "decidedly post-realistic period" (Weber 1980, 11). The result of such a conclusion had different implications for novelists than it did for journalists. For novelists, the idea that the nature of language made realism impossible spurred the impulse to explore what language *could* do in fiction, if it could not construct an accurate picture of the world as it is. What emerged are the much-discussed experimental metafictions of authors such as John Barth, John Barthelme, Robert Coover, Kurt Vonnegut, and Kathy Acker. Included in such experiments, of course, were the autofictional depictions of authorial characters that I examine in this book.

In terms of journalism, these poststructuralist ideas about the vexed relationship between language and reality resulted in the experiments of the New Journalists. Perhaps somewhat surprisingly, these experiments were often diametrically opposed to the novelistic ones. For example, to Tom Wolfe, New Journalism (or what he calls the "social novels" that emerged from that movement) represented an emphatic turning *away* from literary experimentation and an embrace of traditional literary realism combined with journalistic reportage. What literary fiction would no longer do, Wolfe decreed, New Journalism would do with a vengeance. Wolfe describes how literary critics of the 1940s began to talk about the "death of the novel," as they disdained the realistic novel as a genre written to legitimate and cement the values and worldview of the bourgeois class. Wolfe disagreed that literary realism was bourgeois, although he did agree that the novel was dead. Realism, he argued, while increasingly rejected by literary writers, had been embraced by journalists and put to use in service of the general public rather than the literary elite. For Wolfe, the New Journalism represented the apotheosis of journalistic "lumpenproles" to the ranks of cultural prominence once inhabited by vaunted literary novelists, as journalists appropriated for themselves the stylistic elements of literary realism:

> And so all of a sudden, in the mid-Sixties, here comes a bunch of these lumpenproles, no less, a bunch of slick-magazine and Sunday-supplement writers with no literary credentials whatsoever in most cases—only they're using all the techniques of the novelists, even the most sophisticated ones—and on top of that they're helping themselves to the insights of the men of letters while they're at it—and at the same time they're still doing their low-life legwork, their "digging," their hustling, their damnable Locker Room Genre reporting—they're taking on *all* of these roles at the same time—in other words, they're ignoring literary class lines that have been almost a century in the making (1972, 25).

To Wolfe, the New Journalists appropriated the techniques of novelists, just as the novelists were abandoning those styles for more experimental ones; thus, he asserted, while the novel was dead or dying, the New Journalism was rising from its ashes, ready to claim the readership and the cultural cachet heretofore reserved for literary fiction.

Journalism, in Wolfe's view, was destined to replace the novel as the primary mode of written expression, just as the novel had replaced poetry a century earlier. He argued in 1973 that only literary journalism could convey the intense social impact of contemporary American life. Just as the genre of poetry once reigned as the pinnacle of literary endeavor and then gave way to the novel, which was more accessible to the average reader, now the novel, which was becoming far too experimental and complex for the average reader, was surrendering its primacy to literary journalism, a more democratic form that could speak more directly about and to real people.

Wolfe's oft-cited yet somewhat logically flawed 1989 article about the contemporary novel, "Stalking the Billion-Footed Beast," makes the case that it is only through traditional literary realism that readers' emotions can be evoked.[7] While literary critics and theorists were proclaiming that realism did not represent actual mimesis and was a literary device like any other, Wolfe disagreed emphatically: "It was realism that created the 'absorbing' or 'gripping' quality that is peculiar to the novel, the quality that makes the reader feel that he has been pulled not only into the setting of the story but also into the minds and central nervous systems of the characters" (1989, 50). To Wolfe, evoking emotion in the reader is literature's most important calling, and only a realistic approach can do it. According to this argument, the New Journalism, with its engaging and frenetic prose style, its fully realized characters, and its lengthy passages of dialogue, was a reaction against the increasing experimentation of the postmodern novel and a sign that the kind of reportage Wolfe espoused is better able than the novel to convey the spirit of turbulent times. Indeed, as he asserts in the introduction to *The New Journalism*, "the work they would do over the next ten years, as journalists, would wipe out the novel as literature's main event" and "[start] the first new direction in American literature in half a century" (1973, 9, 3). While time has not exactly borne out Wolfe's thesis, the new direction Wolfe saw journalism—and therefore important literature in general—taking would be a return to realism and a turn away from postmodern experimentation.

It is interesting to note, however, that other scholars and practitioners of the New Journalism have posited that, instead of a return to literary realism, this mode of journalism in the late 1960s and early 1970s represented a turn toward similar forms of literary experimentation that were emerging in the novel. Critics have typically posited one of two ways to interpret the rejection of traditional views on objectivity that marked the work of the New Journalists: as a return to the tenets of literary realism extolled by Wolfe, or as an embrace of the literary experimentation that is considered one of the hallmarks of modernism and postmodernism. David L. Eason, for example, writing just a few years after Tom Wolfe's *New Journalism* manifesto appeared, argues that the New Journalism "reflects a self-consciousness of its mode of presentation, the act of writing, not found in traditional journalism" (1979, 13). Eason's point is that by foregrounding the act of writing, New Journalism implicitly addresses the nature of journalism itself: "In making manifest the 'novelistic' practices at work in the report, the nonfiction novel performs a metajournalistic function, making journalism itself part of the subject of the report" (16). To this way of thinking, the vivid literary styles used by these journalists call attention to the text as a text, causing the reader to reflect on the nature of the language and, subsequently, on the nature of the entire journalistic endeavor. And, of course, this is precisely the terminology used to describe the experimental metafiction that was en vogue then and, I argue, continues in the autofiction of today. To Eason, New Journalism serves not merely as an alternative to traditional journalism but as a more or less tacit critique of it, an idea that was not lost on the traditional journalists who emerged as vocal critics of New Journalism.

Furthermore, this metajournalistic tendency often manifested itself in more overt ways than the implicit ones Eason articulates, particularly in the various modes of narration these writers employ. As Robert Augustin Smart has put it, "The nonfiction novel requires a subjective, clearly identified narrative perspective different from the unidentified, omniscient perspective of the conventional realistic novel" (1985, 3). For example, Wolfe discusses his innovative style of narration as being one not limited to a particular perspective, even an omniscient one. Instead of following what he calls a "century-old British tradition" of effacing the narrator's presence by using a bland and understated voice, Wolfe developed what he calls the "hectoring narrator" who calls attention to his presence through his expansive rhetorical style and direct address to both characters and readers. As he explains, "I liked the idea of starting off a story by letting the reader, via the narrator, talk to the characters, hector them, insult them, prod them with irony or condescension, or whatever. Why should the reader be expected to just lie flat and let these people come tromping through as if his mind were a subway turnstile? But I was democratic about it, I was. Sometimes I would put myself into the story and make sport of me" (1973, 17). Wolfe outlines a variety of narrative experiments in this passage, including entering the narrative himself in order to comment on his presence there. Indeed, his trademark "ice-cream suits" suggest that Wolfe seeks not to efface but rather to foreground himself in any situation. For example, in this passage from *The Electric Kool-Aid Acid Test*, the narrator speaks both to the reader and to the character who makes fun of his clothing: "Back in New York City, Black Maria, I tell you, I am even known as something of a dude. But somehow a blue silk blazer and a big tie with clowns on it and . . . a . . . pair of shiny low-cut black shoes don't set them all to doing the Varsity Rag in the head world in San Francisco" (1968, 5). While this authorial intrusion is, as Wolfe says, a marked departure from traditional journalistic tenets, it is most certainly *not* a rejection of postmodern experimentation as he so adamantly claims; rather, Wolfe's description of his narratorial style could be used to describe the styles of many fictional novels of the same period. Vladimir Nabokov's *Pale Fire* (1962), Ronald Sukenick's *Up* (1968), and Kurt Vonnegut's *Slaughterhouse-Five* (1969) are only three examples of novels employing this sort of "hectoring narrator" who intrudes upon the narrative to direct the reader's interpretation of it. Paradoxically, this particular trait of New Journalism is similar to one exhibited by the experimental postmodern novels that Wolfe supposedly disdains.

This connection between New Journalism and postmodernism is made more vividly when we consider the work of Hunter S. Thompson, another New Journalist who practiced these forms of narratorial direct address and authorial intrusion. By immersing himself in his subject in order to perform his method of "participant journalism" or what he called "gonzo journalism," Thompson became the central character in the resulting narratives, in which he referred to himself both by name and by the pseudonym "Raoul Duke." Somewhat tellingly, when the narrator in *Fear and Loathing in Las Vegas*, arguably Thompson's most famous work, refers to "Thompson," it is to deny that he is that man. The narrator tells someone holding a picture of Thompson, "'That's not me,' I said. 'That's a guy named Thompson. He works for *Rolling Stone* . . . a really vicious, crazy kind of person'" (1998, 195). This clever maneuver both equates the narrator with Thompson but also evokes a recognition that the narrator and the author are *never* the same person, even in a work of journalism; this kind of ironic claiming yet denying of authorial identity is also indicative of autofiction.

Fear and Loathing in Las Vegas showcases Thompson's trademark frenzied style, a style that is ostensibly meant to be reportorial, but is far more impressionistic and hallucinatory than that of traditional journalism. For example, instead of describing the occupants of a hotel lobby as reptilian, Thompson claims they are actual lizards, whose long claws are scraping the walls and carpet, indicating that Thompson is aiming for truths that run deeper than documentary-style accuracy can convey, truths we might term literary rather than journalistic. Thompson describes his style of reporting this way: "Probably the closest analogy to the ideal would be a film director-producer who writes his own scripts, does his own camera work, and somehow manages to film himself in action, as the protagonist or at least a main character" (1982, 120). In this conceptualization, the figure of the journalist is central to the story, responsible for all parts of it, including the "scripting" of the action. For this reason, Thompson's gonzo journalism has been criticized for the fact that, despite—or perhaps because of—its innovative yet solipsistic style, one learns very little about the ostensible topic of the story (in *Las Vegas*, a vintage car race) and more about the state of the narrator's somewhat disturbed mind. Thompson's writing is less about depicting a scene than about depicting his narrator's impressions of that scene: Thompson not only rejects traditional journalistic objectivity; he embraces its polar opposite, resulting in a text that is more novelistic due to its interiority than journalistic in describing external events.

Arguably the most famous New Journalist who engaged in authorial intrusion into his own narratives was Norman Mailer, who rendered himself in the third person as the central character in many of his essays and the three narratives published as historical novels. "Mailer," as will be seen, is even more overt in asserting his presence in his ostensibly journalistic narratives than "Thompson." Indeed, "Mailer's" charactorial presence, much like his actual one, often threatens to overwhelm the material he is meant to cover. Mailer's use of authorial intrusion, although different in method from Wolfe's and Thompson's, is similar to them in the way it metafictionally calls attention to the constructed nature of the narrative. When discussing his style of narration, Mailer echoes Wolfe when he says that he refuses to kowtow to the dictates of literary modernism; he has "yet to submit to the prescription laid down by the great physician Dr. James Joyce: 'silence, exile, and cunning'" (1981, 5). Another way of saying this would be that Mailer refuses to adhere to the high modernist dictate of impersonality of artistic endeavor, espoused by T. S. Eliot, in which the role of the artist is not to depict his own personal emotions but to channel his emotions toward an ideal, abstract creation that encapsulates the universality of human experience.

To achieve this impersonality, Eliot argues, the artist must completely obliterate his own identity from the work of art, for "the more perfect the artist, the more completely separate in him will be the man who suffers and the mind which creates" (1919). According to Eliot, in a work of art there ought to be no trace of the individual identity of the artist; rather, art should be an impersonal expression of universal and abstract truths. In this sense, the elimination of artistic personality meant to be achieved through this high modernist process eerily echoes the idea of journalistic objectivity, which requires the eradication of the observer's perspective in the effort to render a purely objective and factual account. The journalistic concentration on objectivity that became paramount in the early twentieth century can be connected to a similar strain in high modernism that emerged during the same period.

It makes sense, then, that it is both the rarified atmosphere of high modernist literary endeavor as well as the notion of journalistic objectivity that the New Journalists scoffed at and tried to counter through their vivid and visceral depictions of real-life events and people. It is perhaps no coincidence that the cultural moment that saw the evolution away from these modernist ideas toward the authorial intrusions evident in postmodernism is the same moment in which the New Journalists be-

gan to challenge the adherence to pure objectivity evinced by traditional journalism. Thus, by rejecting the artistic tenets of high modernism,
the New Journalists were embracing the experiments that came to characterize postmodernism.

It may seem counterintuitive that some writers saw this mode of journalism as in keeping with the experimental literary forms of the emerging postmodernism, since Wolfe—arguably the New Journalism's most
famous practitioner and certainly its most vocal exponent—saw it as a
return to traditional literary realism. But both arguments have merit,
just as one could see in writers like Joyce and Faulkner's use of interior
monologue either a hallmark of modernist experimentation or an extension of the kind of psychological realism exemplified by the later works
of Henry James. The best way, writers like Joyce and Faulkner believed,
to depict the inner workings of the human mind was to dive as deeply
into it as possible in order to translate as best they could the confusing
and contradictory nature of human thought into written language. The
resulting stream of consciousness is both a literary experiment and an
attempt to provide a capital-R Realistic view of human consciousness.

A similar idea occurred to the New Journalists who, despairing of
ever achieving true objectivity, thought that the best way to depict a particular situation or event realistically and accurately was to dive as deeply into it as possible. By this logic, the closest a writer could come to objectivity was to embrace his/her own subjective relationship to the story
and—by admitting to and depicting that subjectivity—to convey, if not
the universal and objective truth, at least an accurate depiction of that
single participant's individual truth. In other words, if it was impossible
to see *the* truth by witnessing from without, the New Journalists would
provide *a* truth as seen from within. Hollowell puts it this way: "By revealing his personal biases, the new journalist strives for a higher kind
of 'objectivity'" (1977, 22). My argument goes quite a bit further than Hollowell's to suggest that "saturation journalists" do not just openly admit
their biases but also attempt to immerse themselves (and thus their readers) in the milieu upon which they report. Wolfe writes about the Merry Pranksters and possibly indulges in his own acid trip (Wolfe has been
cagey about admitting or denying this).[8] Mailer crafts his entire narrative of a march on the Pentagon around his own participation in it, starting with the friend's phone call that got him involved, and Thompson

actually joins the Hells Angels, telling their story from within the exclusive group, not from an observer's viewpoint.

As Robert Scholes argued at the time (calling the New Journalists by his neologism, "hystorian," which refers to one who is a historian of those hysterical times): "The hystorian fights this tendency toward formula with his own personality. He asserts the importance of *his* impressions and *his* vision of the world. He embraces the fictional element inevitable in any reporting and tries to imagine his way toward the truth" (1968, 37). Again, I would take this idea further to argue that, both in this form of New Journalism and the postmodern novels that emerge, these writers are not wending their way toward "the truth" but finding a single version of the truth by delving deeply into one particular perspective.[9] As Mailer describes his role as the central character in *Armies of the Night,* an ambiguous incident (the 1967 march on the Pentagon to protest U.S. military action in Vietnam) requires an ambiguous protagonist: "An eyewitness who is a participant but not a vested partisan is required, further he must be not only involved, but ambiguous in his own proportions" (1994, 53).

Not all New Journalists engaged in this level of active participation in their subject matter. For example, Joan Didion comes to mind here as an example of a New Journalist who sometimes inserted herself into her work, "but only as a dispassionate observer; she never recorded her own impressions in Maileresque fashion, leaving that for her personal essays" (Weingarten 2006, 122). In her 1984 autofiction, *Democracy,* "Joan Didion" enters the work to explain how difficult it is to tell the story she is telling, highlighting the inherent metafictional component in the New Journalistic practices. She writes: "Call me the author. Let the reader be introduced to Joan Didion, upon whose character and doings much will depend" (1984, 16). As the novel's plot unfolds, "Didion" frequently highlights her presence as the observer/storyteller and relates not only the story but also her reasons for needing to tell it. She says she began the novel "at a point in my life when I lacked certainty, lacked even that minimum level of ego which all writers recognize as essential to the writing of novels, lacked conviction, lacked patience with the past and interest in memory; lacked faith even in my own technique" (17). *Democracy,* then, in addition to being the story of characters named Inez Victor and Jack Lovett, is also the story of a writer interrogating the potential for truthful and relevant writing. At one point, "Didion" ponders the role of the writer to convey information objectively and the difficulty of doing so: "I was trained to distrust other people's versions, but we go with what we have. We triangulate the coverage. Handicap for bias. Figure in leanings, predilections, the special circumstances which change the spectrum in which any given observer will see a situation. Consider what filter is on the lens" (124). Here she engages with the questions of New Journalism, recognizing that pure objectivity is impossible and coming to a conclusion similar to those of Wolfe and Mailer: the only real objectivity comes through overtly recognizing the subjectivity of the observer, who triangulates, handicaps, and considers what filter is on the lens. As John C. Hartsock has argued, "Didion is attempting then to close the gulf between herself and an objectified world and her method of doing so is what comes closest to home: her subjectivity" (2000, 153). Thus Didion's intrusive narration demonstrates that this form of immersion journalism hinges upon the overt acknowledgment of the presence of the observer, both as active participant and as active shaper of the resulting narrative.

Norman Mailer employs similar strategies in *Armies of the Night,* in which "Mailer" describes his writing process this way: "Then he began his history of the Pentagon. It insisted on becoming a history of himself over four days, and therefore was history in the costume of a novel" (1994, 241). Chris Anderson describes Mailer's strategy as "metadiscursive": "The frame thus impinges on the picture. The process of writing the book becomes the subject of the book," becoming an instance of "language turning away from its inexplicable object and back onto itself. Or, to put this another way, the actual demonstration of Mailer's subject is impossible: the emphasis thus naturally shifts to the subject of the writer and his relationship to the audience" (Anderson 1987, 92). Because language is not sufficient to explain the subject, the writer's focus trains itself on that conundrum, and the nature of writing itself becomes the subject of the book. What this suggests, once again, is that the employment of what is often considered to be a postmodern, metafictional experiment could also be viewed as an effort to portray realistically the only thing that can be portrayed: the experience of the observer and not the objective reality of the situation being described.

Thus, I attempt to reconcile Wolfe's adamant claim that New Journalism marks a return to realism with the postmodern experimentation employed by many of its practitioners, including Wolfe himself. This is easily done if we recognize the extent to which the kind of authorial intrusion and direct-address narration New Journalists like Wolfe, Thompson, and Mailer employ actually *are* gestures toward realism, similar to the way that the stream of consciousness employed by "Dr. Joyce" could be seen as a development of the psychological realism honed by Henry James and others. Today we might consider the visceral language and direct address of New Journalism a form of "hyperrealism," realism taken to an extreme in which it becomes impossible to discern reality from fiction through the web of language with which we are presented.[10] Indeed, I posit that much of what has long been considered postmodern experimentalism could more accurately be thought of as the only form of realism possible in the face of poststructuralist ideas about the nature and possibilities of language to represent the world.

Of course, the notion I just articulated runs counter to many of the postmodern theorists of the time: "The dominant feeling, articulated by such influential critics as Richard Poirier, Richard Gilman, Robert Scholes, and Ihab Hassan, was that realism was no longer a vigorous literary mode and that the pressing question was where fiction should go, if it was to continue at all, in a decidedly post-realistic period" (Weber 1980, 11). My argument is that, instead of representing a "post-realistic period," postmodern literature is rather a continuation of Realistic principles informed by the poststructuralist theory that suggests that literature is not a mirror reflection of reality but rather a construction of it. What has changed is not the impulse of literature to portray the real world but the emergent belief that language is not transparent enough to do so with any accuracy. What I advocate here is an adjustment to Scholes's edict that "There is no mimesis, only poiesis," to say instead that, in the postmodern wake of poststructuralism, poiesis *is* mimesis. In this interpretation, contemporary postmodern writers are no different from the Realists of the nineteenth century who used language to hold up a mirror to the world; the difference is that postmodern writers hold up that mirror and see only language reflected back.

This relationship between postmodernism and realism further cements the connection between the New Journalism and the postmodern autofiction that I am discussing here. Instead of the former being a re-action against the latter, the two genres arise as simultaneous and sim-ilar responses to poststructuralist ideas about the efficacy and power of language. As Shelley Fisher Fiskin puts it: "In the sixties, reporters, im-patient with the rigid conventions the press had adopted in the name of facilitating the objective reporting of the news, started to borrow tech-nical devices from the novel; novelists, dissatisfied with the realm of the 'sea bottom of the id' that fiction writers had claimed as their natural habitat, began to borrow research methods and subjects from journal-ism" (1985, 207). Leonora Flis has made this connection more recently in her book *Factual Fictions: Narrative Truth and the Contemporary Amer-ican Documentary Novel*, in which she discusses the relationship between experimental novels and what she calls "documentary novels": "The com-mon denominator that connects both types of narrative is the fact that they both stem from the same, postmodern epistemological base, deny-ing the absolute nature of truth and reality, questioning the grand nar-rative of history" (2010, 22). And the connection between the New Jour-nalism and postmodern fiction most important for my discussion is "the central role of the author as transforming agent. . . . In both forms the author is often visibly present as either a narrator or a character or both" (Hellmann 1981, 14–5). It is through the figure of that narrator-character that the connections between the New Journalism and autofiction—and postmodern fiction more generally—can best be demonstrated.

In order to articulate that connection in more detail, I will examine several autofictions in relation to the nonfiction novels to which I have already made reference. What emerges from such a comparison is that, just as the intrusive narrator in New Journalistic texts causes the reader to recognize the constructed nature of the journalistic narrative, the author-character in autofictional texts causes the reader to reflect upon the possibility that the fictional event being depicted could possibly refer to an extratextual reality. In other words, New Journalism calls attention to the potential fictionalization of the real events it depicts, while auto-fiction calls attention to the potential nonfictional elements of the fiction-al events that it depicts. By homing in on its writer and his/her writing process, the New Journalism calls the truth of its narratives—and subse-quently all journalism—into question. Autofiction uses the same tech-niques with the opposite result: by focusing attention on its writer and writing process, autofiction calls the fictionality of its narratives—and subsequently all fiction—into question.

J. G. Ballard's 1973 novel *Crash* emerged just two years after *Fear and Loathing in Las Vegas* in the heyday of the New Journalistic movement. Although a British author, Ballard's prose style and subject matter seems drawn directly from Thompson's brand of gonzo journalism. *Crash* depicts a man gravely injured in an automobile crash in which the other driver is killed and his wife left a widow. Both the man, James, and the widow, Helen, become oddly obsessed and even sexually attracted to the myriad possibilities for injury and death associated with car crashes. James realizes that "this obsession with the sexual possibilities of everything around me had been jerked loose from my mind by the crash," as though the accident had provided "the keys to a new sexuality born from a perverse technology" (1973, 29, 13). James and the widow begin an affair but are unable to engage in any sexual activity unless it takes place in a car of the same make and model as the one in which the original crash took place. The pair soon discover there are many others similarly sexually attracted to accidents and crash sites, and they find themselves drawn into a mysterious, crash-obsessed subculture led by a man named Robert Vaughan. James is erotically drawn to the guru-like Dr. Vaughan, who has been disfigured by his own experience with car crashes and who now listens to the police scanner in order to get to crash sites and photograph them before medical personnel can arrive.

Much like Thompson with the Hells Angels, James abandons his job and neglects his wife in order to spend more and more time with Vaughan, driving recklessly around London while Vaughan has sex with prostitutes in the backseat, paying the women to take the positions of different crash victims from Vaughan's photographs. Due to the crash, James becomes someone willing to put his life, his marriage, and perhaps his sanity on the line to engage fully with this charismatic figure and with this new brand of sexuality.

While surreal and disturbing, the novel takes the form of a chronicle of James's experiences with Vaughan, a chronicle that becomes even more unsettling when, midway through the novel, someone refers to James as "Mr. Ballard," and the reader is jolted into the realization that "James" is a representation of the author himself. Readers are suddenly forced to reckon with the idea that this is perhaps not a novel after all, not an account *resembling* a piece of gonzo journalism, but an actual piece of gonzo journalism. I am not arguing that readers, upon seeing that the protagonist's name is "James Ballard," would actually believe that the book they are reading is true and that the actual Ballard engages in this strange form of auto-eroticism.[11] Rather, by invoking the author's name, the novel elicits from readers a shock that temporarily shatters the complacency that accompanies the reading of fiction. The use of the actual author's name draws a distinct, if fictional, line from the events in the novel to elements outside it. The fictional world of the novel might be reasserted if a reader recognizes that Ballard never had a wife named Catherine and that there never was such a person as Vaughan. Other readers might not dig so deeply, but would rather rest assured that the narrative is indeed a fiction based on how the book is shelved or on the fact that the events depicted therein are outlandish enough to be deemed clearly fictional. And perhaps some readers might believe that the events actually took place and that the book is indeed a factual account. However, reader response is not particularly important to the argument I am making. What is important is to note that giving the protagonist the same name as the author makes a particular kind of gesture toward the world outside the text—a gesture that precludes the reader from seeing the book only as a somewhat allegorical commentary on contemporary life but also as a potentially factual chronicle of that life. The onomastic connection of protagonist to actual author-figure draws the reader, however temporarily, out of the textual world and into the extratextual one.

Critics have referred to this kind of self-referentiality as breaking or violating the convention of the fourth wall, referring to the tradition in realistic theater of assuming that the audience views the action on stage through an invisible fourth wall of a room. Playwrights like Berthold Brecht and Samuel Beckett had been employing this gambit of violating the fourth-wall convention for decades before it began to appear with any regularity in fiction, and autofiction represents only one of many means by which this fourth wall is breached. What is striking about autofictions such as *Crash,* however, is the comparison between the authorial intrusion employed by Ballard and that employed by journalists like Thompson. When "Thompson" refers to himself by name in his journalism, it has the effect of emphasizing the subjective nature of the account and calling into question the nature of journalistic objectivity. When "Ballard" makes an appearance in his novel, we question not the objectivity of the account but the subjective reality of the fictional world in which we have been immersed. In other words, by drawing our attention to a figure with a valence outside the world of the novel, a figure who is actually responsible for creating that novelistic world, we are left to question whether or not that world is indeed fictional. And this ultimately leads to the realization that all fiction actually does refer to elements outside the text; it must do so in order to be at all comprehensible.

In terms of *Crash*, the gesture toward the world outside the novel causes a recognition of the extent to which the themes of the novel might be resonant in the extratextual world as well as the one contained within the narrative. The novel depicts characters whose lives and loves are so sterile and rote that they have become devoid of meaning. Coming into direct and intimate contact with death, injury, pain, and the automobile as the technological instrument that caused the first three revives feelings that the victims' mediated, industrialized existence had deadened. James says, "The crash was the only real experience I had been through for years. For the first time I was in physical confrontation with my own body, an inexhaustible encyclopedia of pains and discharges, with the hostile gaze of other people, and with the fact of the dead man" (1973, 39). The novel suggests that, as technology has removed the characters from visceral contact with the physical world, so it can bring them abruptly back into contact with it. I argue that the evocation of Ballard's name in the narrative and the resulting breaking of the fourth wall brings about the same abrupt reconnection with the external world that "James" experiences in his accident. In this sense, autofictional authorial intrusion jolts a reader out of the fictional world in a powerful and visceral way, if only momentarily.

As the New Journalists became more established, some critics began to speculate that the increasingly widespread inclusion of the characterized versions of the writers themselves served less of a narrative or journalistic purpose and more to aggrandize the figure of the writer. The fear among traditional journalists is that journalistic authorial intrusion "would replace the hard-won tradition of objectivity with a cult of mere egotism" (Hollowell 1977, 45). Hollowell continues: "By turning attention upon himself and how he 'got the story,' the new journalist has himself become a product in this image-making world" (49). And, to some extent, this was so, as some journalists actively participated in marketing their personae: Tom Wolfe's trademark white "ice-cream suits," Truman Capote's willingness to appear on any and all talk shows, and Norman Mailer's boorish public bullying of critics that often devolved into fisticuffs and in his running for mayor of New York City. In the case of Hunter S. Thompson, John Hellmann argues that "he has purposely emphasized and exaggerated certain of his traits in order to create a fictive version of himself which is essentially a self-caricature, not an in-depth representation of a complex human being. Nevertheless, a further confusion arises from Thompson's having carried this creation of a persona over into his lectures, interviews, and general public exposure" (1981, 72). In this current age, when writers and even journalists are expected to turn themselves into "brands" and market themselves by tirelessly flogging their work on digital media, it is perhaps difficult to remember a time when a so-called journalist was meant to stay above the fray of the marketplace in order to maintain objectivity. Some New Journalists, however, seemed to fall into the trap Hollowell articulated, of writing themselves into the story in order to *become* the story. As Wolfe joked at the time, "Reporters didn't want much . . . merely to be *stars*! and of such minute wattage at that!" (1972, 44). So while poststructuralist theory was positing the death of the author, the New Journalists were becoming celebrity writers, actively engaging in the construction and marketing of their personae in addition to the selling of their writing.

In his discussion of literary celebrity, Joe Moran has argued that "celebrity in the United States has been conferred on authors who have the potential to be commercially successful and penetrate into mainstream media, but are also perceived as in some sense culturally 'authoritative'" (2000, 6). The fact that some New Journalists achieved this kind of widespread notoriety is indicative of the challenge they posed to the cultural authority previously enjoyed by novelists. Indeed, some novelists—most notably Norman Mailer—embarked on journalistic efforts, perhaps as a means to garner some of that authority. Mailer was far more successful as a journalist than he was as a novelist, a fact that rankled him in no small way. Mailer wanted to have his cake and eat it, too: to use his journalistic writing as a means to fame (and fortune), but to conveniently repudiate journalism for what he perceived to be the greater cultural respectability of being a novelist.

Although already well known in literary circles for novels like *The Naked and the Dead* (1948), Mailer emerged into mainstream fame largely through his journalistic efforts. Mailer provides perhaps the best example of a writer including himself in the story, then emerging as a crossover celebrity based in part on that inclusion, and then the nature of this celebrity, in turn, becomes once again the fodder for the story. The culmination of this cycle is arguably Mailer's "historical trilogy," which includes *The Armies of the Night* (1968), *Miami and the Siege of Chicago* (1968), and *Of a Fire on the Moon* (1971). Ostensibly meant to be journalistic accounts of historical occurrences, they are rather accounts of Mailer's experience of those occurrences. The narratives have as much to say about how Mailer felt about the events in question and his subsequent shaping of the narrative of those events as they do about the events themselves. This is by design, and the books were quite popular and critically successful: *Armies of the Night*, possibly the most self-conscious of the three, won both the National Book Award and the Pulitzer Prize.

In *Armies*, Mailer refers to himself in the third person by different monikers, such as "your protagonist," "the Novelist," "the Participant," and at times simply "Mailer." The book is an account of the 1967 march on the Pentagon in protest of U.S. military action in Vietnam. However, because he is writing quite soon after the march, "Mailer" claims that he cannot provide a definitive report of its meaning. This is a moment "whose essential value or absurdity may not be established for ten or twenty years, or indeed ever" (1994, 53). He is equipped only to offer his own view of what the march was and what it meant to him, and this perspective forms the first part of the book (the second part is a more objective view of the context of the march). While this perspective is in keeping with the New Journalism's tenet that pure objectivity is impossible, it also demonstrates the potential that Holloway warned about for this kind of narrative to devolve into narcissism. *Armies* provides a masterful comic depiction of "Mailer" as a garrulous, bombastic, and self-important drunkard, living in "the sarcophagus of his image" (5), "admirable, except that he was an absolute egomaniac, a Beast—no recognition existed of the existence of anything beyond the range of his reach" (13). Admittedly, this is a highly entertaining and self-aware portrait of the artist as a narcissist; however, the story of "Mailer's" living spectacularly up to his public image during the march tends to take over the narrative, suggesting that just because someone realizes he is an egomaniac does not justify it or make it worth reading about in and of itself.

In some respects, this version of "Mailer" embodies Virginia Woolf's lamentation in *A Room of One's Own* about the ubiquity in some men's writing of the shadow of the "I," for it becomes at times difficult to see around "Mailer" to view the scene he is describing. He bristles when the poet Robert Lowell, also in attendance at the rally before the march, tells him he is the best journalist in America. After a narratorial tirade against Lowell, Lowell's wife, writer Elizabeth Hardwick, and negative book critics, "Mailer" responds to Lowell: "There are days when I think of myself as being the best writer in America" (1994, 22). *Armies* thus not only describes the march but also provides an opportunity for personal axe grinding. "Mailer's" authorial presence—his celebrity—is often foregrounded in the piece, rather than being merely the basis upon which the piece is founded. And it is Mailer's celebrity that makes such a text as *Armies* interesting or even possible. If Mailer had not already been a household name, such ruminations on "Mailer's" literary abilities and grudge holding would hold little appeal. As Christopher Lasch so famously argued about Mailer: "what begins as a critical reflection on the writer's own ambition, frankly acknowledged as a bid for literary immortality, often ends in a garrulous monologue, with the writer trading on his own celebrity and filling page after page with material having no other claim to attention than its association with a famous name" (1978, 17). In this kind of authorial intrusive journalistic narrative, celebrity becomes an end in itself; for Mailer, when the reporter enters the story, the reporter becomes the story. But, as Lasch points out, "Mailer" with quotation marks is an interesting character only insofar as Mailer without quotation marks is a celebrity in the world outside the text.

In parodic response to this kind of narcissistic narrative,[12] Mark Leyner's 1992 autofiction, *Et Tu, Babe?* portrays "Mark Leyner" as a celebrity writer of rock-star status surrounded by assistants, sycophants, and fans who hang on his every move, to the extent that "Team Leyner" has replaced the Times Square jumbotron with a sign that "simulates positron emission tomography images of Leyner's brain function as he writes, laid over a magnetic resonance image of his brain anatomy—so pedestrians below can actually observe glucose metabolism at various sites within Leyner's cerebral cortex as he's producing one of his critically acclaimed best-sellers" (1992, 164). In other words, *Et Tu, Babe?* describes "Leyner's" fame as so widespread that his fans demand to know him on a molecular level. Indeed, he is so important in the world of this novel that the universe itself is described as consisting of "one continuous teleological process leading inevitably to the birth of Mark Leyner" (168). The story about this writer's daily life is important because "Leyner" is, and while Mailer is not self-aggrandizing to this extreme, the satiric connection is clear.

Et Tu, Babe? opens with "Leyner's" fame skyrocketing as he travels the country holding writing workshops (at which he "takes into custody" any writer who claims to be as good as he is) and adding to his entourage by inviting people he likes to come work for "Team Leyner." The novel serves as a clever and often biting parody of the celebrity autobiography. But in addition, it seems to provide an almost direct satiric reference to works of the new journalism, as "Leyner" has the flamboyant personality of a Tom Wolfe or Norman Mailer, and the novel is written in a feverish style reminiscent of Thompson's. Indeed, one episode in *Et Tu, Babe?* is a direct reference to *Fear and Loathing in Las Vegas*. In the latter, Thompson (or "Raoul Duke") takes a hit of adrenochrome, a drug supposedly gleaned from the adrenal gland of a living human donor. In *Et Tu, Babe?* "Leyner" has a similar experience with a vial of "Lincoln's Morning Breath," which he steals from the National Museum of Health and Medicine. The description of the astounding high he achieves from this "drug" clearly recalls Thompson's, poking fun at the gonzo notion of pushing the boundaries of health and sanity to create fodder for the story.[13]

Most important for my argument, the autofictional author-character of "Mark Leyner" in *Et Tu, Babe?* once again draws a connection between the character and the extratextual figure of the author. The supposed equation between Leyner the writer with a small but loyal cult following and "Leyner" the über-celebrity evokes a consideration of the nature of fame and the extent to which our culture worships the famous. It also causes serious readers to chuckle as they ponder the clearly fictional idea that a literary writer would ever be lionized in the way "Leyner" is. The autofictional connection to the novel's extratextual author-figure further emphasizes the absurdity of an already absurd novel about a self-aggrandizing writer.

In addition, "Leyner," much like some of the more famous New Journalists and like many contemporary writers as well, markets himself relentlessly, even within the text itself. He films numerous ads in the novel and even does a textual product placement for Pepsi (1992, 78). "Leyner" takes self-marketing to a new extreme, however, when his Team develops software that can automatically alter his novels to include the local colloquialisms of each region in which the novel is being sold. In other words, "Leyner" makes it clear that the fame and money are important above all else, including the integrity of the writing. "Leyner" sells out unapologetically and with gusto. Once again, this commentary about contemporary authorship as it relates to celebrity is all the more trenchant given that it is a characterized version of the "actual" author of the novel being depicted here.

Bret Easton Ellis's 2005 novel, *Lunar Park*, also plays with authorial celebrity, and in this case the celebrity is actual rather than fictional, for Ellis was, in the 1980s, the closest thing to a literary celebrity that our culture allows. Ellis is most famous for fictional portrayals of the young, selfishly brutal rich in novels like *Less than Zero* and *American Psycho*. *Lunar Park* makes fun of Ellis's notoriety and of readers' tendencies to equate the writer with his work, as "Bret" careens through disastrous life choices and escapades that are clearly fictional, not real. For example, the novel is a ghost story, yet "Bret" tells us at the outset that everything depicted in the novel actually happened. Indeed, enough actual biographical material about Ellis's life and career is included in *Lunar Park* that it is difficult at first for a reader to determine what is true and what is fiction, although many early reviews of the novel attempted to do just that. However, differentiating fact from fiction is not the point of autofiction. Rather, these novels exist by design in a liminal state between fact and fiction: they depict events that did not take place outside the text, but do so through a characterized version of someone (in this case "Bret") who has an extratextual existence. Through this liminal state, autofiction—like New Journalism—is less wedded to portraying real events and more invested in conveying the deeper capital-T Truths we expect from literature. As "Bret" says, he considered writing a memoir, but "I could never be as honest about myself in a piece of nonfiction as I could in any of my novels" (2005, 24). *Lunar Park*, then, holds out the tantalizing possibility that, although fictional, it contains some kind of ineffable Truth about the world in general and about celebrity author Bret Easton Ellis in particular. And in this, autofiction simply makes manifest what is latent in all fiction: the attempt to depict "truth" through fictional means.

Another contemporary autofiction that is absurdly self-aggrandizing, but sincerely and unsatirically so, is *Windows on the World* by French writer Frédéric Beigbeder. This novel, first published in French in 2003 and in English in 2004, contains two intertwining narratives: a fictional account of a Texan businessman and his two young sons trapped in the World Trade Center restaurant Windows on the World on 9/11, juxtaposed with the story of "Beigbeder" himself, attempting to make sense of that event while sitting at the top of Le Ciel de Paris, the highest building in Paris. The novel, arguably the first to take 9/11 as its main subject, alternates back and forth between the two narratives, one completely fictional and one based on the supposedly real experiences of "Beigbeder." Each chapter of the novel provides a time marker, as the action moves from 8:30 a.m. to 10:30 when the characters jump from the burning building right before its collapse.

Windows on the World resembles a New Journalistic text in several suggestive ways. One, it unflinchingly depicts the death of Yorston Carthew and his two young sons as one son asphyxiates in the smoke of the burning World Trade Tower, and the other eventually jumps with his father from the burning building while holding the body of the dead child between them. The descriptions of the intense heat and smoke are realistic, but they are, of course, also fictional, since no one from that restaurant survived the 9/11 attacks and so a writer can only surmise the details of their deaths. The novel thus represents "an attempt—doomed, perhaps—to describe the indescribable" (Beigbeder 2004, 55). This kind of imaginative depiction of details that are impossible to know is the proper role of literature, according to "Beigbeder": "The role of books is to record what cannot be seen on television. . . . Even if I go deep, deep into the horror, my book will always remain 1,350 feet below the truth" (83, 119).

"Beigbeder" refers to the novel in which he appears as "hyperrealist" because since 9/11 "reality has not only outstripped fiction, it's destroying it" (2004, 8). In other words, the post-9/11 times in which he writes are so extreme as to be more intense than any fiction; this sentiment is almost exactly that of the New Journalists of the late 1960s, who also believed that their times were too turbulent for traditional journalism to do them justice. I have already registered my skepticism, both that any particular time period is more volatile than any other and that any period is more or less amenable to being represented in fiction. However, it is telling that the ideas expressed in *Windows on the World* are so similar to those of the New Journalists, for in both cases writers argue that writerly innovations are necessary in order to do justice to the events being depicted.

In "Beigbeder's" case, the innovation required apparently involves inserting his own perspective and experience into the narrative, interspersed with that of his fictional characters. So while Yorston Carthew and his sons struggle to escape, "Beigbeder" struggles to understand their experience by drinking café-crème in Le Ciel de Paris. If this description sounds snide or dismissive, it is because "Beigbeder's" presence in his novel becomes annoying and increasingly difficult to justify, even to himself. A reader could be forgiven for wondering what the author-character's presence adds to the novel, as "Beigbeder's" ruminations become more and more self-serving and further and further removed from the issues raised by 9/11. One insight "Beigbeder" eventually stumbles upon, while exploring his feelings about 9/11, is that he loves his girlfriend and wants to marry her, and perhaps this is meant to serve as an optimistic counterpoint to the tragedy described in the novel's other narrative. And perhaps there is some solace to be found in the fact that the tragedy is, in terms of this narrative, fictional (Carthew and his sons are made-up characters), and the optimistic part of the story is "true" ("Beigbeder" is a characterized version of a real person who did subsequently marry his girlfriend). But the opposite also holds: 9/11 did take place, while "Beigbeder" is, in some sense, a fictional character. Furthermore, the reader is left with an awareness, shared by "Beigbeder," that the fictionalized narrative about his characterized self would have little value and hold little interest, were it not yoked to the very real and momentous event that is 9/11. As "Beigbeder" himself puts it: "I am also obliged to concede that in leaning on the first great hyper terrorist attack, my prose takes on a power it would not otherwise have. This novel uses tragedy as a literary crutch" (2004, 295). In this sense, the novel demonstrates the point I have been making about autofiction, in that it derives much of its power from gesturing outside itself toward extratextual events and people through the author-character. And just as "Mailer" is only interesting insofar as Mailer is a celebrity, "Beigbeder's" story garners any significance it might have from its oblique connection to the 9/11 tragedy.

Both New Journalism and autofiction use fictionalization techniques to make direct connections to the nonfictional world outside the text, often making these worlds difficult to tell apart. But while New Journalism and autofiction emerge at roughly the same time in the United States from similar philosophical and political underpinnings, they provide contrasting perspectives on the nature of conveying truth through language. The authorial intrusion of New Journalism serves to make an actual account seem more like fiction, while the same trope in autofiction serves to connect the fictional text to the world outside it. Considered together, the two trends demonstrate both the constantly and ambiguously shifting line between fictional and nonfictional narrative and the increasing cultural recognition and acceptance of that ambiguity.

4 Trauma Autofiction, Dissociation, and the Authenticity of "Real" Experience

Kurt Vonnegut, Raymond Federman,
Tim O'Brien, and Jonathan Safran Foer

The process of doubling or expressing two states of consciousness
can occur when the traumatic past is brought into conflict with
the present in order to portray the character's emotional struggle.

— Michelle Balaev, *The Nature of Trauma in American Novels*

A trauma is typically understood to be an experience or event so overwhelming that its sufferer is unable to process it immediately; trauma narratives represent the written accounts of survivors' struggles to put the experience into comprehensible language. In the 1990s, a body of theory emerged that employed the strategies of psychoanalysis and deconstruction to explain the effects that trauma can have on the survivor's life and psyche and to apply those explanations to trauma narratives. This body of trauma theory has established trauma narrative and trauma fiction as distinct literary modes and has developed important strategies for explicating those narratives.

Trauma narratives are chronicles of trauma survivors' attempts, through telling the story of what happened, to impose order and meaning upon the experience. With the often implicit understanding that a trauma cannot be accurately depicted in a mimetic fashion, trauma narratives tend to eschew strategies of traditional realism in favor of experimental strategies and structures that better convey the horror and confusion indicative of a traumatic experience. As Laurie Vickroy puts it: "Trauma narratives go beyond presenting trauma as subject matter or character study. They internalize the rhythms, processes, and uncertainties of traumatic experience within their underlying sensibilities and structures" (2002, 3). Trauma fiction is a subcategory of trauma narrative and is just what its name suggests: fiction that depicts a trauma and its aftermath. And although it is sometimes written *about* rather than *by* trauma survivors, trauma fiction also tends to employ experimental narrative strategies similar to those in more memoir-esque trauma narratives. Autofiction is sometimes one of those strategies, but trauma autofiction, as a subset of trauma fiction, is a form of trauma narrative that has yet to be critically explored. This chapter will discuss how autofictional strategies provide both fictional license and factual legitimacy to the trauma narratives that employ them. Through the inherently split subjectivity of its author-character, autofictional strategies allow for the depiction of a critical distance from a heretofore unrepresentable traumatic event. The author-character becomes both an avatar for the extratextual author and a fictional character whose depiction need not adhere to the strict tenets of truth-telling. In other words, the "fiction" part of autofiction allows for a departure from a strict adherence to referentiality in order to shape the story that is difficult to tell. At the same time, and somewhat ironically, the onomastic connection between author and author-character (the "auto" part of autofiction) lends a kind of credibility—whether deserved or not—to the trauma autofiction.

Trauma narratives are often memoirs and as such are meant to be historically and autobiographically accurate accounts of one person's experience of trauma. However, with some exceptions, trauma theorists tend to elide trauma memoirs with trauma fiction or to focus their attention on the similarities rather than the differences. Part of the reason for this elision is that, in the traditional concept of what a trauma narrative is, the factual accuracy—often referred to as the "authenticity"—of the story being told is a vital factor in determining its storytelling power. Thus trauma *fictions* are often held to the same or similar standards of truth-telling as memoirs, at least in terms of their depiction of the historical details of the traumatic event: in order to be deemed a "trauma narrative," both fictions and memoirs must adhere faithfully to the facts. For example, novels depicting the horrors of slavery (Toni Morrison's *Beloved*), the aftermath of the Vietnam conflict (Tim O'Brien's *In the Lake of the Woods*), or 9/11 (Jonathan Safran Foer's *Extremely Loud and Incredibly Close*) represent characters' post-traumatic stress disorders with almost clinical accuracy. What makes trauma studies relevant to my project, however, is that this mandate for factual accuracy is frequently complicated by the experimental narrative strategies employed by writers of trauma narrative. They often reject pure mimesis as less appropriate to their purposes, preferring instead to tell it slant. In the process, events and situations are shaped and reshaped, sometimes resulting in varying amounts of fictionalization.

This fictionalization is one of the major elements of autofiction, as the distance between the extratextual author and the author-character tends to increase as the novel progresses, so that the author-character continues to evoke, but is certainly distinct from, the extratextual author of the novel. Authors like Raymond Federman, Kurt Vonnegut, Tim O'Brien, and Jonathan Safran Foer employ various intricate autofictional techniques in order to depict traumatic events and their effects. But whereas the extant body of theory and criticism that focuses on trauma narrative tends unproblematically to equate the author with the author-character, I want to argue that the somewhat controversial power of trauma autofiction lies precisely in the *distance* between the author and his onomastic author-character. This distance enables autofiction to represent a traumatic event in ways that may not be historically factual but that may provide access to the deeper narrative truths characterized by works of fiction, while still facilitating the putative claim to authenticity that the onomastic author-character enables.

Cathy Caruth, standing at the forefront of trauma studies in 1996, deemed hers a "catastrophic era" (1995b, 11), while Nancy Miller and Jason Tougaw claimed in 2002 that "ours appears to be the age of trauma" (2002, 1). I am reluctant to deem our age any more or less catastrophic than previous ones; instead, I would suggest that one reason for the contemporary interest in and preponderance of trauma theory is the combination of the traumas of our time with the hindsight provided by contemporary psychology. Health care practitioners are only now beginning to understand how to treat the psychic repercussions of traumatic experience, and literary scholars are bringing these new clinical insights to bear on narratological analysis. A traumatic event, according to Caruth, "is not assimilated or experienced fully at the time, but only belatedly, in its repeated *possession* of the one who experiences it" (1995a, 4). Or as Kai Erikson argues, "Above all, trauma involves a continual reliving of some wounding experience in daydreams and nightmares, flashbacks and hallucinations, and in a compulsive seeking out of similar circumstances" (1995, 184). In this sense, the person suffering through a trauma does not or cannot understand the event as it happens, but afterward repeatedly returns viscerally and often unwillingly to that event in his/her memory. Indeed, one of the primary symptoms of post-traumatic stress disorder is this vivid reliving of the traumatic moment or moments, in either dreams or waking life. Lawrence Langer deems this constant reliving of a single moment a "durational" mode of time rather than a "chronological" one, arguing that a trauma survivor shifts back and forth in time and continues to experience the trauma as a contemporaneous moment, even if that moment is long past. In Langer's estimation, the trauma has lasting duration, even though it has receded in chronological time (1991, 14–15). Thus the event takes on greater and greater significance after the fact, as time is essentially put out of joint and the trauma survivor is often unable to set it right.

This temporal distortion often manifests itself in the narratives that trauma survivors construct about their experiences. Trauma, according to Anne Whitehead, "implicitly repositions the relation between language and the world" (2004, 13). Roger Luckhurst argues that for many trauma survivors, the urge to narrativize their experience becomes paramount: "In its shock impact trauma is antinarrative, but it also generates the manic production of retrospective narratives that seek to explicate the trauma" (2008, 79). So as the traumatic event returns to their consciousness again and again, survivors often attempt to narrativize it as a way to make meaning from the apparent meaninglessness of their experience, to impose order on chaos. But imposing that order often requires a seemingly disordered narrative. The disjointed sense of time and the tumultuous feelings evoked by the trauma are often best depicted by a variety of nonreferential narrative experiments. Anne Whitehead points out one such experiment: "If trauma is at all susceptible to narrative formulation, then it requires a literary form which departs from conventional linear sequence" (2004, 6). Just as the trauma survivor re-experiences the trauma repeatedly and long after it occurred, trauma narratives often eschew straightforward temporal linearity and are characterized by repetitions and jumps forward and back in time.

Whitehead goes on to argue that the experimental nature of many trauma narratives is in keeping with contemporary literary traditions: "Trauma fiction emerges out of postmodernist fiction and shares its tendency to bring conventional narrative techniques to their limit. In testing formal boundaries, trauma fiction seeks to foreground the nature and limitations of narrative and to convey the damaging and distorting impact of the traumatic event" (2004, 82).[1] Paul Crosthwaite posits the converse when he argues that trauma serves as an excellent means through which to understand postmodern literary traditions: "Trauma, as a paradigm of the historical event, possesses an absolute materiality, and yet, as inevitably missed or incompletely experienced, remains absent and inaccessible. This formulation offers a way of conceptualizing postmodernist culture's effacement of the referent or the originary moment, whilst at the same time affirming its sensitivity to the reality of historical experience" (2009, 1). Clearly, there is an affinity between trauma narratives and postmodern literary traditions. Like postmodern literature, trauma narratives (western ones, at any rate) tend to use language in innovative ways in order to convey the unusual and life-altering nature of the event. To that end, Michael Rothberg has coined the term "traumatic realism" to describe the somewhat ironic need for trauma writers to move away from the usual realist traditions in order to convey trauma realistically. Rothberg argues that trauma—particularly the horror of the Holocaust—"is not knowable or would be knowable only under radically new regimes of knowledge and that it cannot be captured in traditional representational schemata" (2000, 3). Thus Rothberg and others posit that depicting trauma with any accuracy requires nonmimetic, nonreferential narrative strategies.[2]

It is important to point out that trauma theorists do not go so far as to suggest that such experimental narrative techniques would render a traumatic experience with complete clarity; in this sense, trauma scholars find their forebears in the poststructuralist theorists who argue that language can never be a completely transparent mode of communication. However, if trauma possesses, as Crosthwaite claims, an "absolute materiality" (2009, 1), then this materiality cannot be ignored or denied as poststructuralist textuality. Instead, critical consensus suggests that the goal of a trauma narrative is to use innovative linguistic strategies to depict that materiality as accurately as possible, in order to facilitate psychological closure to a horrible event: "For traumatic memory to lose its power as a fragment and symptom and for it to be integrated into memory, a form of narrative reconstruction or reexternalization has to occur" (Felman and Laub 1991, 69). This focus on narrative reconstruction leads to a focus on the process of narrativization. Trauma narratives often concentrate on the process of their construction and, therefore, on the one who constructs. Thus they are frequently concerned as much with the writer thereof as with the event itself. It is perhaps no wonder, then, that authorial-intrusive autofictions have a vital role to play in the consideration of trauma narrative. Furthermore, trauma autofiction forces a similar consideration of the author's actual lived history by evoking an author-character who constantly gestures toward his/her extratextual counterpart. Autofiction's continual acknowledgment of the author-figure outside the text serves as a continual reminder of the historical and material reality that exceeds representation within the text.

It is important to differentiate at this point between trauma narratives written by or about actual survivors of trauma, which mostly take the form of memoirs, and the so-called trauma fiction that depicts fictional characters suffering and surviving trauma. The latter may or may not have been written by someone who has actually experienced the trauma being depicted. In this sense, Elie Wiesel's Holocaust memoir *Night* fits the former category, while Toni Morrison's *Beloved* fits the latter. Because they employ psychoanalytic terms and traditions in their analyses, some trauma studies theorists ignore or gloss over the distinction between fictional and nonfictional trauma narratives. Instead, they focus an analytical lens on author and character alike, irrespective of the supposed historical accuracy or admitted fictionality of the narrative. Trauma autofiction contributes to this elision by straddling the two genres of trauma memoir and trauma fiction, as it draws upon some referential and fictional elements and twists the two together in ways that are sometimes impossible to unravel. And of course, despite the efforts of some critics to do so, unraveling the fact from the fiction is decidedly not the point of autofiction. Rather, autofiction's narrative power lies in the overall effects of the blending of the extratextual world and the fictional one within the text.

This is not to say that the difference between reality and fiction is not important—particularly regarding traumatic historical events—just that such a distinction is outside the purview of trauma autofiction. However, because of its connection to actual extratextual figures, autofiction cannot be completely severed from referentiality and reframed as pure fiction. Furthermore, this connection to extratextual reality is important for any narrative touted as a memoir and is perhaps particularly important for a trauma narrative. For example, a Holocaust memoir or autobiography by an actual Holocaust survivor serves as a means of psychological catharsis for its writer and as a compelling and edifying story for its reader. It also serves as evidentiary documentation of an important historical event. Viewing narrative as an important link to history "implicitly repositions the relation between language and the world, so that the text shifts from a reflective mode—based on a position of self-awareness and self-understanding—to a performative act, in which the text becomes imbricated in our attempts to perceive and understand the world around us" (Whitehead 2004, 12). Thus the accuracy of such an account has repercussions extending beyond the experience of the reader, a fact made abundantly clear from the widespread cultural approbation that is aroused when a Holocaust narrative—or any memoir for that matter—is found to be a fiction rather than a factual account written by an actual survivor.[3]

On the other hand, despite trauma studies' frequent focus on the level of factual accuracy in trauma narratives, trauma studies practitioners like Rothberg recognize that such a focus conflicts with the widespread embrace of "the now commonplace insistence on the omnipresence of discourse and the disinterest in questions of reference" (2000, 3). In his book *Traumatic Realism,* Rothberg discusses the conflicting need to position the Holocaust as an actual event within verifiable historical contexts, and the recognition of how the sheer horror of the event renders it incomprehensible and in some senses unrepresentable in the referential modes traditionally employed by historians. As Roland Barthes contends in his wide-ranging argument that language cannot provide direct access to the real, "Historical discourse is presumably the only kind which aims at a referent 'outside' itself that can in fact never be reached" (1970, 153). Subsequently, to the extent that trauma narratives are meant to serve as historical records, there is an inherent paradox in the simultaneous insistence that trauma narratives adhere strictly to a factual account of an event and the sense that horrific events are impossible to depict using traditional strategies of verisimilitude.

The autofictions I discuss resonate with this paradox. By spanning the line between fact and fiction, trauma autofictions demonstrate that, despite the deconstructive arguments about the inability of language to convey a sense of reality, literary gestures toward nonfictional accuracy are still powerful. Autofiction manipulates that power by yoking the eponymous author-character to a mostly—but not completely—fictional narrative. So trauma autofiction, in a manner similar to more traditional trauma narratives, employs fiction—in combination with the nonfictional evocation of the author's name—as a nonmimetic strategy to convey as accurately as possible the truth, if not strictly the facts, of a traumatic event. Tim O'Brien explains this concept much better when he differentiates between happening-truth and story-truth. "Happening-truth" refers to a historically accurate account of what happened; "story-truth" refers to the narrativization of the event that often takes liberties with or alters actual events, but does so in the service of rendering a deeper "truth" about the event than the happening-truth could ever convey.[4] *The Things They Carried,* one of O'Brien's autofictional accounts of his experience in Vietnam, puts it this way: "By telling stories, you objectify your own experience. You separate it from yourself. You pin down certain truths. You make up others. You start sometimes with an incident that truly happened . . . and you carry it forward by inventing incidents that did not in fact occur but that nonetheless *help to clarify and explain*" (2009, 152; emphasis mine). Thus, conveying the reality or "truth" of a horrific event sometimes requires fiction. Story-truth, to O'Brien and to the other autofictionists I will discuss in this chapter, provides a deeper understanding of trauma than could a blow-by-blow chronological, referential account. Thus, in an echo of Barthes's ideas about historical narrative, autofiction aims at a referent outside itself, but with the implicit knowledge, shared by the reader, that this aim will miss and in some instances miss on purpose because, in literary terms, a fiction can be more "truthful" than the facts.

Some of the author-characters—"Kurt Vonnegut," "Raymond Federman," "Tim O'Brien," and "Bret Easton Ellis"—are depicted as trauma survivors, while others—"Jonathan Safran Foer" and "Michael Chabon"—serve as chroniclers of trauma suffered by people close to them. Note that I focus on the author-characters here, not the actual authors. It is less important to my study of autofiction whether or not the extratextual authors have actually suffered the traumas depicted in their novels; sometimes they have, sometimes they have not. What *is* important for my argument, however, is the fact that the onomastic connection between author and author-character implies that the authors have indeed suffered a trauma. This connection imbues the narrative with an authenticity that a traditional trauma narrative requires, even if that authenticity turns out to be ironic or false.

The novels in question here have the patina of factual accuracy about them, as the author-characters place themselves in the rhetorical position of someone authorized to tell a story of trauma. Readers may or may not be aware of the biography of the author and whether or not he actually suffered the trauma being depicted in the text. But whether or not the trauma being depicted is fictional, the autofictional elements in the novel infuse the narrative with the rhetorical force of a nonfictional narrative. At the same time and unlike a trauma autobiography or memoir, trauma autofictions derive a truth-telling power from their fictionality, from the ways in which they shape the world in narrative. Whereas a memoir derives its narrative authority mostly through the authenticity it achieves by providing specific and factual details about an actual event, a novel's authority stems not from the facticity of its account but from the larger philosophical and existential Truths that can be drawn from its plot, structure, and language. When done well, trauma autofiction draws its authority from *both* sources: it is fictional and therefore has access to the depth and universality of story-truths, but it remains yoked to referentiality through the author-character's onomastic connection to the author. No matter how fictional the autofiction becomes, it always gestures metafictionally toward the extratextual world outside itself and the extratextual author of the narrative.

By so doing, autofictions convey a sense of trauma made more immediate and visceral by the depiction of the "actual" author experiencing them. The deployment of an author-character in a trauma narrative serves the purpose of defining the character's authenticity as one who has indeed suffered a trauma and therefore serves as a claim to authority. The author-character's claim to authenticity also demonstrates the extreme subjectivity I discussed in chapter 3. Much like the New Journalist, the trauma fiction writer-character, by making manifest his particular position, demonstrates the impossibility of objectivity. This extreme subjectivity provides a clearer and seemingly more truthful depiction of the traumatic event than an objective account ever could. Thus the biographical connection evoked by the eponymous author-character enables trauma autofiction to explore issues of identity and reality, in addition to plumbing the narrative possibilities and challenges inherent in narrativizing trauma and the potential for truth-telling narratives more generally.

There is a great deal of trauma criticism about works by authors like Kurt Vonnegut, Tim O'Brien, and Jonathan Safran Foer, but this criticism rarely overtly addresses the autofictional nature of their work. Although trauma theory often discusses the difficulties inherent in using words to depict a horrific experience with any accuracy, it tends to take at face value the equation between narrator and author. Most trauma theory does not differentiate between Vonnegut and "Vonnegut," between O'Brien and "O'Brien," even when the text itself suggests or even demands such a distinction. The reasons for this equation of author to character are understandable, since trauma narrative often takes the form of a memoir or mimics that form. There is a particular kind of narrative power that emerges from a factual story told by a real person rather than a character; a similar power emerges, therefore, from the putative equation of author to character. What is striking is the extent to which critics maintain this equation in their discussions of trauma *fiction*—texts that depict traumatic events and experiences but that do so in a clearly fictional format. Traditionally in scholarship about fiction, there exists a clear demarcation between the author and the narrator (or, in poetry, the poet and the speaker); in studies about trauma fiction, that demarcation is less clearly drawn, if drawn at all.

This elision of character and author results in critics suggesting that Vonnegut the author may be able to find some personal peace by writing about his experiences in World War II in *Slaughterhouse-Five*: "*Slaughterhouse-Five* features a fusion of autobiography and fiction that helps the author to keep the distance from the text and its implications, that is to say, to work through his own traumatic condition" (Collado-Rodriguez 2011, 134); and "Vonnegut tries not to face his suppressed memories directly but to get to the core by slowly uncovering layer after layer. The novel reflects this process of narrowing in on himself through the two trauma stories. . . . Removing himself from the factual to the fictional plane by creating the narrator allows Vonnegut a degree of distance from himself and his experiences. Consequently, the final point of recovery in this process of self-therapy is not achieved in the novel but rather comes with its completion" (Vees-Gulani 2003, 182). What encourages both of the critics quoted here to psychoanalyze Vonnegut himself, despite the fact that "Vonnegut" is a fictional character, is the onomastic connection between the author of the novel and the author-character. The autofictional nature of the novel tempts critics to equate author with character in a manner not customary in most literary criticism and despite the fact that this equation is contraindicated by the decidedly fictional nature of a text that involves time-traveling aliens from a distant planet.

Part of my argument in this chapter is that works like *Slaughterhouse-Five* are fictions, but they are fictions complicated by the fact that their narrators have both suffered a trauma and they share a name with their authors, thereby inevitably implying that these authors have also suffered that trauma. To me, it is not important whether or not the extra-textual authors have suffered this trauma; rather, I am interested in the narrative situation created when the onomastic author-character implies that they have. Although such texts as O'Brien's *The Things They Carried* and *In the Lake of the Woods* and Foer's *Everything Is Illuminated* depict some events that actually took place, they also contain much that is overtly—sometimes admittedly—fictional. For trauma autofiction, drawing a distinction between author and author-character is warranted for the same reasons it is warranted with other forms of autofiction: there is a marked and conscious ironic distance between the author outside the text and the author-character within it.

For example, the distance is clear between the Kurt Vonnegut who wrote *Slaughterhouse-Five* and the authorial narrative voice who appears within it. In addition, *Slaughterhouse-Five* employs many of the other narrative experiments endemic to trauma fiction, such as fragmentation and temporal distortion, using a structure that jumps backward and forward in time. Indeed, *Slaughterhouse-Five* not only manifests these temporal shifts but also renders them a significant thematic element, since the aliens who kidnap protagonist Billy Pilgrim do not experience time in a linear fashion but can see time as a sort of landscape where all moments are visible at once: "All moments, past, present, and future, always have existed, always will exist. The Tralfamadorians can look at all the different moments just that way we can look at a stretch of the Rocky Mountains, for instance. They can see how permanent all the moments are, and they can look at any moment that interests them. It is just an illusion we have here on Earth that one moment follows another one, like beads on a string, and that once a moment is gone it is gone forever" (1994, 34). This passage is telling, in terms of trauma theory, because it casts light upon the way that some trauma survivors experience time, for while victims of trauma may not be any more able than anyone else to view time in the Tralfamadorian way, they may be doomed to relive a traumatic moment again and again. This reliving of trauma can take place both viscerally through the flashbacks commonly experienced by those suffering from post-traumatic stress disorder and through the survivors' own unconscious seeking out of the same or similar circumstances (as Erikson articulated above). Trauma survivors, then, are stuck in Langer's "durational" time in a way somewhat similar to Billy Pilgrim, who has come "unstuck in time" as he begins making unexpected and uncontrollable temporal leaps, moving backward and forward in time without warning. Becoming "unstuck in time" provides an apt description for the way in which some trauma survivors experience Langer's idea of durational time. This makes sense, since traumatized former prisoner of war Billy Pilgrim begins to experience these temporal shifts even before his encounters with the aliens, who also experience time that way.

In addition to disjointed temporality, one further narrative experiment and the one most relevant for my discussion here is the common usage in trauma narrative of a fragmented or dissociative narrative voice. By "dissociative," I mean a narrator who, due to trauma, becomes a split subject unable to reconcile the various parts of himself. According to Laurie Vickroy, this "multiple subject positioning" creates "a dialogical conception of witnessing" (2002, 27). Vickroy goes on to argue that this multiple subject positioning is rendered in narrative through multiple first-person narrators whose stories, taken together, provide an account of a traumatic event. But this effect can also be achieved in narratives with a single first-person narrator. For example, memoirs often construct what Philip Lopate has called "double perspective," which simultaneously provides "the experience as it was lived (the confusions and misapprehensions of the child one was, say), while conveying the sophisticated wisdom of one's current self" (2005). Trauma narratives, however, tend to focus on depicting the rawness of traumatic experience rather than the sophisticated wisdom afforded by cool reflection after the fact.

In addition to the dissociation depicted in individual characters, sometimes an entire trauma narrative can be characterized as dissociative. In psychological terms, dissociation is a condition, coined by Pierre Janet, in which a person experiences an altered state of consciousness, a feeling of separating from oneself and reality. The feeling can be mild, as in daydreaming, or extreme, as in memory loss or fragmented identity or multiple personality. Narrative dissociation involves conveying that dissociative experience through writing, using the experimental strategies I have already discussed. Michelle Balaev provides a succinct and useful description of the forms narrative dissociation may take: "Strategies of expressing dissociation include the disjunction of time through the use of repetition and negation; imagistic scenes of violence that lack emotional description; syntactical subversion and rearrangement; atemporality; and a doubled consciousness or point of view. These narrative techniques show the multiple sites of tension that arise within the protagonist and highlight the personal and cultural spheres of action that inform the emotional experience" (2012, xvi). Dissociation in narrative serves to demonstrate the many different senses of self that are exhibited by a trauma survivor. As O'Brien says, "By telling stories, you objectify your own experience. You separate it from yourself" (2009, 152). In terms of trauma autofiction, the conscious and ironic distance between author and author-character could be said to mirror the out-of-body sensation that many trauma victims experience as they feel separated from themselves. Thus the autofictional author-character itself can be viewed as a symptom of that dissociation.

Furthermore, the dissociation of the author-character from the extratextual author introduces a quality of fictionality to the narrative that provides the distance necessary to tell the story, and this fictionalization allows for the telling of story-truths. Aharon Appelfeld has also made this point in an interview with Philip Roth as to why he writes Holocaust-related fiction rather than a true account of his experiences at that time: "I tried several times to write 'The story of my life' in the woods after I ran away from the camp. But all my efforts were in vain. I wanted to be faithful to reality and to what really happened. But the chronicle that emerged proved to be a weak scaffolding. The result was meager, an unconvincing imaginary tale. The things that are most true are easily falsified" (2001a, 128). The result, for Appelfeld, is fiction that often only obliquely refers to the Holocaust as a historical or traumatic event. *Slaughterhouse-Five* provides an example of how an autofictional strategy can help convey this dissociation: within that novel, "Vonnegut" claims that, directly after the war, "I thought it would be easy for me to write about the destruction of Dresden, since all I would have to do would be to report what I had seen. And I thought, too, that it would be a masterpiece or at least make me a lot of money, since the subject was so big. But not many words about Dresden came from my mind then—not enough of them to make a book, anyway" (1994, 2). It is not until years later when he finds a way to fictionalize the story—to separate himself from it by relating the story of Billy Pilgrim— that Vonnegut can begin to tell it at all. He also fictionalizes the story by autofictionally separating himself from *himself* by separating Vonnegut from "Vonnegut." The dissociative autofictional author-character is one more mode of separation and fictionalization.

Balaev explains that dissociation often takes the narrative form of a "doubling" of the consciousness of the protagonist, which is an idea similar to Lopate's of a later self narrating the journey of an earlier one. According to Balaev, "Two states of consciousness can occur when the traumatic past is brought into conflict with the present" (2012, xvii). By drawing a distinction between the author and the eponymous yet differentiated author-character, autofiction represents a distinct mode of narrative dissociation. This is another reason why autofiction often becomes a useful vehicle for depicting trauma: the post-traumatic stress of the author-character can take any fictional form necessary while the novel still retains the narrative authority of being connected to a person (the author) existing outside the narrative. The author-character maintains the connection to the extratextual author regardless of how outrageously fictional the narrative becomes. So *Slaughterhouse-Five* can have its Tralfamadorians and *Breakfast of Champions* can involve "Vonnegut" entering into his novel and confronting his literary creations in order to "set them free," while still maintaining that link with the outside world through the author-character. The novels are clearly fictional, but the metafictional gesture outside themselves requires the reader to consider the novels' relationship to the actual world by implying that the trauma being described has a clear basis in fact or, at the very least, that the author-character in the novel is connected to the author-figure outside it.

Sometimes the autofiction does maintain a basis in fact. For example, Raymond Federman writes mostly about his own life, notably about his experiences as a Jew during the occupation of Paris, where he barely escaped the concentration camps while his immediate family did not. When soldiers came to arrest his family, his mother pushed fourteen-year-old

Federman into a closet and cautioned "chut" (shush). Federman's father, mother, and sister were taken away while he remained hidden for several hours. This experience is impressionistically portrayed in Federman's novel *Voice in the Closet*, in which a writer named "Federman" struggles to tell the story of a young boy hiding in a closet, while the boy rejects the older man's storytelling efforts, frustrated at the narrative liberties the older man takes in the telling. As he relates the defining trauma of his life, the extratextual Federman is doubled twice, as the older "Federman" and as the boy. Subsequently, this narrative exacerbates traumatic dissociation and demonstrates the difficulty of depicting trauma with any accuracy, because the voice of the present ("Federman") cannot reconcile his story with the voice of the past (himself as a boy).

Federman often employs this kind of double-doubling in his novels. Another example is *Aunt Rachel's Fur*, which chronicles "Federman's" experiences after the war, returning to Paris to find that his extended family had moved into his immediate family's apartment after their arrest; when he returns, they treat him like a squatter rather than a beloved family member. *Aunt Rachel's Fur* alternates between this story and the account of novelist "Federman" writing a novel about a man named "Namredef" ("Federman" spelled backwards) who is also writing a novel. Once again, the originary author-figure is twice dissociated, able through this separation to tell his characters' stories, which may or may not resemble his own. And as is often the case with autofiction, it is impossible to be sure what is factual and what is fictional. At times, "Federman" refers to the text we read as fiction, admitting that as he writes his novel, he borrows or "plagiarizes" from his life: "The work of fiction is always a form of recovery of the past, even if that past has to be falsified to seem real. The act of recalling the past in what we write doesn't mean knowing the way it really was, but rather becoming the master of memories as they burn in the perilous instant of creation" (2001, 35, 99). At other times, however, "Federman" claims to be telling his referential, historically accurate life story, albeit with some embellishments: "What the hell, what's the point of writing your life if you can't improve it a bit, one can only tell the truth, I mean the real truth, with detours and lies, it's an old dictum, and besides the only way a life can pass for literature is through exaggerations" (18). These intricate posturings and doublings make for a complex and metafictional text and provide the dissociative cover necessary to convey the author-character's sense of confusion and displacement. At the same time, the author-character's connection to the extratextual Federman, in addition to certain biographical details that match that author's life, provide a kind of authenticity and authority to the stories of his wartime experiences that they would not have if they were admittedly purely fictional. By onomastically connecting author-figure Federman to the events being described, the author-character "Federman" suggests that they are factual, whether they actually are or not.

Furthermore, although the historical accuracy of the story is a part of what makes a trauma narrative important, it is not the only important element, for even a factual story might not be "true." Tim O'Brien expounds upon this idea by trying to define what he calls a "true war story": "You'd feel cheated if it never happened. Without the grounding of reality, it's just a trite bit of puffery, pure Hollywood, untrue in the way all such stories are untrue. Yet even if it did happen—and maybe it did, anything's possible—even then you know it can't be true, because a true war story does not depend upon that kind of truth. Absolute occurrence is irrelevant. A thing may happen and be a total lie; another thing may not happen and be truer than the truth" (2009, 79–80). Here O'Brien articulates the fine line that a trauma narrative must balance upon: being "true" is not sufficient in and of itself, for some "true" stories seem like lies and some fictions seem "truer than the truth." At the same time, if the story is not "true"—if it never happened—then the reader feels cheated and the story becomes trite. Or, as Ruth Klüger has argued, connection to extratextual fact is necessary in a trauma narrative or that narrative "deteriorates to kitsch" (quoted in Yagoda 2009, 246).

O'Brien demonstrates this idea that fiction might tell a truer story than nonfiction in his story from The Things They Carried entitled "On the Rainy River," which depicts author-character "Tim," after receiving notice of being drafted to serve in Vietnam, going fishing with his kindly employer. The old man takes "Tim" in his boat to the middle of a Minnesota lake, stopping a short, swimmable distance away from the Canadian border. The two men sit there silently, understanding the decision "Tim" must make about whether or not to defect to Canada to avoid the war; the old man provides the opportunity for escape but says nothing, allowing

"Tim" to make up his own mind. As "Tim" sits weeping in the boat, thinking of the shame his family would feel and the dishonor he would bring to his small town if he were to run to Canada, he realizes he does not have the courage to face those consequences. He decides to report for duty, framing his decision as cowardly rather than heroic. Later in the collection, however, "Tim" reveals that this fishing trip never happened, but claims that the fictional story—of an older, wiser man quietly forcing him to make a conscious decision either to escape the war or to choose to fight in it—distilled the situation to its essential meaning. In this sense, then, the story is fictional and simultaneously "true." Furthermore, the onomastic connection between the character and the author provides the grounding in reality necessary to keep the story from devolving into triteness or kitsch, even though the fishing trip did not take place. Furthermore, it is important to note that, even though Tim O'Brien did serve in Vietnam, it is not necessary for him to have done so for the autofictional strategy to be evocative of narrative authenticity. The onomastic connection between author and author-character implies that the story being told is factual and that implication influences the way we read the text: this would be the case whether the extratextual author did or did not experience a trauma. The metafictional gesture to the extratextual world would obtain regardless of the extratextual accuracy of the trauma depicted therein.

For this reason, narrative dissociation can be a useful strategy even in autofictions in which the author-character has no direct experience of the trauma being depicted. For Jonathan Safran Foer, the dissociation of author and character is extreme enough that his novel *Everything Is Illuminated* renders "Jonathan" in the third person through the eyes of seventeen-year-old Alex, a Ukrainian tour guide hired to take "Jonathan" to his grandfather's childhood village. This level of dissociation, in which the author-character is rendered in third person rather than first, disallows the kind of intimate connection between reader and author-character that autofiction typically affords, yet still maintains the aura of nonfictionality provided by the onomastic connection between author and character. "Jonathan's" term for this self-distancing is to live "once-removed" (2002, 96), by which he means to live self-consciously. Subsequently, the first-person narrator with whom the reader identifies is Alex, whose naiveté and English-language malapropisms are endearingly comic. This added layer of third-person separation from the autofictional author-character mirrors the fact that "Jonathan" has come to Ukraine to investigate not his own but another person's trauma: his Grandfather Safran's persecution by the Nazis. During the trip, "Jonathan" learns less about his own grandfather's traumatic history than about Alex and his grandfather.

As seen through Alex's eyes, "Jonathan" is a finicky and somewhat ignorant American tourist prima donna. Alex knows "Jonathan" is writing a book about his experience in Ukraine and contributes his own perspective to the effort. The two later work together on the resulting narrative, sending their respective chapters back and forth and making recommendations for shaping and altering those chapters as they go. Alex discusses his ideas about what happened on their trip and about the nature of writing in general. He echoes "Federman," telling him, "I relish writing for you so much. It makes it possible for me to be not like I am, but as I desire. . . . I can repair my mistakes when I perform mistakes. . . . With writing, we have second chances" (2002, 144). And, to a certain extent, this is so. Indeed, in some instances, even "Jonathan" is not averse to changing the details of the story; he wants to remove Alex's dog from the narrative, for example, because he worries that Alex's descriptions of "Jonathan's" fear of dogs make him look foolish.

But the story they tell becomes more and more painful as Alex's grandfather becomes directly implicated in the death of his Jewish friend Herschel at the hands of the Nazis. Alex begs Jonathan to avoid revealing the devastating aspects of his family's story in their collaborative writing. Indeed, instead of just asking to alter the narrative slightly, the way "Jonathan" had by wanting to erase the dog, Alex begins to want to make substantial changes to how the boys will represent the horrific events from Alex's Grandfather's past. After all, Alex argues, they have already been taking some small liberties with actual events or, as he puts it, they are "being very nomadic with the truth" (2002, 179). In that case, Alex suggests, he and "Jonathan" could continue in that vein to correct the much larger mistakes of the past, to seize on those second chances that writing affords: "If we are to be such nomads with the truth, why do we not make the story more premium than life? . . . I do not think that there are any limits to how excellent we could make life seem" (179–80). But "Jonathan" is unyielding: the pivotal parts of the story must be told the way they happened, and Alex must tell them, even though doing so profoundly alters Alex's life and destroys the boys' friendship. In writing the story, Alex is forced to confront the continued legacy of violence spawned by the Holocaust. And in this way, *Everything Is Illuminated* demonstrates that relating the story of trauma can itself constitute a trauma, despite the narrative distance afforded by depicting the author-character in the third person.

Furthermore, *Everything Is Illuminated* demonstrates the limits we place on narrative "shaping" when telling a story that connects to an important historical event. While "Jonathan" thinks it is perfectly acceptable to alter some of the less significant events of the story to make himself look better (removing the dog, for instance), there are some aspects he refuses to alter, even though his friend Alex begs him to do so. The story of how Alex's grandfather betrayed his Jewish friend to save his own family is, to "Jonathan," a story that cannot be erased or even softened but must be told uncompromisingly. This story must be told even though Alex's grandfather is so grieved at revealing the story to Alex that he takes his own life, writing the story down causes Alex such pain that he ends his friendship with "Jonathan" and gives up his dreams of coming to America, and knowing the story forces Alex to confront his abusive father and take leadership of his family.

The message here seems to be that when it comes to something as profound as the Holocaust, no quarter must be given to fictionalizing: the facts must be accurately represented (even when those "historic" facts are fictional, i.e., they happen within the world of the novel *Everything Is Illuminated*). This is important because, as Alex's emotional letter to "Jonathan" puts it, in addition to those who actually lived—and died—in it, we are all implicated in the Holocaust and its aftermath: "The truth is that I also pointedatHerschel and I also said heisaJew and I will tell you that you also pointedatHerschel and you also said heisaJew and more than that Grandfather also pointedatme and said heisaJew and you also pointedathim and said heisaJew" (2002, 252, spacing Foer's). By betraying his friend to save his family, Alex's grandfather betrayed the coming generations of that very family, so his grandson is implicated in Herschel's death, too: Alex also pointed at Herschel. During that time, Alex's grandfather says, "You had to choose, and hope to choose the smaller evil" (246). But escaping the larger evil is impossible, Alex argues, for even "Jonathan," a Jewish American descendant of two Holocaust survivors, pointed at Herschel and, by implication, so did we all. To Alex, writing that story spurs him to try to end the cycle of violence his grandfather and the Nazis set in motion by standing up to his abusive father. To "Jonathan," even though telling that story hurt Alex and his grandfather, that story needed to be told for the sake of historic accuracy. This latter argument is particularly compelling in the context of the Ukrainian countryside, where the travelers were met with stony silence whenever they asked about the location of shtetls destroyed by the Nazis. The villagers deny these towns ever existed and yet ask the searchers, "Why now?" implying that they know of these places and want to forget what they know (2002). And as more and more mass Jewish graves are discovered in Ukraine and other Eastern European countries, a history begins to emerge that local citizens had long tried to deny, possibly even to themselves. *Everything Is Illuminated* makes the case that stories like Alex's must be told—and told accurately—so that what happened to those towns and those people is not forgotten.

And yet, of course, despite "Jonathan's" advocating historical accuracy, *Everything Is Illuminated,* and therefore Alex's story, are fictitious. True, the novel has the feel of historical accuracy because the autofictional connection between "Jonathan" and Foer causes us to draw connections between what happens within and outside the novel. But while the shtetls did exist and most of the Jews in them were murdered by the Nazis, the stories in the novel about these individuals are patently fictional. What "Jonathan" refuses to do within the novel, Foer unabashedly does: he invents, taking liberties with historical accuracy for the sake of fictional truth. As Alex would put it, the novel is more concerned with being "faithful" than with being "actual" (2002, 240). Or, as I would argue, the novel is concerned with being both "faithful" and "actual," and both modes are made possible by the novel's autofictional structure.

Tim O'Brien's novel *In the Lake of the Woods* engages in a distancing process distinct from the one employed by *Everything Is Illuminated.* O'Brien's author-character emerges only in the footnotes of the narrative. The novel tells the story of Vietnam veteran John Wade, whose campaign for U.S. senator from Minnesota is derailed when allegations emerge about his participation in the My Lai Massacre. Soon after his defeat, John's wife, Kathy, goes missing, and much of the evidence points to John as the culprit. But due to the fugue state often brought on by his Vietnam-induced post-traumatic stress disorder, even John is unsure whether he is guilty of killing her. The chapters of the novel alternate between the present-day situation, quotations from various sources about Vietnam and other wars, and chapters describing a variety of scenarios of what might have happened to Kathy. These possibilities range from her running away from John, taking a boat out on the lake and drowning or getting lost, or John killing her by pouring boiling water on her face while she sleeps. The novel never provides a definitive answer as to what happened, but rather meditates on the ephemeral nature of memory and the impossibility of truly knowing another person or completely understanding a moment of history.

Instead of concrete answers to the novel's mysteries, or perhaps because there are no concrete answers, the author-character is conjured, or even compelled, to emerge in footnotes to remark upon John and Kathy's story. These authorial comments appear only in the footnotes, seemingly so as not to interfere with the primary narrative. But as the novel progresses, the footnotes increase in number and become longer and longer, sometimes taking up almost the entire page; the authorial voice threatens at times to drown out the novel proper. Even though the novel remains ambiguous about what happened to Kathy, the author-character provides his opinion and thereby inflects our reading process. Much like "Bret" in *Lunar Park*, this author-character wants both to maintain the novel's indeterminacy and to provide his authoritative opinion on the proceedings. He "rejects" the idea that John could murder someone he loved so much (2006, 300n4), but ends by saying that there is no hope for "tidiness" and that "all secrets lead to the dark, and beyond the dark there is only maybe" (301n6). "O'Brien" insists that a novel about trauma cannot provide closure to that trauma, cannot provide comfort or even a definitive understanding. What *can* such fiction provide? "O'Brien" suggests the following: "My own war does not belong to me. In a peculiar way, even at this very instant, the ordeal of John Wade— the long decades of silence and lies and secrecy—all this has a vivid, living clarity that seems far more authentic than my own faraway experience. Maybe that's what this book is for. To remind me. To give me back my vanished life" (298n10). Writing a novel about fictional character John Wade gives "O'Brien" the perspective he cannot find while thinking about his own life. The dissociation provided through a fictional character and a fictionalized representation of the author make possible a portrayal of traumatic events that, although far removed from it, illuminate the life of the author-character, while still avoiding the possibility for complete healing or even comprehension. Constructing the story about John Wade provides the author-character "O'Brien" with a fuller, if not complete, understanding of his own traumatic experiences. Connecting "O'Brien" onomastically to O'Brien allows readers to imagine that this understanding extends to the world outside the text, even as they differentiate between the author and the author-character.

In these myriad ways, autofiction emerges as one of the narrative experiments particularly suited to the depiction of trauma and its aftermath. Through temporal shifts, fictionalization, and dissociation, the author-character provides sufficient narrative distance from the unrepresentable realities of trauma in order to make it possible to represent them. The combination of referential and fictional elements affords a kind of flexibility in narrativization that is often necessary in the depiction of traumatic events, and yet it also provides a veneer of nonfictional historical accuracy through the onomastic connection of author to author-character.

5 : Memoir vs. Autofiction as the Story of Me vs. the Story of "Me"

Philip Roth, Richard Powers, Bret Easton Ellis, and Ron Currie Jr.

> *It is* not *myself. It is* far *from myself—it's play, it's a game, it is an* impersonation *of myself! Me* ventriloquizing *myself.*
>
> —Phillip Roth, *Deception*

I stated in my introduction that the terms "autofiction" and "memoir" often seem interchangeable, depending upon one's definition of autofiction. In this book, I have adhered more closely to Gérard Genette's concept of autofiction as a fictional narrative helmed by a characterized version of the author. And although it maintains some connection to extratextual truth, this author-character is often largely—and sometimes flamboyantly—fictional. "*True* autofictions," according to Genette, are "authentically fictional," because the author implies (or states): "I, the author, am going to tell you a story of which I am the hero but which never happened to me" (1993, 77, 76). It is that "never happened to me" part of the sentence that differentiates autofiction as Genette defines it from memoir as traditionally conceived.[1] Nevertheless, as I described in chapter 3, American autofiction also has ties to the truth-telling traditions of journalism, particularly with the emergence in the late 1960s and early 1970s of the highly personal and subjective New Journalism. In this chapter, I will move forward several decades to make a related argument that, although autofiction is distinct from the memoir genre, it draws upon the truth-telling traditions and expectations (not to mention the current popularity) of memoir to achieve its rhetorical purpose.

For decades scholars of life writing have struggled to categorize texts that purposely straddle the line between fiction and nonfiction. Sidonie Smith and Julia Watson point out that "many contemporary writers deliberately blur the boundary between life writing and the kinds of stories told in the first-person novel that some call 'faction,' others 'autofiction'" (2010, 10).[2] Such works have also been called "nonfictional novels," "autobiographical novels," "factual fictions," and "fictional autobiographies" (Adams 1990, 6). I have been using the term "autofiction" to refer to texts that, through their author-character, are somewhat referential but that also feature decidedly fictional components. Because of the onomastic author-character, autofiction is often similar to, and sometimes initially mistaken for, memoir. The term "memoir" seems to have emerged as the catchall term used "to describe various practices and genres of self life writing" (Smith and Watson 2010, 3). "Memoir," then, is the term of art for a text that is referential or mostly so, but which may at times venture into narrative that borders on, but does not quite become, fiction. Timothy Dow Adams has argued that memoirs have grown in prominence because contemporary writers wanted to "regain the ambiguity that naturally surrounded the novel at its beginnings" in an effort to "keep the reader guessing about the precise degree of fictionality within their text" (1990, 8). As I have argued throughout this book, Adams's statement could be employed rather seamlessly as a way to explain the rise of autofiction. Indeed, I would take issue with Adams to note that the recent popularity of memoir is more likely due to readers' desire for a "true story" and not because they want to be kept guessing about the degree of fictionality.

To wit, G. Thomas Couser defines memoir as a text which "presents itself, and is therefore read, as a nonfictional record or re-presentation of actual humans' experience" whose primary function is "to make identity claims" (2012, 15, 13). Memoir is usually conceived of as an autobiographically accurate story told from a highly particularized and personal perspective; it is *one* person's side of *one* story, rather than an objective history or a comprehensive account of an entire life. But although a memoir may tell a small story, it nonetheless tells a referential one, that is, a story based in biographical and historical fact; in this it differs from autofiction. However, as both autofiction in France and memoir in the United States have become more and more widespread, the definitions of both have evolved to include more creative and often fictional elements. In terms of autofiction's relationship to factual events, Doubrovsky himself has noted that autofiction often "assembles them in a radically altered presentation disorderly or in an order which deconstructs and reconstructs the narrative according to its own logic with a novelistic design of its own. It can recount, and I personally do so constantly, past events or feelings, long gone situations, in the present tense, as if they were just happening" (2013, i). The fact that "enhanced material," "novelistic techniques," and "radically altered presentation" are now allowable in a putatively referential narrative demonstrates the extent to which both autofiction and memoir have shifted away from being purely factual accounts and forged a closer—and for memoir a somewhat more problematic— relationship with fictional traditions.

Furthermore, many recent memoirs have adopted a highly self-conscious or even metafictional style. Smith and Watson posit that contemporary memoirs often focus not just on the memories being depicted but also on the process of their depiction: "The categorization of memoir often signals autobiographical works characterized by density of language and self-reflexivity about the writing process, yoking the author's standing as a professional writer with the work's status as an aesthetic object" (2010, 4). In other words, contemporary memoirs are often chronicles of their own production; this self-referential yoking of the author to the work signals a rejection of modernist impersonality, and it is the primary similarity between contemporary memoir and autofiction.

In fact, because they feature characterized versions of their authors, autofictions tread by design upon ground already occupied by the contemporary memoir. Of course, autofictions are *not* pure fictions. They are adulterated by constant, if deceptive, connection to the world outside themselves. Autofiction's onomastic connection between author and protagonist can confuse readers as to whether such texts are fictions or memoirs, and they contain elements of both. This readerly confusion is part of the point: authors of autofictions are consciously eliding reality and fiction when they construct a fictional narrative around a character who also has a real-life, extratextual existence. Readers of these autofictions are faced with questions about whether the depiction of the author-character also represents an accurate portrayal of the real-life author. Even if, as is the case for me, a reader does not particularly care about the actual life of the actual author, the mere fact that the narrator/protagonist shares a name and some biographical characteristics with the author necessitates a different kind of reading process than one would undertake with a purely unreferential fiction.

This chapter will explore the effects of novels that gesture overtly and repeatedly to the world outside themselves, while simultaneously constructing obviously fictional worlds in which obviously fictional events take place. In other words, this chapter will address autofictions that masquerade as memoirs but then depart radically from an extratextual reality into a decidedly fictional one. A study of these novels demonstrates that autofictions require a flexible reading stance that shifts continually between the different expectations inherent in reading fiction and nonfiction. These autofictions consciously play with readerly expectations regarding memoir and fiction, thwarting both and thereby forcing a recognition that, although we maintain an important line of distinction between truthful and fictional narratives, the line is at times rather permeable.

The novels discussed in this chapter seem at the outset quite similar to memoirs; they are written in first person and contain some accurate biographical information about the author. Often, uninitiated readers and some critics at first mistake these autofictions for memoirs. But, in addition to any factual material they contain, these novels also portray events that simply could not have actually taken place. Richard Powers's *Galatea 2.2* depicts a computer that achieves human consciousness; Philip Roth's *Operation Shylock* has "Philip" engaging in a covert mission for the Israeli Mossad; Bret Easton Ellis's *Lunar Park* is replete with ghosts and demons; Arthur Phillips's *Tragedy of Arthur* involves his father discovering a heretofore unknown Shakespeare play; and Ron Currie Jr.'s *Flimsy Little Plastic Miracles* recounts how "Ron" faked his death while his novel, published posthumously, became an international best seller. Readers easily recognize that none of these events has actually taken place outside the text, yet the onomastic connection of protagonist to author requires constant interpretive code switching so that both the referential and fictional elements can be comprehended simultaneously.

For example, Richard Powers's *Galatea 2.2* follows "Rick," a fiction writer just returning from the Netherlands after breaking up with his girlfriend of many years. "Rick" has been given a yearlong residence in "U" during which he finishes the final draft of his latest novel and grapples with writer's block which precludes him from beginning the next one. These details of "Rick's" life mirror those of Powers's, who did live and write for many years in the Netherlands and did subsequently work as professor and writer-in-residence at the University of Illinois in "U"r-bana. So the details of Powers's life are the same as the novelistic ones for "Rick." The same could be said for Philip Roth's *Operation Shylock,* which opens with "Philip" living in New York with his wife, Claire (Roth was married to actress Claire Bloom at the time of that book's publish-ing), planning a trip to Israel to interview writer Ahron Appelfeld. These interviews did take place and were published by Roth in 1998 in the *New York Times Book Review.*

Another similar example of a novel that seems—at the outset—like a memoir is Bret Easton Ellis's 2005 *Lunar Park,* which opens with a thirty-page description of "Bret's" rise to fame as a member of the "Literary Brat Pack" of the 1980s. However, the vigilant reader tracing the connections between Ellis the author and "Bret" the character will notice that, while Ellis went to Bennington College, "Bret" attended the fictional Camden College. While small, that detail is important, for it makes clear very ear-ly on that "Bret" and Ellis are *not* the same person and that significant portions of *Lunar Park* are fictional, not referential: overall, *Lunar Park* is more fiction than memoir.[3]

What is curious are the lengths to which these autofictions go to give the impression that their narratives represent a biographically accurate chronicle of the lives of their authors. Even as the narratives veer off in clearly fictional directions, they still maintain ties, to varying extents, to the real-life identities of their authors. The question at issue is why auto-fictions would overtly draw upon readers' expectations of memoir by fea-turing an authorial protagonist, but would then knowingly thwart those expectations by embroiling that author-character in a clearly fictional narrative. What is to be gained by this narrative maneuver, and why have such works become so popular?

In order to approach these questions, it is helpful to examine what these autofictions actually do, what expectations they elicit from readers, and how they play with and frustrate those expectations. For my purpos-es, it is not important to determine the exact moment or moments when these novels shift from fact to fiction. Rather, what interests me is the nar-rative effect these novels achieve by evoking the traditions of memoir and exploiting them for fictional ends. Autofiction occupies a liminal space between fiction and nonfiction. This is a space that requires the reader to perform continuous adjustments to the reading process, as the novel vacillates between biographical fact and outright fiction. This unsettling of the reading process obviates the possibility for narrative suture by calling repeated attention to the presence of the author-figure external to the text whose life may or may not be accurately depicted within it. This denial of narrative suture—of becoming so deeply involved in the world of the novel that one "loses oneself"—is a characteristic of all metafiction. It is of particular interest in autofiction, however, for the ways in which it draws upon the traditions and expectations of memoir in order to call readers' attention to its own fictionality. In so doing, autofiction forces a recognition that, as much as we like to believe that a novel can create a purely fictional world of its own, novels instead continually make reference to the extratextual world. These references might be the explicit ones made by autofiction or the implicit ones evinced in more traditional realistic fiction.

Furthermore, autofiction represents the extent to which awareness and tacit acceptance of poststructuralist theory has reached a mainstream audience. Poststructuralist narrative theory decrees that any attempt at narrativization is fictional by its very nature, for whenever words are arranged in order to convey information, the shaping of events into a verbal format and a narrative structure necessarily requires the reconstruction and therefore the fictionalization of those events. Language and narrative are not transparent modes of communication; rather, they inherently impose a screen between the audience and the reality being depicted. Dorrit Cohn quotes several writers making this argument in *The Distinction of Fiction*:

> "The mere selection, arrangement, and presentation of facts is a technique belonging to the field of fiction" (Arnold Toynbee); "All accounts of our experience, all versions of 'reality,' are of the nature of fiction" (Ronald Suckenick); "There is no fiction or nonfiction as we commonly understand it: there is only narrative" (E. L. Doctorow); "If it is true that narratives give us no reliable knowledge of what they purport to relate, they are all fictions, including those of history" (Wlad Godzich). (Cohn 2000, 8)

Hayden White provides perhaps the most notable articulation of this opinion, claiming that even historical accounts are "verbal fictions," in much the same way novels are (1978, 82). And while Cohn herself and other theorists like Paul Ricoeur and Marie-Laure Ryan have taken issue with the idea that all narrative is inherently fictional (a phenomenon that Ryan has termed "panfictionality"), that notion has had a widespread effect on narrative theory as well as on the general reading public.

Whether one accepts the notion of panfictionality or not, it is clear that memoir is similar to fiction in substantial ways: any work that narrativizes real-life events must, to a certain extent, reconstruct those events, and that reconstruction often greatly resembles a fiction. The term "memoir" itself implies memory, and memory is notoriously inaccurate, so the argument goes. Although the author of a memoir may try to hew as closely as possible to a factual representation of what happened, all he/she can do is convey a close approximation. The resulting narrative is perhaps fictive, if not completely fictional. Because some might see this as a distinction without a difference, the idea might be better expressed by saying that memoir involves the creative construction of a narrative in order to relate events that actually took place, rather than the fictional invention of events that did not. Thus, although readers of memoir are somewhat forgiving of authors who must operate within the vicissitudes of memory, they also expect the memoirist to present accounts of historic or personal events as factually as possible.

This connection to factual accounts differentiates memoir—if only somewhat—from the autofictional novels I discuss. As Couser suggests, "While the memoir and the novel may mirror each other in *form*, in *force* they may be quite different" (2012, 13). In other words, novels and memoirs are similar in structure and content, but the memoir's connection to supposed "truth" brings about a difference in the effect a memoir can have on its reader. This difference in force between a memoir and a novel, even while they employ a similar form, is precisely what autofictional novels are exploiting. By ironically pretending to be memoirs ("ironically" because few readers actually mistake these novels for genuine memoirs), autofictions construct a fictional situation that readers pretend to take as fact. The reading process for autofiction, therefore, is somewhat different from that for traditional novels, for while readers recognize that much of what is depicted in an autofiction is fictional, the onomastic connection of author to protagonist implies that *some* of what is depicted is nonfictional. Readers of autofiction engage in only a partial suspension of disbelief, knowing that the text is a novel, but engaging with it for the nonce as a memoir.

Like autofiction, memoir as a genre has become increasingly popular over the past several years, even decades. Perhaps the current popularity of the memoir genre is one reason why such memoir-esque autofiction is also increasingly widespread. The popularity of both genres is indicative of the already close relationship between the memoir and the novel. Couser argues, "In the West, memoir developed in tandem with the novel; in English, at least, the two genres have enjoyed a symbiotic relationship for some two hundred years. And they remain intertwined" (2012, 15). He then points out that "most novels (at least until about 1900) took the *form* of life-writing genres" (15), such as diaries, journals, or series of letters. The memoir and the novel continued along much the same path until the advent of modernist fictional innovations such as internal dialogue or stream of consciousness, which Couser suggests presented a set of fictional strategies that were not available in the same way to the memoir writer. I have my doubts about this part of his argument, for it seems as though contemporary memoir calls upon all the devices employed by fiction, including stream of consciousness. Suffice it to say, his point about the vital role the memoir played in the development of the novel is important to consider in this exploration of contemporary autofiction that self-consciously evokes the characteristics of a memoir in a decidedly fictional milieu.

The current popularity of the memoir forces a reexamination of the extent to which we can say that the nature of all narrative is fictional (and therefore forces a reconsideration of much of what Hayden White and others argued above). And the case could be made that the rise of memoir demonstrates that contemporary American readers do perceive a difference between fiction and nonfiction and have recently developed an avid taste for the latter. In other words, while contemporary critics and theorists seem to have accepted the idea that a narrative cannot convey truth, but only a partial and not impartial version of it, a more general readership may not have accepted that idea and may, in fact, be actively resisting it by embracing the memoir as a genre. The individual versions of truth known as memoirs have in recent years become one of the most widely read forms of narrative being published today. Ben Yagoda, in *Memoir: A History*, points out that between 2004 and 2008, total sales in some categories of memoir increased more than 400 percent. Furthermore, "Memoir has become the central form of the culture: not only the way stories are told, but the way arguments are put forth, products and properties marketed, ideas floated, acts justified, reputations constructed or salvaged" (2009, 28).[4] With the advent of new media outlets in which someone's personal blog can develop into a widely read (and potentially lucrative) publication, Yagoda's statement is even more applicable.

Many writers have speculated as to why the memoir genre has become and remains so popular, while the popularity of fictional works has waned. Some have attributed the increased interest in writing memoir to our psychologized, confessional culture, and this preoccupation with the personal narrative no doubt is an important reason that autobiographical writing has been popular throughout the novel's history. However, Yagoda contrasts Sylvia Plath's "semi-autobiographical" work *The Bell Jar* from 1963, in which she changed the names of characters and institutions (and even used the pseudonym "Victoria Lucas" for its publication), with Susanna Kaysen's 1993 memoir, *Girl, Interrupted*, which not only uses real names but also includes a photocopy of her case file (Yagoda 2009, 228). So while rendering one's own experiences into narrative is nothing new, the urge to reveal intensely personal, often unsavory information and experiences and proudly claim them as one's own is seemingly a contemporary phenomenon and one that is strengthening with the increasing ubiquity (and popularity) of social networks and personal blogs.[5] As Yagoda says about the explosion of memoirs on the contemporary publishing scene, "Something was in the air" (13).

But what was—or is—that "something?" While the above explains somewhat why so many writers feel compelled to write memoirs and personal narratives, it does not explain their popularity. What is it that readers want and get from memoirs that more traditional fiction does not supply? One possible answer lies in the ways in which a memoir promises to lay bare the identity of the author. Philip Lopate has argued that "the trick" in writing memoir is "to establish a double perspective, that will allow the reader to participate vicariously in the experience as it was lived (the confusions and misapprehensions of the child one was, say), while conveying the sophisticated wisdom of one's current self." J. Nicole Jones argues something similar when she says that memoir provides "a unique dialogue that happens only in memoir between the present and the past." However, while I would agree that a good memoir does employ this "double perspective," I would take issue with the notion that such a dialogue is unique somehow to memoir. There are scores of great works of fiction that make use of an older, wiser narrator reflecting upon events of his/her past, and therefore there is little in these definitions of memoir to differentiate it from fiction. Neither do these definitions answer the question of why, in this current moment, memoir is so popular in relation to fiction.

One element that memoir provides and fiction does not, of course, is a referential gesture toward extratextual fact. Perhaps this is an increasingly important factor to readers in a "post-truth" age in which doubts abound about whether objective truth is accessible or if it even exists. To demonstrate the contemporary desire for a historically and biographically accurate narrative, Yagoda cites Holocaust survivor Ruth Klüger's reaction to a Holocaust memoir that turned out to be a hoax, as it was written by someone with no personal connection to the Holocaust:[6] "However valid it may be that much of this may have happened to other children, with the falling away of the authentic autobiographical aspect and without the guarantee of a living first-person narrator identical with the author, it [the memoir] merely becomes a dramatization that offers no illumination" (Yagoda 2009, 246). Writers and readers of fiction might object to the contention that nonautobiographical narratives offer no illumination, but Klüger goes on to make the point that when a narrative employs "naïve directness" to portray "naïve suffering," a connection to autobiographical fact is necessary, or else the narrative "deteriorates to kitsch" (246). The unstated but implicit point she seems to be making here—one that writers like Neil Genzlinger and other reviewers have also made—is that because a memoir is an ostensibly referential narrative, the bar for the quality of writing seems lower. If a fictional narrative is well written, it can be moving; if a narrative can make claims to truth, it can be moving without being particularly well written.[7] If that "true" narrative is later discovered to have been false, the poor writing instantly becomes more evident, rendering the narrative "kitsch" or, as Yagoda terms it, "schlock" (246). This is not, of course, to say that all memoirs are written poorly, just that the extent to which memoirs engage with a referential story affords them a short-cut to depth and poignancy to which fiction does not have access.

Couser suggests that the reason the quality of writing is less important for a memoir than for a fiction is that a memoir performs a different sort of "cultural work" than a fiction does. Memoir, he says, "entails moral and political force rather than, or as well as, literary form" (2012, 53). Thus a memoir that is proven to be false cannot retain the same force, because that force emits not from the quality of the writing nor from the power of the narrative world it constructs (as it does in fiction) but from the connection the memoir makes to an extratextual reality. Thus whereas fiction creates a rarified and self-contained universe of its own (a universe that *may* but need not greatly resemble the actual one), much of a memoir's power derives from the accuracy of its correspondence to the world outside itself. This is why the question of whether a narrative is "true" becomes so important for a memoir: if it is not historically accurate, a memoir loses that direct connection with the actual world that constituted an important part of its appeal. What autofiction demonstrates, however, is that the cultural force of a work of fiction is also, if to a lesser extent, determined by its connection to the world outside the text.

Ron Currie Jr.'s 2013 novel, *Flimsy Little Plastic Miracles: A True Story**, provides a good example of what I mean. In it, "Ron" has escaped to a tropical island to write his next novel. Despairing over how badly it is turning out and mourning a lost relationship, he decides to kill himself, but he survives and flees to Afghanistan. His friends and family believe that he is dead; his unfinished novel is found and published to great acclaim, partly due to the supposedly tragic suicide of its author. "Ron" describes the publishers' and public reaction like this: "My botched ode to Emma, my incomplete hymn to obsessive love, my literary flipper baby, was quite simply, as far as they were concerned, a hugely compelling piece of art—well nigh a masterpiece" (2013, 256). Once "Ron" emerges from hiding, however, a James Frey type of controversy ensues. The novel is considered a masterpiece when its author has killed himself for love, and it becomes an instant catastrophe once he is revealed to still be alive. *Flimsy Little Plastic Miracles* suggests that what is the case with memoirs is true for fiction as well: the quality of the narrative is determined in no small part by the identity and circumstances of its author. In other words, context matters, both for memoir and for fiction.[8] In terms of memoir, the context is that the author is telling an ostensibly "true" story; this element of autobiographical accuracy is part of the meaning readers glean from the text and, therefore, inextricably part of the aesthetic value they assign to it. For fiction, the context can be more complicated to suss out, for the identity of the author (what Foucault calls the "author-function") helps determine how a book is read. For "Ron," this means that a novel with a tragic backstory is somehow considered better than one without.

The fact that memoirs are supposedly autobiographically accurate narratives, and that this factor is partly why they are popular, suggests that, poststructuralist theory aside, there remains in our culture a deep attraction to the idea of "truth." Even in the face of the understanding that all writing is artificially shaped, memoirs' claims to truth are their prime selling points, indicating that, despite some narrative theorists' protestations, we are not actually ready to cede all narrative to the category of fiction: something there is that doesn't love panfictionality. Apparently, a factual story still has an important cultural valence, perhaps in direct reaction to the very theories that posit the impossibility of language to convey the truth. That is to say, a particular *form* of truth is increasingly important to readers: the specific and highly personal narrative evinced by most memoirs (as opposed, say, to the kind of historical accuracy provided by a more traditional biography or a historical narrative). Clearly, there is something about a referential narrative, now more than ever, that engages readers in a time when the popularity of other forms of published narrative seems to be declining. Jill Ker Conway has ironically argued that "the only prose narratives which are accorded the suspension of disbelief today are the autobiographers' attempts to narrate the history of a real life or the biographers' carefully documented historical reconstructions of lives in times past" (1998, 5). It might be more accurate to say that the appeal of biography or autobiography lies in the fact that suspension of disbelief is not necessary if the events being chronicled actually took place. And perhaps that is what is at issue: readers are less interested in suspending disbelief than they are in reading about the "truth."

Will Self, in his autofictional novel *Walking to Hollywood*, suggests that it is not an unwillingness but an inability to suspend disbelief that is damaging his ability to enjoy narrative fiction. In this novel, protagonist "Will Self" laments, "I'd had these difficulties with theatre since my late teens . . . then, when I began writing myself, narrative fiction was the next victim—hauling on the strings of my own puppets meant I couldn't help seeing everyone else doing the same tricks. Film and TV remained plausible. . . .

But then—it must've been ten years ago or so—I began to be insistently aware of the sound recordist hovering out of shot, his furry boom mike dangling above the frame. So I started looking for it all the time" (2010, 134–35). Being able to see the mechanics involved in the construction, first of theater, then fiction, then film and television, has stripped from "Will" the ability to lose himself in narrative. The current preoccupation with metanarrative—by calling attention to the structures of narrative that I discussed in the introduction—are clearly at the root of "Will's" problem. "Will" sees this inability to suspend disbelief as a widespread phenomenon and goes on a pilgrimage to Hollywood to determine what caused it or, as he says, to figure out what "killed the movies."

"Will's" conclusion is that the technological advances that facilitate ever more amazing cinematic special effects have caused audiences to lose their ability to suspend disbelief. The movies are so realistic looking—even when depicting the physically impossible—that viewers no longer have to supply their own sense of wonder because the film supplies it for them. Thus, according to "Will," contemporary audiences (and, implicitly, readers) have lost the capacity for imaginative viewing (or reading). *Walking to Hollywood*, an autofiction, provides some possible insight into the popularity of the memoir: if readers were no longer able or willing to suspend disbelief, then fiction would lose much of its appeal. Such readers would logically embrace the insight into authentic experience that memoir ostensibly provides. This reaction would suggest that readers are wedded, perhaps even more than ever, to the possibility of accessing truth through narrative because the hyperreal world of CGI and reality television has atrophied readers' imaginations, rendering them unable to enjoy a fictional narrative.

Admittedly, this conclusion is provocative and rather harsh, but there is another way to understand the burgeoning popularity of the memoir. Rather than a reaction *against* poststructuralist ideas of language's fallibility and the impossibility of objective truth, it could be argued that the popularity of memoir is due in large part to an *acceptance* of those very ideas. The more mainstream poststructuralist ideas about the nature of language and its shortcomings as a mode of communication become, the more popular narrative forms like memoir—which purport to tell a true story—become. As readers grasp the notion that the truth is not out there, or not accessible to us if it is, they become more and more invested in knowing a particular version of the truth. It is important to note that it is memoir, not autobiography, that has become so widespread. An autobiography purports to tell *the* story of an entire life, while a memoir tells *a* story—a personal and highly specific story—about a particular episode or aspect of a person's life. In other words, a memoir by definition gives a single perspective on a single event or issue; it does not purport to tell the entire story. And this, perhaps, is why this genre has become so popular. Memoirs provide readers with the sense of access to the "truth" that they crave, while evincing an awareness that such truth is not universal or eternal, but fleeting and in the eye of the beholder. Thus the memoir rises in popularity not despite but because of the increasing awareness that language does not merely convey meaning but constitutes it, language does not merely depict reality but shapes our perceptions of it, and the reality of a situation is highly dependent upon the perspective of the observer. Read this way, the explosive popularity of memoir reflects a culture that recognizes that one's reality is wholly contingent upon one's point of view. In this sense, the burgeoning memoir boom and the attendant development in creative writing curricula of the "Creative Nonfiction" genre—what Mark McGurl calls "the fascination of the conversion of memory into felicitous expression"—can be traced to ideals similar to those that informed the New Journalism (2009. 19).

McGurl goes on to argue convincingly that the postwar democratization of the American university system eventually resulted in the widespread establishment of creative writing programs. From this emerged the near-religious tenet exhorting would-be writers to "Write What You Know," an exhortation which, while it probably does not relate directly to the self-reflexive turn of mid-twentieth-century American fiction, could partially explain the rising popularity of memoir writing in this country. It is also possible to draw a more or less direct line of descent from the gonzo journalism of a Hunter S. Thompson or the "participatory journalism" of a George Plimpton to the kind of experiential memoir typified by writers who devote a year to living "bibically," "sugar free," cooking like Julia Child or learning to dunk a basketball.[9]

The popularity of such books (which sometimes even get made into major motion pictures starring Julia Roberts (*Eat, Pray, Love*) or Meryl Streep and Amy Adams (*Julie and Julia*) suggests that readers embrace narratives depicting "true" experience while at the same time recognizing the impossibility of language to convey the whole truth of any experience. This contradiction at the heart of the popularity of memoir is amply illustrated by the Oprah Winfrey/James Frey affair. James Frey's putative memoir, *A Million Little Pieces* (2003), was featured in Winfrey's powerful Book Club in 2005, after which it reached number one on Amazon's best-seller list. At the height of the book's popularity, allegations emerged that some of the incidents described in it were fabricated, and a national scandal ensued. Frey later admitted to misrepresenting the work as a memoir, saying that he had been unable to find a publisher for the book when he called it a novel. When Frey changed its designation to memoir, the book was almost immediately accepted for publication by Random House (who had rejected it in its novel form). As it unfolds, Oprah Winfrey's multifaceted response to the incident is indicative of our ambiguous and complicated cultural stance toward the memoir and its capacity for truth-telling.

Winfrey's first public reaction to the revelation that the memoir she had so enthusiastically touted was, in fact, a fiction occurred on January 11, 2006, when she called in to respond to the situation when CNN's *Larry King Live* had Frey as a guest. At that point, Winfrey still defended Frey and his book, saying that, regardless of the controversy, "the underlying message of redemption in James Frey's memoir still resonates with me. And I know that it resonates with millions of other people who have read this book and will continue to read this book." Here Winfrey seems to be saying that what is important in a text is its power to move a reader, regardless of whether it is factual or fictional. At this point, Frey's book had not yet devolved in her mind into "kitsch," even though key parts of it were found to be fabrications.

A few moments later in the same exchange, however, Winfrey altered her stance somewhat to say, in reference to one of the events that had been fabricated: "Whether he hit the police officer or didn't hit the police officer is irrelevant to me. What is relevant is that he was a drug addict who spent years in turmoil, from the time he was ten years old, drinking and . . . and tormenting himself and his parents. And, out of that, stepped out of that history to be the man that he is today, and to take that message to save other people and allow them to save themselves. That's what's important about this book and his story." Here, then, Winfrey refers not to the power of the *narrative* but to the identity of its *au-*

thor. What is important, she argues, is that, although some of the specifics of the story might have been invented, the most important details have not. Frey really was an addict, he truly was in recovery, and therefore his story was still effective and still had the potential to help others. Her argument shifts significantly to posit that the factual accuracy of the *story* is not important as long as the biographical accuracy of the *author* remains untarnished. She implies that the vital component of a memoir is not the story but the lived reality of the person behind the story. In suggesting that the power of the narrative lies not within the text but within the life of its writer, Winfrey joins the long line of those giving the lie to Barthes's well-known requiem to the author.

This iteration of Winfrey's argument goes as follows: a certain amount of fictionalization would be acceptable in a memoir, but too much fictionalization would render the book invalid. A further implication is that a novel—a completely fictional story—about addiction, perhaps written by a nonaddict, would not have had the same value as a "true" story written by an actual addict. Couser's take on this issue is that, as a recovering addict, Frey engages in an implicit pact with his readers based on "the ethics of recovery, in which the candid acknowledgment of one's failings is considered a crucial step" (2012, 82). By lying about those failings, Frey violated those ethics, rendering his work invalid as a narrative of confession and redemption, because a memoir's power emerges not from the strength of the writing but from the accuracy of the confession and the sincerity of the request for redemption. Thus, according to Couser, another difference between a memoir and a fiction is that authorial intention is more immediately relevant in a memoir than it is in a fiction: "It matters whether a memoirist is confessing, boasting, defending, witnessing, or accusing. Each action involves a different stance toward past experience and the audience; therefore, reading involves identifying the author's stance" (177). Once again, the power of the memoir arises externally, not internally. It comes not from within the narrative but from without, from the identity and the intentions of the one who wrote it. And those intentions are instrumental in determining how we read memoir.

The point I am trying to make in this discussion is that this distinction between fictional elements that a reading audience will tolerate in a memoir and ones they will not accept demonstrates not only that the author is not dead—at least in relation to the genre of memoir—but also that the adherence to a belief in the intentional fallacy that still drives much literary criticism of the novel simply is not relevant with regard to the memoir. Ultimately, and in a similar manner, autofiction demonstrates that authorial intention also matters for fiction, since that is what informs a reader how to read a work as fiction in the first place.

How one ought to determine an author's legitimacy and how much fictionalization is too much in a memoir are questions that Winfrey, Frey, and King do not tackle. But after her appearance on Larry King, Winfrey received a great deal of blowback from disgruntled readers of Frey's book, upset with his misrepresentations and angry that she had supported him. She subsequently had Frey on her own show on January 26, 2006, so that he could face her audience's wrath. At this point, Winfrey's reaction, tempered by that of her viewers, had shifted once again: "I regret that phone call," she said, in reference to her call to *Larry King Live*. "I made a mistake, and I left the impression that the truth does not matter, and I am deeply sorry about that. That is not what I believe. . . . To everyone who has challenged me on this issue of truth, you are absolutely right" (Memmot 2006). Here Winfrey's opinion had evolved to the point that the factuality of Frey's narrative actually did matter, so much so that she spent most of that episode of her show ripping into Frey, eliciting several in-person mea culpas from him and his editor, Nan Talese, whom she chided for not fact-checking Frey's book more carefully or, as the editor herself admitted, not fact-checking it at all.

Oprah Winfrey's evolution of opinion on the James Frey episode reveals our contentious relationship with narrative in general and memoir in particular. On one hand, readers of memoir realize that memory is fleeting and often inaccurate and that rendering real-life experience into language requires shaping and, yes, taking some liberties with the facts. But, as Winfrey made clear to Frey, a good memoir must ultimately hew rather closely to historical and biographical fact, at the very least in order to pass muster with debunking websites like *Smoking Gun*, which is the site that originally investigated and called into question Frey's claims to having been imprisoned. What emerges is the idea that the story a memoir tells can be unrealistic but must be mostly "true," for as Leigh Gilmore puts it, "Autobiography draws its authority less from its resemblance to real life than from its proximity to discourses of truth and identity, less from reference or mimesis than from the cultural power of truth telling" (2001, 3).

As I mentioned earlier, some narrative theorists look quizzically upon this controversy, given that poststructuralist criticism has long purported that writing—and language in general—is always an artificial screen upon which ideas are projected. Writing is unable to convey direct experience or reality and is, according to these scholars, fictive if not fully fictional. Arnaud Schmitt represents this sentiment when he says, "The James Frey affair is actually a simple matter and there is no way one could have predicted it (outside the author's personal sphere). It is just a text shifting from one modality to another simply because it has been abruptly recontextualized" (2010, 133). What the Frey controversy demonstrates, however, is the extent to which a rather large segment of the population does *not* see a discredited memoir as simply requiring a shift in modality or a recontextualization. And furthermore, given the response to other disproven memoirs, it is evident that this situation could very well have been predicted. Clearly, "truth" still matters in narrative, at least in some contexts and among some readers. The question for me is, how are the novelists I examine employing this penchant for truth-telling and truth-reading in their highly fictional works?

And I think the answer can be found in an examination of the differences between the way we read memoirs and the way we read novels. At the heart of those differences is that concept of what constitutes "truth" in narrative. Couser argues that being "tethered to the real world," while limiting what a memoir can say or do, also allows it "to enlist—to conscript" the reader to its particular stance (2012, 176, 170). In other words, the memoir's reference to and putative correspondence with the world outside itself elicits a different kind of response from the reader than does fiction, through its construction of a hermetically sealed world of its own. Thus an autofiction—a novel with an eponymous author/protagonist—would elicit much the same reader response as a memoir, at least at first. This kind of fictional autofiction implies that it maintains a memoir-esque connection with the outside world and then conveys a story that is so obviously fictional that it seems to sever that connection. However, the fact that the author and the protagonist have the same name and many of the same biographical characteristics disallows a complete severing of their connection.

Autofictions are consciously departing from the "truth" of their author-characters' extratextual lives in order to test the limits of the connection to the external world that memoirs maintain. The result is a group of novels that take Philip Lopate's idea of "double perspective" to an even greater extreme, for instead of merely a wiser narrator describing an earlier, less knowledgeable self, there is the added layer of the "actual" writer outside the text who is clearly not identical to his character. And of course, this is a marked departure from memoir, in which the narrator is meant to be equated to the real-life author; this equation is ultimately rendered impossible in autofiction.

Part of the effect of the autofictional novel is that it demonstrates the continued relevance of the author, despite theoretical arguments about his (and sometimes her) death. Far from being dead to these novels, the author is the protagonist. Furthermore, by requiring a constant adjustment and readjustment of reader expectations as to what is factual about the author-character and what is fictional, autofiction requires a continual recognition of the presence and authority of the actual author. In other words, the figure of the extratextual author maintains a presence within the novel by requiring the reader to determine—or at least to wonder—to what extent the author is equivalent to the author-character. With each increasingly unlikely plot development, the reader is forced to reconsider the relationship between the author and the eponymous protagonist. One might say that the extratextual author-function "haunts" these texts, not fully appearing in his biographical reality, but making his presence felt through the eponymous character who resembles him and shares his name.

These novels lead inevitably to questions from readers about how much of what they depict is biographically factual. Indeed, one of the first articles published about *Lunar Park*, "A Fact-Finding Tour of 'Lunar Park,'" is exactly that: an attempt to delineate which elements of the novel are factual and which are fictional. And authors like Ellis often play up the idea that their fictions are referential narratives, even though they are published, marketed, and shelved as novels. For example, "Bret" the character admonishes: "There's one thing you must remember as you hold this book in your hands: all of it really happened, every word is true" (2005, 30). And perhaps the argument could be made that, while much of it did *not* really happen, every word still is, in a literary sense, "true."

Promotional materials for autofictional novels often play upon that uncomfortable relationship between reality and fiction. When *Lunar*

Park was first published, the publisher's website for the novel featured a split screen with two representations of "Bret Easton Ellis," with one side representing the author and the other side representing the character. The character side included photos of Bret's supposed wife, actress Jayne Dennis (who does not exist outside the text). The website made it clear that *Lunar Park* was a novel, not a memoir, by differentiating between the two Ellises, thus cluing readers in to the autofictional "joke." By contrast, Philip Roth went to great lengths to try to convince readers that *Operation Shylock* was a true story in a March 7, 1993, article for the *New York Times Book Review* that appeared near the time of its publication. In the article, "A Bit of Jewish Mischief," Roth describes his recent experience challenging a man impersonating him in Jerusalem, claiming that the experience imbued him with sympathy for his frustrated readers: "I now understand a little more subjectively something of the disorienting extremes of distress with which my books are said to bedevil these readers." Roth's claims that the events in his autofictional novel actually happened caused a bit of confusion, and some bookstores called the publisher because they were having trouble determining whether to shelve the book as fiction or nonfiction.

"Philip" the autofictional author-character goes even further than Roth to assert that *Operation Shylock* is a referential narrative, as he claims to have omitted the chapter that chronicled his work as a representative for the Israeli secret service, the Mossad, because of the threat to international relations such revelations would cause. Thus both Roth and "Philip" claim that the story actually took place, but they imply that they must call it a fiction to avoid revealing vital Israeli secrets and getting into legal trouble—or worse. Near the end of the novel, "Philip" calls attention to the traditional disclaimer at the beginning of any novel: "This book is a work of fiction. . . . Any resemblance to actual . . . persons, living or dead, is entirely coincidental" (1994, 361). He thereby implicitly invites the reader to compare this disclaimer to the actual disclaimer found at the end of *Operation Shylock*, which is nearly identical to the one included within the novel, except it has an extra line at the end: "This confession is false." But which confession is the false one, the disclaimer or the novel itself, which has *A Confession* as its subtitle? If the confession of the disclaimer is false, then the novel is "true," but if the confession that constitutes the novel is false, then the entire narrative is a fiction. Within the novel, protagonist "Philip Roth" vows to us that every word is true and that the disclaimer is false. Through these labyrinthine confessions and misdirections, "Philip" forces readers to examine the text they hold, to acknowledge it as a written artifact. That is to say, the author-character within the novel overtly evokes the paratextual world outside it, exhorting readers to take notice of the construction of the book itself. The autofictional nature of the novel—the fact that "Philip Roth" is its main character—demands that the reader pay attention to both the textual and the extratextual worlds. Even if one reads the text as a fiction, its metafictional and autofictional elements place limits on the possibility for narrative suture.

In a similar manner, Michael Chabon pushes the boundaries of autofictional memoir in *Moonglow: A Novel*, which, despite its title, masquerades as a family history. As a masquerade within a masquerade, the novel reveals that "Mike's" grandmother lied about being a Holocaust survivor. But the fiction of "Mike's" grandmother's life story is, of course, contained within the fiction of the novel, whose paratextual disclaimer assures us: "This is a work of fiction. Names, characters, places, and incidents are products of the author's imagination or are used fictitiously and are not to be construed as real. Any resemblance to actual events, locales, organizations, or persons, living or dead, is entirely coincidental. Scout's honor" (Chabon 2016). Thus the stunning revelation about a member of "Mike's" family both does and does not carry the weight of truth: it is true within the novel and fictional outside it.

Ron Currie Jr.'s *Flimsy Little Plastic Miracles: A True* Story* evokes the opposite effect, as he claims that his novel is "true." The asterisk by the word "True" in the title directs the reader to the lengthy disclaimer at the beginning of the text which says that the novel is "based on real events": "If you, like me, get goose bumps whenever you encounter those magic words . . . I promise, on my father's grave, that that is exactly the sort of story you'll find in this book" (Currie 2013). David Foster Wallace's posthumously published unfinished novel, *The Pale King*, also plays with disclaimers, although this time within the actual text: "Author here. Meaning the real author, the living human holding the pencil, not some abstract narrative persona. . . . David Wallace, age forty, ss no. 975–04–2012, addressing you from my Form 8829–deductible home office at 725 Indian Hill Blvd., Claremont 91711 CA, on this fifth day of spring, 2005, to inform you of the following: All of this is true. This book is really true" (2011, 66). The "author," "David Wallace," really wants to convince us he is the real authorial deal, even going so far as to provide us with his address and Social Security number. In a very real sense, the gestures toward "truth" that these novels evince are possible only because of their autofictional nature—because they employ protagonists with the same name as their authors. As I said, the author-character draws an explicit connection between the world within and the world outside the text, a connection encouraged by the continual claims that the story we are reading is "true," or, as "Ron Currie Jr." puts it, "capital-T True" (2013, 1).

These autofictions take on the patina of memoir in order to titillate and intrigue, but they also do so ironically, for the louder the truth claims, the more explicit the invitation to compare the fictional truth claims with the extratextual facts. These overt claims to truth have the opposite effect, as they serve to convince readers of the text's fictionality. Furthermore, when a reader is repeatedly asked to evaluate a novel's truth claims, this calls into question the extent to which any narrative can be completely nonfictional (since all writing involves some amount of reconstruction) or completely fictional (since all narrative is drawn in some ways from life itself). Autofictions, then, cause a reconsideration of the impossibility of a completely fictional narrative as well as a completely truthful one.

And it is in that gesture toward nonfiction—that gesture toward memoir—that the autofictions I focus on become relevant here. It is my contention that the same cultural forces that contribute to the increasing popularity of the memoir genre also contribute to the rapid increase in contemporary autofictions. The contemporary American preoccupation with a "true story"—or the impossibility thereof—has led both to the rise in prominence of the literary memoir and to the widespread proliferation of autofiction. In an era in which the heretofore dominant literary genre of fiction is potentially being overthrown in importance and marketability by the memoir, some autofiction could be viewed as "fictional memoirs"— as literary efforts to capitalize on the popularity of the memoir and to experiment with it as a literary form. As a corollary, I would point to Arnaud Schmitt's discussion about the rise in the nineteenth and early twentieth centuries of autobiographical novels such as *David Copperfield, A Portrait of the Artist as a Young Man,* and *In Search of Lost Time.* Schmitt argues,

"Originally, autobiographical novels stemmed from the author's will to enjoy the rising social status of fiction writers" while still allowing the author to write about his own life (2010, 123). As writers of fiction gained status, Schmitt continues, those writers who wanted to include autobiographical elements in their writing began to do so in the guise of fiction, hence the autobiographical novel. In current times I would turn Schmitt's argument around to say that one reason writers often evoke charactorial versions of themselves in their fiction is so they can take advantage of the rising social status of the memoirist—and challenge the limits of the memoir genre at the same time.

The insecurity of novelists in the face of the waning popularity of the novel—what Kathleen Fitzpatrick has called "the anxiety of obsolescence"—is made further evident in the ways these texts address authorial authority (or the lack thereof) on both a structural and thematic level (2006, 20). For example, "Rick" in Powers's *Galatea 2.2* grapples with writer's block for the entire novel, until the last sentence depicts him as suddenly feeling able to write about the events that have just taken place. The ultimate result of this unblocking is, ostensibly, the novel we are reading. The plot of *Galatea 2.2* involves "Rick" working with scientists to create a computer construct that is complex enough to mimic human consciousness. As the writer of several critically successful novels, "Rick" contributes to the project by trying to teach Helen, the computer network, about the human condition by infusing her with literary texts; he is, in a sense, trying to "author" her. In that process, he develops fodder for a new novel, essentially ending his writer's block. Thus the novel deals both thematically and structurally with the reassertion of authorial power and authority. The fact that the protagonist is "Richard Powers" is significant because *Galatea 2.2* thereby becomes the story of its own creation, or what Steven G. Kellman calls a "self-begetting novel."[10]

The goal of the experiment depicted in *Galatea 2.2* is to test whether a computer construct could be formulated to imitate human consciousness well enough to fool a person into thinking it was human, a gauge known as the Turing Test.[11] "Rick's" job is to introduce the computer to the canonical literary texts he had studied as a graduate student at U ten years earlier. Eventually he reads to Helen (the name he gave to the series of computers that he has anthropomorphized into a "little girl") from his own work and letters, and Helen begins to evince something that resembles self-awareness. For a man suffering from writer's block, conjuring a seemingly conscious being from his own words greatly boosts "Rick's" authorial confidence. And even though Helen, discouraged by her inability to understand the human world in which she was "dropped down halfway," shuts herself down at the end of the novel, "Rick" emerges from the experience reinvigorated and empowered to write the novel we are reading. Not only does *Galatea 2.2* constantly call attention to its own construction by featuring an author-character, but it also takes as one of its major themes the restoration of that author's creative power.

For "Philip" in Roth's *Operation Shylock*, the problem of authorial authority takes a different form, as he discovers a man in Jerusalem calling himself "Philip Roth." This impostor attempts to use Roth's reputation as an internationally renowned Jewish author to bring about a mass migration of Ashkenazi Jews from Israel back into Europe, in order to rescue them from what the impostor argues will be a second Holocaust, this time caused by Middle Eastern strife. In other words, "Moishe Pipik" ("Philip's" derogatory name for this impostor)[12] attempts to usurp "Philip's" (and, therefore, Roth's) extratextual authorial authority for distinctly nonauthorial and somewhat dubious and possibly anti-Semitic aims. *Operation Shylock*, then, depicts *two* authorial doubles, two constructed characters pretending to be the "real" Philip Roth: Pipik and "Philip" himself. "Philip" represents the character-ized version of Roth, built out of words, while Pipik tells "Philip" he is "the you that is not words" (1994, 87).

Operation Shylock explores the extent to which Pipik is able to exploit "Philip's" authorial persona for an agenda that has nothing to do with his writing: it addresses the question of what kind of real-world authority an author can legitimately (or illegitimately) claim. Pipik's attempts to wield the authority of the author Philip Roth mirrors the way the author Philip Roth attempts to wield that authorial authority through the character of "Philip." Pipik is not "authorized" to use the influence of Philip Roth in Israel, just as the extratextual author Philip Roth—according to the traditions of fiction—is not authorized to impose his intentions or interpretations on readers of his fiction. Thus the novel's content reflects its structure, as both explore the boundaries of an author's extratextual authority.

The novel further explores these boundaries by depicting Pipik attempting to do something with "Philip's" persona that Jewish leaders have often chided Roth himself for *not* doing: using his considerable fame and influence to support Jewish causes. On the contrary, Roth's work has often been criticized for being anti-Semitic in its depiction of Jews, since some of his characters are unpleasant or morally compromised. Pipik, perhaps, represents Roth's response to this criticism, as this rather mentally unstable character travels the world using Roth's persona to advocate a preposterous idea: the removal of Jews from Israel in order to save them from Arab aggression, a plan which, as Debra Shostak points out, "effectively erases Israel as the geographical sign and ethical center of Jewishness" (1997, 743). Pipik could be compared in this way to "Philip," who complains, "When I was younger my Jewish betters used to accuse me of writing short stories that endangered Jewish lives" (1994, 186). Now in *Operation Shylock*, there emerges a Philip Roth imposter who claims to be trying to save Jewish lives, but who, by arguing for the removal of Jews to Europe, is effectively arguing for the symbolic, if not literal, destruction of Israel. Meanwhile, the "real" "Philip" (who is, of course, also not real but a character in the novel) tries, rather lamely at first, to persuade Pipik to cease and desist, demonstrating the difficulty an author faces when he tries to curate his public persona.

Roth has faced this difficulty repeatedly, as he has had to grapple with a variety of biographical accounts that paint widely disparate portraits of him, some, like the memoir of his ex-wife Claire Bloom, quite negative. In this sense, then, the autofictional text draws an interesting parallel to the extratextual reality faced by the extratextual author. While "Philip" finds it difficult to maintain control over his extratextual authorial persona, Roth is attempting to do just that. According to Loren Glass, Roth is culling and organizing his archives, preparing to turn them over to his chosen biographer, Blake Bailey. He has also instructed that his papers should be destroyed once Bailey is finished with them, so that no unauthorized versions of Philip Roth—or author-characters, in my terms—can be constructed (Glass 2014, 234). All this persona shaping suggests that an important recurrent theme of autofiction, at least in the case of *Operation Shylock*, is an author's desire to participate in and control the construction of his authorial image.

Throughout *Operation Shylock*, the struggle between "Philip" and Pipik is framed as a struggle for authorial as well as personal supremacy, exemplified by this passage in which "Philip" worries that Pipik is getting the better of him: "It would be only natural, to assume that in a narrative contest (in the realist mode) with this impostor, the real writer would easily emerge as inventive champion . . . but instead the Jerusalem Gold Medal for Vivid Realism has gone to a narrative klutz. . . . His artifice is phony to the core, a hysterical caricature of the art of illusion, hyperbole fueled by perversity (and perhaps even insanity)" (1994, 247). The author worries about being bested by the far less artful impostor, much the way memoir as a genre threatens to best more artfully constructed fictional narratives.

Ultimately, "Philip" is able to reclaim his authorial authority in a traditionally masculine way by sleeping with Pipik's girlfriend after it is revealed that Pipik is impotent and therefore, according to "Philip," only "fifty percent of a man" (247). It is by proving himself to be the better *man* that "Philip" is able to assert himself as the real *author*: as the "genuine versus the fake, the responsible versus the reckless, the serious versus the superficial . . . the accomplished versus the unfulfilled . . . the essential versus the superfluous" (249). After "Philip's" assignation with Pipik's girlfriend, Pipik disappears from the narrative, leaving "Philip" free to turn the tables and impersonate Pipik on a secret mission for the Israeli Mossad in order to determine where the monetary support for Pipik's "Diasporism" originated. By the end of *Operation Shylock*, the double has been neutralized and "Philip's" authorial authority restored. Furthermore, the autofictional onomastic connection between "Philip" and Roth serves to restore Roth's authorial authority as well.

Ellis's *Lunar Park* also engages in a complex form of authorial doubling that turns into a sort of "tripling." Not only is the protagonist named "Bret Easton Ellis," but within the novel the character of "Bret" himself becomes further split between the man who wants to be a good father to his son, Robby, and the "writer" who "yearned for chaos, mystery, death" (2005, 212). As "Bret" (unsuccessfully) attempts to reconcile what it means to be a writer with what it means to live a meaningful life—to reconcile the writerly persona with the human one—the reader is invited to try (just as unsuccessfully) to reconcile "Bret" the character with Ellis the author.

At the beginning of the novel, the equation of author with character is fairly straightforward, as "Bret" describes his early career and the facts match up (with the few small exceptions I mentioned earlier) with Ellis's own. "Bret" and Ellis's fame perhaps culminated with the publication of the hugely controversial novel *American Psycho*, an incredibly violent and disturbing portrayal of entitled Yuppie/Wall Street analyst turned serial killer Patrick Bateman. *Lunar Park* describes that time when, upon its publication in 1991, *American Psycho* became an instant best seller, despite attempted boycotts, and Ellis ("Bret") was reviled as a deranged psychopath for having written it. The president of the Los Angeles chapter of the National Organization for Women, Tammy Bruce, said, "Mr. Ellis is a confused, sick young man with a deep hatred of women who will do anything for a fast buck" (Cohen 1991), while Gloria Steinem accused him of being responsible for any copycat crimes that might ensue.[13] So in *Lunar Park*, "Bret" describes how he was charged and convicted in the public imagination with the crimes supposedly committed by his fictional character Patrick Bateman. It is perhaps in response to having been repeatedly equated with one of his protagonists that Ellis decided to actually feature a characterized version of himself in *Lunar Park*.

And within *Lunar Park*, this characterized version of the author takes liberties with his work that are generally not allowed to authors, namely, by providing authorial insights into *American Psycho* and instructing readers on how to interpret it, seemingly in an attempt to mitigate the controversy surrounding that novel. To that end, "Bret" claims that Patrick Bateman "was a notoriously unreliable narrator, and if you actually read [*American Psycho*] you could come away doubting that these crimes had even occurred. . . . The murders and tortures were in fact fantasies fueled by his rage and fury about how life in America was structured and how this had—no matter the size of his wealth—trapped him" (2005, 122). This is indeed a very plausible—and popular—reading of this novel, but contemporary literary criticism does not usually afford an author the opportunity to explain his own work. As an autofictional character, however, "Bret" seizes control of the interpretation and asserts a kind of authority that Ellis the author rarely or never does. (Ellis often refuses to comment on possible interpretations of his work.) The autofictional novel thereby allows for the insertion of authorial interpretation, but under the cover of the author-character rather than the author himself. On the other hand, this interpretation of *American Psycho* takes on a patina of authority that it would not have without "Bret's" onomastic connection to Ellis himself. Thus if an autofictional author were so inclined (and I make no argument about Ellis's authorial inclinations), he could take advantage of the alibi-space that autofiction provides to promulgate his own perspective, but then simultaneously and legitimately call it fiction.

However, at the same time that "Bret" wrests interpretive control of *American Psycho* from the cultural critics who denounced it, he attempts to relinquish the "blame" for having written it in the first place. Furthermore, it is during "Bret's" description of the writing of *American Psycho* that the split between "Bret" and Ellis becomes more and more apparent, for it is at this point that "Bret's" writerly persona emerges as a distinct Other. At this one pivotal—and confusing—moment in the novel, the author splits from his character, and the character further splits into "the writer" and "the father." As "Bret" explains, while he was writing *American Psycho*:

> someone—*something*—else took over and caused this new character to be my only reference point. . . . I kept resisting, but the novel forced itself to be written. I would often black out for hours at a time only to realize that another ten pages had been scrawled out. My point—and I'm not quite sure how else to put this—is that the book *wanted* to be written by someone else. It wrote itself and didn't care how I felt about it. I would fearfully watch my hand as the pen swept across the yellow legal pads I did the first draft on. I was repulsed by this creation and wanted to take no credit for it—Patrick Bateman wanted the credit. (2005, 13)[14]

The demonic Patrick Bateman, then, emerges as a ghostly being within "Bret's" actual world, a being with the power to shape "Bret's" work and, we find later, his life. Just as "Bret" the character is authorized to interpret *American Psycho*, Patrick Bateman asserts a kind of authorial control over "Bret's" life, as he thwarts every attempt "Bret" makes to connect with his wife and child. By the end of the novel, "Bret's" son has disappeared, his wife has divorced him, and he is left alone, but with his writing life intact.

As I have said, one of the primary thematic reasons that these novels call attention to the existence and identity of their authors by deploying eponymous protagonists is to reaffirm the authority of authorship in general and of these specific authors in particular. And what could better demonstrate an author's considerable power than one or more of his characters coming to life? In *Operation Shylock*, a friend first informs "Philip" about a Philip Roth impersonator by remarking, "Philip, I feel that I'm reading to you out of a story you wrote" (1994, 31). In response, "Philip" imagines the impostor as embodying all his previous protagonists and therefore as part of himself: "It's Zuckerman, I thought, whimsically, stupidly, escapistly, it's Kepesh, it's Tarnopol and Portnoy—it's all of them in one, broken free of print and mockingly reconstituted as a single satirical facsimile of me. In other words, if it's not Halcion and it's no dream, then it's got to be literature" (34). In *Galatea 2.2*, "Rick's" authorial prowess is no less impressive, as he is able through his words to arouse consciousness in a computer, while "Bret" is assaulted throughout the novel by demonic attacks, not just by Patrick Bateman, but by several other characters from his previous work. For all these author-characters, their work and words are sufficient to bring textual creations to life, at least within the pages of the novel. And perhaps the most striking evidence of this authorial prowess is that these writers are able to create charactorial versions of themselves.

On the other hand, and to their very great credit, each of these novels evinces an awareness of the narcissism inherent in the idea that one's literary creations—more or less overt manifestations of oneself—are vivacious enough to cross the barrier of fiction to become real. Indeed, an important theme in each of these novels is the extent to which this kind of narcissism is necessary in order to live a writing life. In other words, these novels show the pitfalls of living the too-examined life of the writer. As "Philip" puts it, his kind of life leaves him open to suffering from "Me-itis. Microcosmosis. Drowning in the tiny tub of yourself" (1994, 55). For "Rick," writing had been the tool he used to connect to his girlfriend, C. "I thought I might write my way to a place where my friend C. could live" (1995, 104). His stories, which become his novels, work for a while to cement the couple together, but eventually "Rick" learns that writing is not enough to sustain a romance or a life. From his work with Helen, he realizes, "All human effort, it seemed to me, aimed at a single end: to bring to life the storied curve we tell ourselves" (312). Later, he puts it a different way, viewing life as "the world's Turing Test": "Life meant convincing another that you knew what it meant to be alive" (327). As he goes off to write the novel we are reading, "Rick" discovers that he can both aid and hinder that process.

For "Bret," the events of *Lunar Park* demonstrate to him that, although he enjoys the wealth and celebrity that writing has brought him, there can be drawbacks as well.[15] "Bret" has learned to use his considerable talent as a writer to shape and frame events in his own life so that they are more to his liking. He develops a propensity for imagining his life taking place on a movie screen, onto which he can project events as he wants them to have taken place, altering his memories to suit his desires: "As a writer, you slant all evidence in favor of the conclusions you want to produce and you rarely tilt in favor of the truth" (2005, 146). However, as he tries for the first time to connect to another person—his son, Robby—he realizes that the writerly screen he constructs to shape reality to his liking might also become a trap. He recognizes that "a writer would always be cut off from actual experience because he was the writer" (192). His propensity to project his fictional fantasies onto the screen of reality serves to distance "Bret" from the other people in his life. He refers to himself as "the ghost" because he wanders around his house barely present, almost transparent (at one point he even wraps himself in a bedsheet) as the life of his family goes on around him without his participation. In this sense, "Bret" the character embodies the figurative role we assign to authors: that of a ghostly presence, not quite part of the work but not quite separate from it either. Thus, while authors are unable to exert direct influence over their published work, their indirect influence continues to be felt and felt most acutely in autofiction. The author-characters of autofiction direct our attention to the ghostly presence that is the extratextual author.

In addition to bolstering the perceived diminishing power of the contemporary author, another effect of these autofictions' myriad appropriations of the representational nature of the memoir genre is to make direct reference to the generator of the narrative: to the author himself. By evoking the memoir, the autofictions I have discussed in this chapter explicitly invite readers to focus on the identity of the writer (or in the case of the novels, the writer-character). The reason these books are memoir-esque is that they overtly point outside themselves to their external reality, even if only to ironically deny that reality within the world of the novel through outlandish plotlines and false biographical information. Although these autofictions do develop a fictional world within themselves, their unmistakable reference to the extratextual existence of the author necessitates a double awareness on the part of the reader, who must maintain a distinction between the nonfictional reality of the author and the fictional reality of the author-character. And this double awareness is often mirrored by the split subjectivity of the author-characters depicted within the novels.

Thus *Lunar Park* thematizes the idea that writing exacts its price from an author by alienating him from his own life. "Bret" claims that "when you give up life for fiction you become a character" (2005, 192). Of course, the reader is in on the joke that "Bret" is indeed just that: a character. And instead of only threatening his happiness, "Bret's" writing actually threatens his life and family as his characters come to life as haunting presences. When "Bret" tells himself, "Writing will cost you a son and a wife," we recognize that he is not speaking abstractly but rather that his horrific literary creations are endangering the safety of his family (252). Not only is this a ringing testament to the power of "Bret's" (and possibly Ellis's) writing, but it is a literal representation of the figurative role that writing can play in authors' lives.

The idea that a writer uses his fiction-making ability to reconstruct reality to his own liking and shield himself from actual life is reflected in the structure of the autofictions I have been discussing. In other words, if constantly chronicling one's life builds a screen of words between the writer and that life, these autofictions similarly build a screen of fiction between the author and the character, suggesting that they are the same person while also implying that they cannot be. And the irony here is that it is through this very screen of fiction (as opposed to nonfiction) that the real emotional impact can be felt of the devastation of the writer-character's life.

While I argued earlier that these novels are drawing upon the rising power and popularity of the memoir, it is important to note that they do so in addition to calling upon the continued narrative power of fiction. What I mean to say is the same thing fiction writers have been saying for centuries: fiction can portray truths that nonfiction cannot. As Tim O'Brien famously explains, "Story-truth is truer sometimes than happening-truth" (2009, 171). When "Philip" asks writer Ahron Appelfeld why he never wrote a nonfictional account of his experiences in the Holocaust, he responds: "To create means to order, sort out and choose the words and the pace that fit the work. The materials are indeed the materials from one's life, but, ultimately, the creation is an independent creature" (Roth 1994, 86).[16] "Philip" the character says something similar when he explains that fiction "provides the storyteller with the lie through which to expose his unspeakable truth" (58). And according to "Bret," "I could never be as honest about myself in a piece of nonfiction as I could in any of my novels" (2005, 24). The autofictions discussed in this chapter thus evoke both the "interactivity" of the memoir (Couser 2012, 177) and the "capital-T Truth" of fiction (Currie 2013, 1) in order to engage readers both with the gesture toward reality that memoirs provide and the gesture toward abstract truth that we typically associate with the novel. That this "have my cake and eat it, too" genre of autofiction has become more and more popular is an indication of readers' and writers' expectations of what a literary text can and should provide.

Coda

In this book I have attempted not only to define autofiction in American terms but also to demonstrate its widespread relevance to contemporary literary endeavor. Autofictional echoes can be seen and felt in literary theory and criticism, journalism, history, memoir, and trauma narrative. Indeed, autofiction serves as a nexus for several critical cultural shifts. For example, the burgeoning of autofiction serves as a barometer for the shift from modernist authorial effacement to postmodern literary self-consciousness. The widening employment of autofictional techniques demonstrates an increasing acceptance of the idea that selfhood is mediated and constructed in part by the language we use to convey it; at the same time, autofiction constantly calls attention to that element of selfhood that retains an extratextual valence. In a related manner, autofictional texts suggest a cultural awareness that pure objectivity—in narrative and elsewhere—is impossible, while simultaneously illuminating the important distinction between a fictional and a nonfictional text.

The decades-long burgeoning of contemporary autofiction is a result of a perceived diminishment of the cultural authority of traditional modes of authorship brought about by several phenomena: the civil rights and feminist movements, the advent of literary theory which hypothesized diffused subjectivity over stable identity, and the democratization of authorship made possible by emergent new media. But what this study of autofiction makes clear is that authorship remains a powerful, if often ironically powerful, cultural force, despite authors' beleaguered sense of diminished authority.

Understanding autofiction as a trope requires a recognition that the force of a literary text can be conveyed in a number of ways: (1) in the quality of the writing or the created world of the text; (2) in the real lived experience of the author or the historical context of the work; and (3) in the referential nature of the story being told. The latter two elements require more of an extratextual consideration than the first. In considering traditional fiction, we tend to focus primarily on the quality of the writing, and while quality is important in life writing, memoir and autobiography must also meet the extratextual requirements of authenticity of authorship and truth-telling to be considered valid. So while Toni Morrison's novel about slavery, *Beloved*, is not based on her personal experience, its considerable power derives from her facility with language and the poignant world and characters she creates. And even when Tim O'Brien is not writing about his own experience fighting in Vietnam, the fact that readers know something about his history lends novels like *July, July* an authority they might not otherwise have. And finally, while Elie Wiesel's *Night* is undeniably powerful in terms of writing quality and authorial integrity, it is the fact that he relates his own harrowing experience that makes his work an important cultural record.

In terms of autofiction, writing quality is important, but its true innovation comes from the effects of combining fictional and referential elements and from toying with authorial authenticity. The uncertainty in these texts provides a certain titillation to the reader. But the most striking element at work in autofiction is its emphasis on the relationship between the text and its context. Autofiction demands a consideration of authorial intention (what has been called "the intentional fallacy"): we must ask *how* the author intended this book to be read, whether as a fiction, a memoir, or an odd amalgam of the two. And while we must do this for any text we read, in the case of autofiction, the conclusions readers draw about authorial intention must often change as they read. Autofiction evokes frequent code-switching from fictional to life-writing modes of reading. Furthermore, because such texts cause a repeated consideration of the author's intentions, they cause a repeated recognition of the author's continued relevance to the text. Autofiction will not allow us to forget or ignore the authorial presence inherent in any text; autofictional authors refuse to die.

As the first study of its kind, this book is necessarily broad in scope, as it attempts to provide a wide-ranging view of the literary and cultural landscape that gave rise to the autofictional trend in the United States. One avenue of potential further study is the extent to which autofictional elements have inflected film and television, so that right now some of the most popular visual texts involve ironic representations of real people.

Autofiction in these media represents a rich and as yet unmined area for critical analysis. Indeed, the onomastic relationship between television stars and their on-screen avatars reverberates throughout contemporary television and adds a layer of satirical comedy, as viewers recognize the unspoken difference between the two figures. Autofictional elements can even be found in so-called reality TV, in which participants consciously ramp up their outlandish behavior and fabricate conflicts in order to make "good viewing," while viewers implicitly understand the inherent fictionality of these spectacles. Thus, even though it has not always been named as such, autofiction continues to have extensive cultural influence in both literary and popular contexts.

Appendix
American Autofictions

Titles appear in chronological order: List is as comprehensive as possible, and any omissions are inadvertent:

Gertrude Stein: *The Autobiography of Alice B: Toklas* (1933)

Henry Miller: *Tropic of Cancer* (1934)

Henry Miller: *Tropic of Capricorn* (1939)

Vladimir Nabokov: *Bend Sinister* (1947)

Norman Mailer: *Armies of the Night* (1968)

Tom Wolfe: *The Electric Kool-Aid Acid Test* (1968)

Frederick Exley: *A Fan's Notes: A Fictional Memoir* (1968)

James McConkey: *Crossroads* (1968)

Ronald Sukenick: *Up* (1968)

Ronald Sukenick: *Death of the Novel and Other Stories* (1969)

Kurt Vonnegut: *Slaughterhouse-Five* (1969)

Joyce Carol Oates: *Them* (1969)

George Cain: *Blueschild Baby* (1970)

Gore Vidal: *Two Sisters: A Novel in the Form of a Memoir* (1970)

Nicholas Delbanco: *In the Middle Distance* (1971)

Norman Mailer: *Of a Fire on the Moon* (1971)

Gilbert Sorrentino: *Imaginative Qualities of Actual Things* (1971)

Hunter S Thompson: *Fear and Loathing in Las Vegas* (1971)

John Barth: *Chimera* (1972)

Kurt Vonnegut: *Breakfast of Champions* (1973)

Ronald Sukenick: *Out* (1973)

Vladimir Nabokov: *Look at the Harlequins!* (1974)

Frederick Exley: *Pages from a Cold Island* (1975)

Kathy Acker: *Kathy Goes to Haiti* (1978)

John Barth: *Letters* (1979)

Gilbert Sorrentino: *Mulligan Stew* (1979)

Joan Didion: *Democracy* (1984)

Paul Auster: *City of Glass* (1985)

Kathy Acker: *Empire of the Senseless* (1988)

Frederick Exley: *Last Notes from Home* (1988)

Philip Roth: *Deception* (1990)

Mark Leyner: *My Cousin, My Gastroenterologist* (1990)

Mark Leyner: *Et tu, Babe?* (1992)

Philip Roth: *Operation Shylock* (1993)

Tim O'Brien: *The Things They Carried* (1990)

Tim O'Brien: *In the Lake of the Woods* (1994)

Richard Powers: *Galatea 2:2* (1995)

Mark Leyner: *Tooth Imprints on a Corn Dog* (1995)

Raymond Federman: *Double or Nothing: A Real Fictitious Discourse* (1998)

Mark Leyner: *The Tetherballs of Bougainville* (1998)

Charles Baxter: *The Feast of Love* (2000)

Camden Joy: *Boy Island* (2000)

Raymond Federman: *The Voice in the Closet* (2001)

Raymond Federman: *Aunt Rachel's Fur* (2001)

John Barth: *Coming Soon!!* (2001)

Jonathan Baumbach: *B: A Novel* (2002)

Jonathan Safran Foer: *Everything Is Illuminated* (2002)

Ben: Marcus *Notable American* Women (2002)

Charlie Kaufman: *Adaptation* (film) (2002)

Philip Roth: *The Plot against America* (2004)

Percival Everett: *A History of the African-American People [Proposed] by Strom Thurmond as Told to Percival Everett and James Kincaid [A Novel]* (2004)

Bret Easton Ellis: *Lunar Park* (2005)

Michael Martone: *Michael Martone* (2005)

Salvador Plascencia: *The People of Paper* (2005)

Lee Siegel: *Who Wrote the Book of Love?* (2005)

Douglas Coupland: *JPod* (2006)

Raymond Federman: *Return to Manure* (2006)

Chris Kraus: *I Love Dick* (2006)

Gary Shteyngart: *Absurdistan* (2006)

Katherine Taylor: *Rules for Saying Goodbye: A Novel* (2007)

Percival Everett: *I Am Not Sidney Poitier* (2009)

Charles Yu: *How to Live Safely in a Science Fiction Universe* (2010)
Teju Cole: *Open City* (2011)
Arthur Phillips: *The Tragedy of Arthur* (2011)
David Foster Wallace: *The Pale King* (2011)
Ruth Ozeki: *A Tale for the Time Being* (2013)
Ron Currie Jr.: *Flimsy Little Plastic Miracles* (2013)
Iris Smyles: *Iris Has Free Time* (2013)
Percival Everett: *Percival Everett by Virgil Russell* (2013)
Ben Lerner: *10:04* (2014)
Joshua Cohen: *Book of Numbers: A Novel* (2015)
Mark Leyner: *Gone with the Mind* (2016)
Michael Chabon: *Moonglow: A Novel* (2016)

Notes

Introduction

1. I refer here to television shows like *It's Garry Shandling's Show* (1986–90) and *Seinfeld* (1989–98), which feature actors playing themselves or, I should say, fictionalized versions of themselves. To name only a few of many examples, Larry David picked up the *Seinfeld* mantle in *Curb Your Enthusiasm* (2000–2011), Ricky Gervais and Stephen Merchant enlisted numerous cameo appearances by stars playing "themselves" in their shows *Extras* (2005–07) and *Life's Too Short* (2011–13), and Neal Patrick Harris can arguably trace his current superstardom to a virtuoso performance as "himself" in the film *Harold and Kumar Go to White Castle* (2004). Louise Brix Jacobsen has coined the term "vitafiction" to refer to such performances when "celebrities play fictionalized versions of themselves, and their roles cannot be completely separated from who they are as real people" (253). She differentiates vitafiction from autofiction by pointing out that the former is audiovisual in nature and is not necessarily created by the celebrity performer him/herself. By contrast, autofiction features fictionalized versions of authors as characters who are distinct from but also cannot be completely separated from who they really are.
2. Jeff Thoss defines "metalepsis" as "a paradoxical transgression of the line that separates the inside from the outside of a storyworld" (2015, 4).
3. I draw a distinction between American autofiction and the French version, which adheres more closely to the American definition of memoir.
4. Elsewhere, Genette has described Proust's masterwork as an autofiction for much the same reason, imagining the explanation this way: "'In this book, I, Marcel Proust, tell (fictitiously) how I meet one Albertine, how I fall in love with her, how I keep her a captive, etc. I ascribe to myself, in this book, those adventures which in reality did not at all happen to me, at least not in this form. In other words, I invent for myself a life and a personality that are not ("not always") exactly mine.' What to call this genre, this form of fiction, since fiction, in the real sense of the term, is what we have here? The best term would doubtless be that used by Serge Doubrovsky to designate

his own narrative: *autofiction*" (1997, 250–51). Genette here takes liberties with Doubrovsky's definition, saying that the life and personality depicted in an autofiction might *not* accurately reflect its authors', while Doubrovsky repeatedly asserts the continuity between them.

5. A homodiegetic narrator is also a character in the story he/she is narrating, usually its protagonist. This is in contrast to a heterodiegetic narrator who narrates the action but does not participate in the story.

6. Indeed, although I do discuss one French and several English novels, these often focus on primarily American locales or characters, for example, Martin Amis's *Money: A Suicide Note* (1984), Frederic Beigbeder's *Windows on the World* (2004), and Will Self's *Walking to Hollywood* (2010).

1. Masculinity and Whiteness

1. See Kimmel's book and E. Anthony Rotundo's *American Manhood* for much more in-depth history of American masculinity than it is my purpose to provide here.

2. Aaron Jaffe's innovative work, *Modernism and the Culture of Celebrity*, argues convincingly that, although modernist authors claimed to disdain the culture of celebrity and marketing, they engaged quite actively in the creation of their "imprimaturs" or authorial styles and personae. Jaffe almost goes so far as to suggest that the literary dictates of high modernism amounted to little more than a cultural pose: "Impersonality of critical method and autonomy of the objects of criticism . . . in fact disguise deep resemblances between public literary persona and the ideal, magisterial author presupposed in modernist theories of literary production" (2005, 4). While compelling, Jaffe's argument does not actually touch upon my own. Whatever the reason for the embrace of "impersonality of critical method and autonomy of objects of criticism," the resulting modernist fiction does not engage in the self-conscious authorial intrusions I have been discussing here.

3. Seán Burke has argued that this "impersonalist position" was not meant to be interpreted as a theoretical stance toward art, but rather an "aesthetic" one. Impersonalism, he argues, should therefore not be read as a precursor of the "anti-authorial" position of poststructuralist theorists like Barthes and Foucault (1992, 206). I address these issues to a greater extent in chapter 2, but suffice it to say that an "aesthetic" stance is, of course, also a theoretical stance.

4. Another means by which women were seen to be unable to access objectivity was through Lawrence Kohlberg's "Stage of Moral Development," which emerged in the late 1950s and held great sway thereafter and is still used in some contexts today. According to Kohlberg, a truly "moral" person recognizes that one's personal perspective is irrelevant to morality. Rather, true

morality is based on universal ethical principles that apply equally to everyone and to all situations. In Kohlberg's studies, women and girls were often found to fall into lower stages of moral development than men. As Carol Gilligan so famously pointed out in her groundbreaking work *In a Different Voice*, this was due to women's tendency to see ethical situations from a personal standpoint, basing their moral determinations upon the relationship they had with the people affected rather than upon universal ethical principles. Kohlberg determined his moral standards through interviews with men alone. He decided that ethical objectivity was the highest standard of morality possible, and then found women were inadequate when they did not hew to a standard developed without their input. The fact that Kohlberg's theories are still widely taught, particularly in schools of education, is a telling reminder of how entrenched is the idea that objectivity is to be valued and that women have less access to it.

5. This includes Luce Irigaray, Julia Kristeva, and Elaine Showalter.

6. See also Peter Middleton, who, through a reading of *A Portrait of the Artist as a Young Man*, argues that Stephen Dedalus's development into an artist is equivalent to his development into a man: "His arrival at the status of artist, and therefore man, occurs when the novel modulates from this realist objectivity into a new subjectivity signified by the articulate self-reflexive entries of a journal" (1992, 53). Middleton departs from the argument that modernist masculinity is characterized by objectivity, arguing that, for Stephen, manhood is achieved when he is able to move beyond objectivity to write in a self-reflexive manner.

7. Of course, deconstructionists have demonstrated the impossibility of focusing only upon the literary text at hand, without any reference to external, cultural, historical, or paratextual elements.

8. Furthermore, the more recent focus on literary theory in analytical circles threatened a similar foreclosure on consideration of a text's cultural and historical contexts, a point often made by feminist critics and critics of minority literature and typified by the following comment from Gilbert and Gubar, who argue that some theoretical approaches, "radically antipatriarchal as they may seem, ultimately erase the reality of gendered human experience." Instead, Gilbert and Gubar advocate an approach that "define[s] the ways in which texts are as marked by the maker's gender as they are by the historical moment in which they were produced or by the generic conventions to which they adhere" (1988, xiv).

9. One other example is the British novelist Christopher Isherwood, whose 1939 collection *Goodbye to Berlin* contains a characterized version of himself that his German landlady calls "Herr Issyvoo." As autofictions, these

stories take on the flavor of memoir while also presenting fictionalized representations of people and events. The seemingly unproblematic equation of author with protagonist, both here and in Miller's fiction, provides a rather stark contrast to the ways in which later autofictions foreground the author-character as a means to call authorial authority into question. The authorial authority of Miller and Isherwood is never in question—at least, that is, to Miller and Isherwood themselves.

10. See Michael Kimmel, Sally Robinson, and David Savran for a history of the various forms and monikers this "crisis" has taken.

11. Of course, the experiences of men and women of color, particularly African Americans, during this period were vastly different, as they were precluded, often legally, from participating in the postwar economic boom.

12. *Sexual Politics* constituted a part of Millett's PhD dissertation at Columbia.

13. Of course, this review fails to take into account the centuries of feminist philosophy that presaged Millett's book and even seems unaware of the 1949 publication of Simone de Beauvoir's *The Second Sex* or Betty Friedan's hugely influential *The Feminine Mystique* from 1963. I suppose, however, that the latter would fall into this reviewer's category of "intuitive passion."

14. Millett's focus on male writers differentiates that book from much of the feminist literary criticism that immediately followed, which tended to focus primarily on work by women in an effort to trace a distinctive female literary tradition; I am thinking here of scholars such as Elaine Showalter, Sandra Gilbert and Susan Gubar, Nina Baym, Carolyn Heilbrun, and Judith Fetterley.

15. Millett's book made enough of an impression upon its publication that the entire March 1971 issue of *Harper's* was subsequently devoted to Norman Mailer's response. Mailer's piece, later published in book form as *The Prisoner of Sex*, makes the case that, while some aspects of women's liberation deserve attention, essential gender roles are natural: "Women must have their rights to a life which would allow them to look for a mate. And there would be no free search until she was liberated" (1971, 232–33). But it is that search for a mate in order to procreate that must be the primary function of a woman's life: "Finally a day had to come when women shattered the pearl of their love for pristine and feminine will and found the man, yes that man in the million who could become the point of the seed which would give an egg back to nature, and let the woman return with a babe who came from the root of God's desire" (1971, 233–34).

16. It is striking as well that in the review's second part, Lehmann-Haupt ultimately faults the book for being "too masculine" (1970b).

17. This point is aptly demonstrated by the effect the revelation of Millett's bisexuality had on her reputation as a feminist leader. A 1970 *Time* magazine arti-

cle was fairly spot-on when it suggested, "The disclosure is bound to discredit her as a spokeswoman for her cause, cast further doubt on her theories, and reinforce the views of those skeptics which routinely dismiss all liberationists as lesbians" (1970b, 50). Millett's personal life thus supposedly impugns not only her efficacy as a leader but her theories as well, reflecting a different standard than the one male thinkers were typically subjected to at this time.

18. Robert Siegle has essentially equated self-consciousness and self-reflexivity, saying that both use metaphors of selfhood and consciousness that are typically employed in psychological rather than literary contexts (1986, 3).

19. For example, see Harper, *Framing the Margins*; McGurl, *The Program Era*; and Dussel, "Beyond Eurocentrism."

20. However, as the advent of feminist literary theory encouraged both the opening of the literary canon to texts by women and people of color and the effort to recover such works that had previously been lost or ignored, there arose widespread and quite famous efforts to oppose those efforts to "decenter" the so-called Dead White Males from the canon. Published in 1987, both Allan Bloom's *The Closing of the American Mind* and E. D. Hirsch Jr.'s *Cultural Literacy: What Every American Needs to Know* focused primarily on reaffirming the importance of the traditional literary and philosophical canon, consisting almost entirely of works by white men. Both books were *New York Times* best sellers and have been said to be the opening salvos of what has come to be called the "culture wars" or the resistance to "political correctness."

21. As in *Bend Sinister*, there is no overt onomastic connection between the Genie and the extratextual John Barth. But even though the Genie is never referred to using Barth's proper name, the textual cues connecting the two are unmistakable.

22. A productive connection could be made here to Mark McGurl's designation of the largely white and male postmodern experimental novels as "technomodernist" texts that demonstrate "the obvious continuity of much postwar American fiction with the modernist project of systematic experimentation with narrative form" (2009, 42). He posits but does not pursue the idea that "even the 'whitest' technomodernism can function as a discourse of difference, producing a symbolic placeholder for a paradoxically non-ethnic ethnicity" (2009, 62). One could read my study as an attempt to make this whiteness overt as an ethnicity.

23. As Daniel S. Traber puts it, "There is no shortage of nonwhites, women, or homosexuals in the roster of American rebels posed against the status quo, but the necessities of identity politics often force people from those groups into taking on the role of representing their category. White straight males

have not had to carry that burden, they are granted more license—in politics, art and life in general—to focus on the self without a concern for the community" (2007, 6). My argument is that, even with the representation in autofiction of a white straight male character, the particularity afforded that character by his being equated to the "actual" author of the novel means that he still does not have to bear the symbolic weight of representing an entire gender, race, or sexuality.

24. Indeed, some critics have suggested that because the "impresario" is often described in the third person by the first-person narrator, he is a different figure from the narrator. However, during his appearance on the train, the narrator eventually admits that he is the impresario and begins talking about himself in the first person: "Now the question I am asking, as I stare at Charles . . ." (2004, 405).

25. Vonnegut evinces this racial awareness throughout the novel by identifying a character's race when he/she is introduced, even if that character is white. This practice is unusual even today and is evidence of a race consciousness that is far ahead of its time for a white writer.

26. Debra Malina makes a different but related point about metalepsis in general when she says, "It disrupts narrative hierarchy in order either to reinforce or to undermine the ontological status of fictional subject or selves" (2002, 2). However, I believe that autofiction does not either reinforce or undermine authorial authority but does both simultaneously. In this, I agree more with J. Pier, who argues that the nature of metalepsis reasserts "the existence of the very boundaries" it effaces (2009, 195).

27. I discuss *Operation Shylock* in other chapters.

28. Although it is not really relevant to my argument, it is interesting to note that the "lover" here is probably based on British novelist Janet Hobhouse, who is believed to be the model for "Maria," a character in Roth's novel *The Counterlife* as well as here in *Deception*. It is of less interest to me, however, to tease out these connections and more relevant to my argument to discern what effect the autofictional character has on the reading experience.

29. She is not named, but one could assume that the wife is modeled on British actress Claire Bloom, to whom Roth was married at this time.

2. Dying of the Author

1. Indeed, Judith Ryan argues that *The Rhetoric of Fiction* may have primed American audiences for what was at the time a fairly radical argument: "Booth laid the groundwork for what we now call the author-narrator distinction. Barthes's 'Death of the Author' may have seemed less shocking to

some English-speaking readers who assimilated his ideas to those of Wayne Booth" (2012, 24).

2. However, more recent critical trends, in particular the continued popularity of historicism, perhaps signal a move back toward the author as signifier, albeit one signifier among many.

3. Philippe Lejeune, author of "The Autobiographical Pact," commented that *Roland Barthes by Roland Barthes* "seems to be the anti-*Pact* par excellence" (1989a, 24).

4. Furthermore, Burke points out that at the end of the twentieth century, literary theorists "have been accorded all the privileges traditionally bestowed upon the great author. . . . Indeed, were we in search of the most flagrant abuses of critical *auteurism* in recent times then we need look no further than the secondary literature on Barthes, Foucault, and Derrida, which is for the most part given over to scrupulously faithful and almost timorous reconstitutions of their thought" (1998, 178).

5. Indeed, P. David Marshall has compared the cultural conception of celebrity to that of the author-function: "As in Foucault's interpretation of the author, the celebrity is a way in which meaning can be housed and categorized into something that provides a source and origin for the meaning" (1997, 57).

6. Dervila Cooke differentiates between the reading experience of the reader informed about the life of the author and the "yardstick reader" who is aware only of the text at hand and not of any information about the author external to that text (2005, 75).

7. Moran also points out "the irony that the kinds of publicity about authors . . . seemed to emerge at roughly the same time as academic criticism was becoming increasingly suspicious of essentialist notions of the individual author" (2000, 58).

8. As I argued in the introduction, though, autofiction plays with traditional expectations of autobiography, seeming on the one hand to adopt the central tenet of Philippe Lejeune's "Autobiographical Pact," only to shatter it on the other. Lejeune's pact "supposes that there is *identity of name* between the author (such as he figures by his name on the cover), the narrator of the story, and the character who is being talked about" (1989a, 12) and that this implies a correspondence between the life described in the narrative and the life actually lived by the author. However, as these examples demonstrate, autofiction maintains the identity of name between author, narrator, and character, but does so in a narrative that often clearly deviates from the actual life of the author.

9. A scene remarkably similar to this one appears in the 2002 film *Adaptation*. "Charlie Kaufman," the autofictional charactorial representation of screenwriter Charlie Kaufman, cannot resist putting a version of himself into his screenplay. In one reverie, he imagines filming a scene depicting the Big Bang and the evolution of life on earth leading up to his birth and eventual work on this piece of writing. In contrast to "Leyner," however, "Kaufman" is depicted as so solipsistically stuck in his own head as to be unable to write anything decent. On the other hand, the film that *depicts* his self-absorbed anguish is highly inventive and entertaining. This example demonstrates the point I have been making that the impotence of the author-character often thematically bolsters the creative power of the author.

10. This conception is, of course, highly masculinist, not only because Bloom refers only to male writers in his book but also because, as many feminist literary theorists have posited, women writers may have a different relationship to their respective literary traditions—a relationship that may not involve trying to outdo or overcome those who came before. However, given that most autofiction is written by men, Bloom's ideas are quite relevant to an explication of the burgeoning autofictional tradition.

11. The Oedipal narrative of *Notable American Women* is all the more interesting when one considers that the extratextual Ben Marcus is the son of noted feminist scholar of literary modernism, Jane Marcus, so the domineering mother in the novel is a charactorial version of her.

12. For a discussion of the challenges Phillips faced in writing a pseudo-Shakespeare play, see Jonathan Segura. "All Lies: pw Talks with Arthur Phillips."

13. For a fuller discussion of this illusion of options in terms of "Click," see Laura Shackelford. "Narrative Subjects Meet Their Limits."

14. For one of many examples, see Will Self, "The Novel Is Dead."

15. Two other texts I should mention here are Katherine Taylor's *Rules for Saying Goodbye* (2007) and Iris Smyles's *Iris Has Free Time* (2013), both of which feature author-characters rendered in the first person. Although published as novels, these books seem to be thinly fictionalized memoirs of the writers' lives and not the kind of autofiction I have been discussing here, in which the life of the intertextual writer-character deviates from that of the extratextual author. In addition, I should mention that, while texts like Maxine Hong Kingston's *The Woman Warrior* (1975) and Theresa Cha's *Dictée* (1982) are indeed by women of color, they are, according to the definition in my introduction, memoirs rather than autofictions.

16. While Percival Everett and George Cain are the only African American autofictionists that I was able to find (with the possible addition of John

Edgar Wideman's short story "Surfiction"), Everett has written three auto-fictional novels of varying style. I have already discussed *A History of the African-American People [Proposed] by Strom Thurmond as Told to Percival Everett and James Kincaid* and want to mention here the third, a sort of pseudo-memoir from 2013 entitled *Percival Everett by Virgil Russell* in which "Percival Everett's" father, "Virgil Russell," writes the story of his son's life and vice versa. Furthermore, while Everett has clearly embraced the authorial intrusion inherent in autofiction, to date the trope is not nearly as visible in African American fiction as it is in that written by white men.

3. New Journalism as New Fiction

1. Kevin Kerrane (1997, 17) points out that this was by far not the first usage of the term "new journalism": "The term 'new journalism,' in fact, was originally coined by Matthew Arnold in 1887 to describe the style of Stead's *Pall Mall Gazette:* brash, vivid, personal, reform-minded—and occasionally, from Arnold's conservative viewpoint, 'featherbrained.'"

2. Eason rightly objects to differentiating between "fictional" and "journalistic" techniques because the distinction between the two are by no means clear-cut and are often merely a matter of degree rather than difference (1979, 7). I will continue to employ the distinction, however, because the writers I discuss do so.

3. Lennard J. Davis traces the intimate connections between journalism and the novel throughout the novel's history.

4. Hollowell, Hellman, Wolfe, and others have made similar claims that this period was the most turbulent of times. But John C. Hartsock makes the exact same claim about a completely different time period between 1860 and 1890, which he calls "a time of extraordinary social and cultural transformation and crisis" (2000, 57). I mention this only to demonstrate that any era could be characterized as extraordinary; indeed, judging one's own time period as remarkably uncommon turns out to be fairly common.

5. Although critics of the New Journalism generally distinguish between "journalistic" techniques and "fictional" or "literary" ones, David L. Eason makes an excellent point when he says: "The fictional technique distinction obscures as much as it reveals and in effect creates an inadequate framework for the discussion of nonfiction novel [*sic*] even at the level of practice. First, the distinction rests on the assumption that there are 'fictional techniques,' used for making sense out of imaginary situations, as opposed to techniques for making sense out of 'real' situations, thus creating the issue that the nonfiction novel exists in a vague no-man's-land between fact and fiction. Second, the conception reifies the form by remov-

ing it from the process of history and treating it as a disembodied style which has no relationship to perception" (1979, 7–8). This point is well taken and serves to bolster my later argument that there is less of a difference between fictional and nonfictional novels than most critics of New Journalism assume.

6. The most notorious instance at the time of a composite character was Gail Sheehy's "Redpants," a sketch of a prostitute who did not actually exist, but who was representative of many women Sheehy had met doing research for an article for *New York Magazine* in 1971. Sheehy was both criticized and supported for the creation of "Redpants," demonstrating the lack of clear consensus at that time about what the rules of journalism ought to be.

7. I say "logically flawed" for several reasons, some of which I will expound upon a bit later. One reason, however, that bears mentioning here is that, in his defense of literary realism, Wolfe makes the argument that "No one was ever moved to tears by the unhappy fates of heroes and heroines in Homer, Sophocles, Moliere, Racine, Sydney, Spenser or Shakespeare" (49). Wolfe's characteristic penchant for hyperbole notwithstanding, his assertion here that only realism can move a reader is not only false but unnecessary for his argument.

8. Wolfe did not, however, accompany the Pranksters on any part of their famous ride on the "Furthur" bus; it is a testament to the vividness of the writing in *The Electric Kool-Aid Acid Test* that it seems as though he did.

9. I argue in chapter 5 that this perspectival idea also has resonance in the current popularity of the memoir genre.

10. I borrow this term, of course, from Jean Baudrillard, who defined "hyper-reality" as "the generation by models of a real without origin or reality"; in this sense, language generates the models of a reality without any direct access to an original reality, which may or may not even exist (1994, 1).

11. By way of apology for that pun, I can only point out that I am by far not the first person to employ it.

12. I am of course borrowing this term from Linda Hutcheon.

13. There are also veiled references to Thompson and his pharmaceutical excesses in Leyner's 1990 *My Cousin, My Gastroenterologist* in which the unnamed narrator admits to "habitually abusing an illegal growth hormone extracted from the pituitary glands of human corpses" (1990. 3).

4. Trauma and Dissociation

1. Subsequently, trauma theories have been criticized for its western, white (and, I would argue, male) ethnocentrism: "They fail on at least three counts: they marginalize or ignore traumatic experiences of non-Western

or minority cultures; they tend to take for granted the universal validity of definitions of trauma and recovery that have developed out of the history of Western modernity; and they often favour or even prescribe a modernist aesthetic of fragmentation and aporia as uniquely suited to the task of bearing witness to trauma. As a result of all of this, rather than promoting cross-cultural solidarity, trauma theory risks assisting in the perpetuation of the very beliefs, practices, and structures that maintain existing injustices and inequalities" (Craps 2014, 46). While all these are important critiques of trauma theory, these theories seem quite relevant to the autofiction I discuss, which focuses on American and a few British texts largely written by white males. I have attempted, in previous chapters, to address the race and gender implications of the literary strategies I expound upon.

2. In his later work, Rothberg also recognizes the western ethnocentrism in trauma theory as it is traditionally practiced, citing "the limits of classical trauma theory's dislocation of its own context of emergence (i.e., its failure to transcend a Eurocentric frame)" (2014, xii).

3. For example, *Fragments*, published in 1995 supposedly by someone named Binjamin Wilkomirski, was widely reviled when it turned out to have been written by a Swiss Gentile named Bruno Grosjean. But examples abound of memoirs that, once found to contain falsehoods or inaccuracies, have brought public disgrace to their authors. I discuss this issue more fully in chapter 5.

4. This idea is similar to the differentiation Donald Spence makes between "narrative truth" and "historical truth" (1982, 279–97).

5. Memoir vs. Autofiction

1. Serge Doubrovsky, the French author who coined the term, defines "autofiction" more as a memoir than a fiction. In an American context, I feel that Genette's definition is more appropriate than Doubrovsky's.

2. In this, Smith and Watson employ Doubrovsky's rather than Genette's definition of autofiction.

3. However, even some reviewers maintain a careful focus upon what is "true" and what is "fiction" in these novels. See, for example, Karen Holt, "A Fact-Finding Tour of 'Lunar Park.'"

4. Couser makes the case for memoir's increasing acceptance as a legitimate literary genre by pointing out that "memoirs are more frequently and prominently published by prestigious presses and more widely reviewed than ever before. For example, the highly selective *New York Times Book Review* almost always assesses at least one memoir in each weekly issue" (Couser 142).

5. Of course, this kind of confessional narrative hearkens back to *Confessions* by Augustine and later Rousseau, who admit to terribly bad behavior in the hopes of educating readers toward a different path (Augustine) and instructing readers as to what goes into building a man of enlightenment (Rousseau). However, while contemporary memoirs often contain that element of confession as a gesture toward edification, it represents a marked difference from autobiographical works from the nineteenth and early twentieth centuries.

6. Klüger refers here to *Fragments*, published in 1995, which was purported to have been written by a Holocaust survivor named Binjamin Wilkomirski but which turned out to have been written by a Swiss gentile named Bruno Grosjean.

7. I am not the only person to make this somewhat controversial claim. Ben Yagoda has said: "Memoir is to fiction as photography is to painting, also, in being easier to do fairly well. Only a master can create a convincing and compelling fictional world. Anyone with a moderate level of discipline, insight, intelligence, and editorial skill—plus a more than moderately interesting life—can write a decent memoir" (2009, 240). Neil Genzlinger is somewhat less charitable, saying that the best among the contemporary crop of memoirs becomes "lost in a sea of people you've never heard of, writing uninterestingly about the unexceptional, apparently not realizing how commonplace their little wrinkle is or how many other people have already written about it."

8. In his book of essays entitled *The Curtain,* Milan Kundera discusses the importance of context or what he calls "historical consciousness" to our perceptions of a work of art: "Let us imagine a contemporary composer writing a sonata that in its form, its harmonies, its melodies resembles Beethoven's. Let's even imagine that this sonata is so masterfully made that, if it had actually been by Beethoven, it would count among his greatest works. And yet no matter how magnificent, signed by a contemporary composer it would be laughable. At best its author would be applauded as a virtuoso of pastiche" (2005, 4).

9. Jacobs, *The Year of Living Biblically*; Schaub, *Year of No Sugar*; Powell, *Julie and Julia*; Price, *Year of the Dunk*.

10. Kellman defines a "self-begetting novel" as "an account, usually first-person, of the development of a character to the point at which he is able to take up his pen and compose the novel we have just finished reading" (1980, 3).

11. See Alan Turing, "Computing Machinery and Intelligence" for a more in-depth discussion of this test and its implications.

12. "Moishe Pipik" in Yiddish means "Moses Bellybutton," a slang term for an upstart, overweening young boy. But in this context it could be construed as a joke about Philip Roth's continual contemplation of his own navel.

13. Supporters of *American Psycho*, on the other hand, claim that, taken as a whole, the novel acts as an indictment against the Bateman character and the excesses of the American 1980s. See, for example, Elizabeth Young and Graham Caveney, *Shopping in Space*.

14. It is important, of course, to maintain the distinction here between "Bret" and Ellis himself: as part of the plot of the novel *Lunar Park*, "Bret" argues that *American Psycho* was written under the influence of some kind of demonic possession. To my knowledge, the extratextual Ellis has never made such a claim.

15. Once again, please note that I say it is "Bret," not Ellis, who learns these lessons. I do not presume (nor much care) to argue that Ellis has learned or even should learn anything.

16. Originally published in the *New York Times Book Review*, February 28, 1988.

References

Acker, Kathy. 1988. *Empire of the Senseless*. New York: Grove Press.

Adams, Timothy Dow. 1990. *Telling Lies in Modern American Autobiography*. Chapel Hill: University of North Carolina Press.

Alter, Robert. 1975. *Partial Magic: The Novel as a Self-Conscious Genre*. Berkeley: University of California Press.

Amis, Martin. 1984. *Money: A Suicide Note*. New York: Viking.

Anderson, Chris. 1987. *Style as Argument: Contemporary American Nonfiction*. Carbondale: Southern Illinois University Press.

Anson, Robert Sam. 1976. "The *Rolling Stone* Saga, Part II." *New York Times*, December 10, 24.

Auster, Paul. 1990. *City of Glass*. In *New York Trilogy*. New York: Penguin Books. First published in 1985.

Baker, Nicholson. 1991. *U and I: A True Story*. New York: Random House.

Balaev, Michelle. 2012. *The Nature of Trauma in American Novels*. Evanston il: Northwestern University Press.

Ballard, J. G. 1973. *Crash*. New York: Picador.

Barth, John. 1969. *Lost in the Funhouse*. New York: Bantam Books.

———. 1972. *Chimera*. New York: Houghton Mifflin.

———. 1984. "The Literature of Exhaustion." In *The Friday Book: Essays and Other Fiction*. Baltimore: Johns Hopkins University Press. First published in 1967 in the *Atlantic*.

———. 2001. *Coming Soon!!!* New York: Houghton Mifflin.

Barthes, Roland. 1970. "Historical Discourse." In *Introduction to Structuralism*, edited by Michael Lane, 145–55. New York: Basic Books.

———. 1974. "The Writer on Holiday." In *Mythologies*, translated by Annette Lavers, 29–31. New York: Hill and Wang. First published in 1957.

———. 1975. "Introduction to the Structural Analysis of Narratives." *New Literary History* 6 (2): 237–72.

———. 1977a. "The Death of the Author." In *Image, Music, Text*, translated by Stephen Heath, 142–48. New York: Hill and Wang.

———. 1977b. "From Work to Text." In *Image, Music, Text*, translated by Stephen Heath, 155–64. New York: Hill and Wang.

———. 1977c. *Roland Barthes by Roland Barthes*. Translated by Richard Howard. London: Macmillan.

Baudrillard, Jean. 1994. *Simulacra and Simulation*. Translated by Sheila Faria Glaser. Ann Arbor: University of Michigan Press.

Beauvoir, Simone de. 1989. *The Second Sex*. Translated by H. M. Parshley. New York: Random House. First published in English by Alfred A. Knopf, 1953, and in French by Librairie Gallimard, 1949.

Beigbeder, Frederic. 2004. *Windows on the World*. New York: Hyperion.

Beller, Thomas. 2014. *J. D. Salinger: The Escape Artist*. New York: Houghton Mifflin.

Bloom, Harold. 1973. *The Anxiety of Influence*. New York: Oxford University Press.

———. 1998. *Shakespeare: The Invention of the Human*. New York: Riverhead Books.

Booth, Wayne. 1961. *The Rhetoric of Fiction*. Chicago: University of Chicago Press.

Bordo, Susan. 1987. *The Flight to Objectivity: Essays on Cartesianism and Culture*. Albany: suny Press.

Boyle, Claire. 2007. *Consuming Autobiographies: Reading and Writing the Self in Post-War France*. Oxford: Legenda.

Buelens, Gert, Sam Durrant, and Robert Eaglestone, eds. 2014. *The Future of Trauma Theory: Contemporary Literary and Cultural Criticism*. New York: Routledge.

Burke, Seán. 1998. *The Death and Return of the Author: Criticism and Subjectivity in Barthes, Foucault, and Derrida*. 2nd ed. Edinburgh: Edinburgh University Press.

Cain, George. 1970. *Blueschild Baby*. New York: McGraw-Hill.

Caruth, Cathy, ed. 1995a. *Trauma: Explorations in Memory*. Baltimore: Johns Hopkins University Press.

———. 1995b. *Unclaimed Experience: Trauma, Narrative, and History*. Baltimore: Johns Hopkins University Press.

Célestin, Roger. 2001. "Interview with Serge Doubrovsky: Autofiction and Beyond." *Journal of the Twentieth Century/Contemporary French Studies* 1 (2): 397–405.

Chabon, Michael. 2016. *Moonglow: A Novel*. New York: HarperCollins.

Cohen, Roger. 1991. "Bret Easton Ellis Answers Critics of 'American Psycho.'" *New York Times*, March 6.

Cohn, Dorrit. 2000. *The Distinction of Fiction*. Baltimore: Johns Hopkins University Press.

Collado-Rodriguez, Francisco. 2011. "Experimental Fiction and Trauma Studies: The Case of Kurt Vonnegut's *Slaughterhouse-Five*." In *Between the*

Urge to Know and the Need to Deny: Trauma and Ethics in Contemporary British and American Literature, edited by Dolores Herrero and Sonia Baelo-Allue, 129–44. Heidelberg: Universitatsverlag Winter.

Collins, Patricia Hill. 1990. *Black Feminist Thought: Knowledge, Consciousness, and the Politics of Empowerment*. New York: Routledge.

Colonna, Vincent. 2004. *Autofiction et Autres Mythomanies Litteraires*. Auch, France: Tristram.

Conway, Jill Ker. 1998. *When Memory Speaks*. New York: Vintage Books.

Cooke, Dervila. 2005. *Present Pasts: Patrick Modiano's (Auto)Biographical Fictions*. New York: Rodopi.

Corrigan, Maureen. 2014. *So We Read On: How* The Great Gatsby *Came to Be and Why It Endures*. New York: Little, Brown.

Coupland, Douglas. 2006. *JPod*. New York: Bloomsbury.

Couser, G. Thomas. 2012. *Memoir: An Introduction*. New York: Oxford University Press.

Craps, Stef. 2014. "Beyond Eurocentrism: Trauma Theory in the Global Age." In Buelens et al., *The Future of Trauma Theory*, 45–61. New York: Routledge.

Crosthwaite, Paul. 2009. *Trauma, Postmodernism, and the Aftermath of World War II*. New York: Palgrave Macmillan.

Currie, Ron, Jr. 2013. *Flimsy Little Plastic Miracles: A True* Story*. New York: Viking.

D'Amore, Jonathan. 2012. *American Authorship and Autobiographical Narrative*. New York: Palgrave.

Davis, Lennard J. 1997. *Factual Fictions*. Philadelphia: University of Pennsylvania Press.

DeKoven, Marianne. 1991. *Rich and Strange: Gender, History, Modernism*. Princeton, nj: Princeton University Press.

Dennis, Everette E., and William L. Rivers. 2011. *Other Voices: The New Journalism in America*. New Brunswick nj: Transaction. First published in 1974 by Canfield Press.

Derrida, Jacques. 1988. *Limited, Inc.* Translated by Samuel Weber. Evanston il: Northwestern University Press.

Didion, Joan. 1984. *Democracy*. New York: Simon and Schuster.

Doubrovsky, Serge. 1988. "Autobiographie/verite/psychoanalse." In *Autobiographiques*, 61–79. Paris: puf.

———. 1993. "Autobiography/Truth/Psychoanalysis." Translated by Logan Whalen and John Ireland. *Genre* 26 (1): 27–42.

———. 2013. "Autofiction." *Auto/Fiction* 1 (1): i–ii.

Eakin, Paul John, ed. *On Autobiography*. Translated by Katherine Leary, 119–37. Minneapolis: University of Minnesota Press. Originally published in 1982.

Eason, David L. 1979. *Metajournalism: The Problem of Reporting in the Nonfiction Novel*. Ann Arbor mi: University Microfilms International.

Eliot, T. S. 1919. "Tradition and the Individual Talent. *Poetry Foundation*. http://www.poetryfoundation.org/learning/essay/2378681919.

Ellis, Bret Easton. 2005. *Lunar Park*. New York: Knopf.

Erikson, Kai. 1995. "Notes on Trauma and Community." In Caruth, *Trauma: Explorations in Memory*, 183–99.

Everett, Percival. 2004. *A History of the African-American People [Proposed] by Strom Thurmond as Told to Percival Everett and James Kincaid*. New York: Akashic Books.

———. 2009. *I Am Not Sidney Poitier*. St. Paul: Graywolf Press.

Exley, Frederick. 1968. *A Fan's Notes: A Fictional Memoir*. New York: Harper & Row.

———. 1975. *Pages from a Cold Island*. New York: Random House.

———. 1988. *Last Notes from Home*. New York: Random House.

Faludi, Susan. 1991. *Backlash: The Undeclared War against American Women*. New York: Doubleday.

Federman, Raymond. 1979. *The Voice in the Closet*. Madison wi: Coda Press.

———. 1981. *Surfiction: Fiction Now . . . and Tomorrow*. Chicago: Swallow Press.

———. 2001a. *Aunt Rachel's Fur*. Normal il: fc2.

———. 2001b. *The Voice in the Closet*. Buffalo ny: Sharcherone Books.

Felman, Shoshana, and Dori Laub. 1991. *Testimony: Crises of Witnessing in Literature, Psychoanalysis, and History*. New York: Routledge.

Felski, Rita. 1995. *The Gender of Modernity*. Cambridge: Harvard University Press.

Ferrebe, Alice. 2005. *Masculinity in Male-Authored Fiction, 1950–2000*. London: Palgrave Macmillan.

Ferreira-Meyers, Karen. 2012. "Autofiction: 'Imaginaire' and Reality, an Interesting Mix Leading to the Illusion of a Genre?" *Caietele Echinox: Imaginaire et Illusion*, 23:103–16.

Fils, Leonora. 2010. *Factual Fictions: Narrative Truth and the Contemporary American Documentary Novel*. Newcastle upon Tyne: Cambridge Scholars.

Fishkin, Shelley Fisher. 1985. *From Fact to Fiction: Journalism and Imaginative Writing in America*. Baltimore: Johns Hopkins University Press.

Fitzpatrick, Kathleen. 2006. *The Anxiety of Obsolescence: The American Novel in the Age of Television*. Nashville: Vanderbilt University Press.

Flis, Leonora. 2010. *Factual Fictions: Narrative Truth and the Contemporary American Documentary Novel*. Newcastle upon Tyne: Cambridge Scholars.

Fludernik, Monica. 2003. "Scene Shift, Metalepsis, and the Metaleptic Mode." *Style* 37 (4): 382–400.

Foer, Jonathan Safran. 2002. *Everything Is Illuminated*. New York: Houghton Mifflin.

Forter, Greg. 2011. *Gender, Race, and Mourning in American Modernism.* Cambridge: Cambridge University Press.

Foster, John Burt, Jr. 1995. "Bend Sinister." In *The Garland Companion to Vladimir Nabokov,* edited by Vladimir E. Alexandrov, 25–35. New York: Garland.

Foucault, Michel. 1977. "What Is an Author?" In *Language, Counter-Memory, Practice,* ed. Donald Boucahard, 113–38. Ithaca: Cornell University Press.

Fowles, John. 2004. *The French Lieutenant's Woman.* London: Vintage. First published in 1969.

Gallagher, Catherine. 1994. *Nobody's Story: The Vanishing Acts of Women Writers in the Marketplace, 1670–1820.* Berkeley: University of California Press.

Genette, Gérard. 1983. *Narrative Discourse.* Translated by Jane E. Lewin. Ithaca ny: Cornell University Press.

———. 1993. *Fiction & Diction.* Translated by Catherine Porter. Ithaca ny: Cornell University Press.

———. 1997. *Palimpsests: Literature in the Second Degree.* Translated by Channa Newman and Claude Doubinsky. Lincoln: University of Nebraska Press. First published in 1982 by Seuil.

Genzlinger, Neil. 2011. "The Trouble with Memoir." *New York Times,* January 28.

Gilbert, Sandra M., and Susan Gubar. 1988. *No Man's Land.* Vol. 1, *The War of the Words.* New Haven: Yale University Press.

Gilligan, Carol. 1982. *In a Different Voice: Psychological Theory and Women's Development.* Cambridge ma: Harvard University Press.

Gilmore, Leigh. 2001. *The Limits of Autobiography: Trauma and Testimony.* Ithaca ny: Cornell University Press.

Glass, Loren Daniel. 2004. *Authors, Inc.: Literary Celebrity in the Modern United States, 1880–1980.* New York: New York University Press.

———. 2014. "Zuckerman/Roth: Literary Celebrity between Two Deaths." *pmla* 129 (2): 223–36.

Goldman, Jonathan. 2011. *Modernism Is the Literature of Celebrity.* Austin: University of Texas Press.

Hallman, J. C. 2015. *B & Me: A True Story of Literary Arousal.* New York: Simon & Schuster.

Harper, Phillip Brian. 1994. *Framing the Margins: The Social Logic of Postmodern Culture.* New York: Oxford University Press.

Hartsock, John C. 2000. *A History of American Literary Journalism: The Emergence of a Modern Narrative Form.* Amherst: University of Massachusetts Press.

Hellmann, John. 1981. *Fables of Fact: The New Journalism as New Fiction.* Urbana: University of Illinois Press.

Hollowell, John. 1977. *Fact & Fiction: The New Journalism and the Nonfiction Novel*. Chapel Hill: University of North Carolina Press.

Holt, Karen. 2005. "A Fact-Finding Tour of 'Lunar Park.'" *Publishers Weekly*, July 11, 22–23.

hooks, bell. 1990. *Yearning: Race, Gender, and Cultural Politics*. Cambridge, ma: South End Press.

Hughes, Alex. 1999. *Heterographies: Sexual Difference in French Autobiography*. New York: Berg.

Hutcheon, Linda. 1980. *Narcissistic Narrative: The Metafictional Paradox*. Waterloo, Ontario: Wilfrid Laurier University Press.

———. 1988. *A Poetics of Postmodernism: History, Theory, Fiction*. New York: Routledge.

———. 1989. "Historiographic Metafiction: Parody and the Intertextuality of History." In *Intertextuality and Contemporary American Fiction*, edited by P. O'Donnell and Robert Con Davis, 3–32. Baltimore: Johns Hopkins University Press.

Huyssen, Andreas. 1986. *After the Great Divide: Modernism, Mass Culture, Postmodernism*. Bloomington: Indiana University Press.

Jacobsen, Louise Brix. 2015. "Vitafiction as a Mode of Self-Fashioning: The Case of Michael J. Fox in *Curb Your Enthusiasm*." *Narrative* 23 (3): 252–70.

Jaffe, Aaron. 2005. *Modernism and the Culture of Celebrity*. Cambridge: Cambridge University Press.

James, Henry. 1984. *The Bostonians*. New York: Modern Library. First published in 1885.

Jeannelle, Jean-Louis, and Catherine Viollet. 2007. *Genese et Autofiction*. Paris: Academia-Bruylant.

Jones, Elizabeth H. 2009. "Serge Doubrovsky: Life, Writing, Legacy." *L'Esprit Créateur* 49 (3): 1–7.

———. 2010. "Autofiction: A Brief History of a Neologism." In *Life Writing: Essays on Autobiography, Biography, and Literature*, edited by Richard Bradford, 174–84. New York: Palgrave Macmillan.

Jones, J. Nicole. "Becoming Story: The State of Memoir." *Los Angeles Review of Books*. January 10, 2013. http://lareviewofbooks.org/article.php?id=1299.

Joyce, James. 1986. *Ulysses*. Edited by Hans Walter Gabler. New York: Vintage.

Kellman, Steven G. 1980. *The Self-Begetting Novel*. New York: Columbia University Press.

Kerrane, Kevin. 1997. "Making Facts Dance." In *The Art of Fact: A Historical Anthology of Literary Journalism*, edited by Kerrane and Ben Yagoda, 17–20. New York: Scribner.

Kimmel, Michael. 1996. *Manhood in America: A Cultural History.* New York: Free Press.

———. 2013. *Angry White Men: American Masculinity at the End of an Era.* New York: Nation Books.

King, Larry. 2006. "Interview with James Frey." CNN *Larry King Live*, January 11. CNN Transcripts. http://transcripts.cnn.com/transcripts/0601/11/lkl.01.html.

Kohlberg, Lawrence. 1981. *Essays on Moral Development.* Vol. 1, *The Philosophy of Moral Development.* San Francisco: Harper and Row.

Kraus, Chris. 2006. *I Love Dick.* Los Angeles: Semotext(e).

Kundera, Milan. 2005. *The Curtain: An Essay in Seven Parts.* Translated by Linda Asher. New York: HarperCollins.

Langer, Lawrence. 1991. *Holocaust Testimonies: The Ruins of Memory.* New Haven: Yale University Press.

Lasch, Christopher. 1978. *The Culture of Narcissism: American Life in an Age of Diminishing Expectations.* New York: Norton.

Lehmann-Haupt, Christopher. 1970a. "He and She—I." *New York Times*, August 5, 33.

———. 1970b. "He and She—II." *New York Times*, August 6, 31.

Lejeune, Philippe. 1989a. "The Autobiographical Pact." In Eakin, *On Autobiography*, 3–30.

———. 1989b. "The Autobiographical Pact (Bis)." In Eakin, *On Autobiography*, 119–37.

Levinson, Paul. 1997. *The Soft Edge: A Natural History and Future of the Information Revolution.* New York: Routledge.

Leyner, Mark. 1990. *My Cousin, My Gastroenterologist.* New York: Random House.

———. 1992. *Et Tu, Babe?* New York: Harmony Books.

Lodge, David. 1992. *The Art of Fiction.* New York: Viking.

Lopate, Philip. 2005. "Reflection and Retrospection: A Pedagogic Mystery Story." In *The Fourth Genre* (Spring). http://philliplopate.com/2011/08/reflection- and-retrospection-a-pedagogic-mystery-story.

Luckhurst, Roger. 2008. *The Trauma Question.* New York: Routledge.

Lury, Celia. 2002. *Cultural Rights: Technology, Legality, and Personality.* New York: Routledge.

Lyotard, Jean-François. 1984. *The Postmodern Condition: A Report on Knowledge.* Translated by Geoff Bennington and Brian Massumi. Minneapolis: University of Minnesota Press. First published in 1979.

Macdonald, Dwight. 1965. "Parajournalism, or Tom Wolfe and His Magic Writing Machine." *New York Review of Books*, August 26, 3.

Mailer, Norman. 1971. *The Prisoner of Sex.* Boston: Little, Brown.

———. 1981. *Cannibals and Christians*. New York: Pinnacle.

———. 1994. *The Armies of the Night: History as a Novel, the Novel as History*. New York: Plume. First published in 1968.

Malina, Debra. 2002. *Breaking the Frame: Metalepsis and the Construction of the Subject*. Columbus: Ohio State University Press.

Marcus, Ben. 2002. *Notable American Women*. New York: Vintage Books.

Marshall, P. David. 1997. *Celebrity and Power: Fame and Contemporary Culture*. Minneapolis: University of Minnesota Press.

McGurl, Mark. 2009. *The Program Era: Postwar Fiction and the Rise of Creative Writing*. Cambridge, ma: Harvard University Press.

McHale, Brian. 1987. *Postmodern Fiction*. New York: Routledge.

Memmott, Carol. 2006. "Oprah Confronts Frey about Disputed Memoir." usa Today. January 25.

Middleton, Peter. 1992. *The Inward Gaze: Masculinity and Subjectivity in Modern Culture*. New York: Routledge.

Miller, Nancy K., and Jason Tougaw, eds. 2002. *Extremities: Trauma, Testimony, and Community*. Chicago: University of Illinois Press.

Millett, Kate. 1970. *Sexual Politics*. New York: Simon & Schuster.

Moran, Joe. 2000. *Star Authors: Literary Celebrity in America*. Sterling va: Pluto Press.

Nabokov, Vladimir. 1947. *Bend Sinister*. New York: McGraw-Hill.

———. 1989. *Selected Letters, 1940–1977*. Edited by Dmitri Nabokov and Matthew J. Bruccoli. New York: Harcourt.

O'Brien, Tim. 2006. *In the Lake of the Woods*. New York: Houghton Mifflin Harcourt. First published in 1994.

———. 2009. *The Things They Carried*. New York: Houghton Mifflin Harcourt. Originally published in 1990.

Ozeki, Ruth. 2013. *A Tale for the Time Being*. New York: Viking.

Phillips, Arthur. 2011. *The Tragedy of Arthur*. New York: Random House.

Phillips, Jerry. 1997. "Literature in the Country of 'Whiteness' from T. S. Eliot to *The Tempest*." In *Whiteness: A Critical Reader*, edited by Mike Hill, 329–45. New York: New York University Press.

Pier, John. 2009. "Metalepsis." In *Handbook of Narratology*, edited by P. Hühn, J. Pier, W. Schmid, and J. Schönert, 190–203. Berlin: Walter de Gruyter.

Plascencia, Salvador. 2005. *The People of Paper*. San Francisco: McSweeney's Books.

Powers, Richard. 1995. *Galatea 2.2*. New York: HarperCollins.

Price, Asher. 2015. *Year of the Dunk: A Modest Defiance of Gravity*. New York: Crown.

Robinson, Sally. 2000. *Marked Men: White Masculinity in Crisis*. New York: Columbia University Press.

Rosen, David. 1993. *The Changing Fictions of Masculinity*. Urbana: University of Illinois Press.

Roth, Philip. 1993. "A Bit of Jewish Mischief." *New York Times Book Review*, March 7.

———. 1994. *Operation Shylock: A Confession*. New York: Vintage.

———. 1997. *Deception*. New York: Vintage. First published in 1990.

———. 2001a. "A Conversation in Jerusalem with Aharon Appelfeld." In *Shop Talk: A Writer and His Colleagues and Their Work*, 18–39. New York: Houghton Mifflin.

———. 2001b. "Writing American Fiction." In *Reading Myself and Others*. New York: Farrar, Straus and Giroux. First published in March 1961 in *Commentary*.

Rothberg, Michael. 2000. *Traumatic Realism: The Demands of Holocaust Representation*. Minneapolis: University of Minnesota Press.

———. 2014. "Beyond Tancred and Clorinda—Trauma Studies for Implicated Subjects." In Buelens et al., *The Future of Trauma Theory*, xi–xviii.

Rother, James. 1976. "Parafiction: The Adjacent Universe of Barth, Barthelme, Pynchon, and Nabokov." *boundary 2* 5 (1): 21–43.

Rotundo, E. Anthony. 1993. *American Manhood: Transformations in Masculinity from the Revolution to the Modern Era*. New York: HarperCollins.

Russell, John. 2000. *Reciprocities in the Nonfiction Novel*. Athens: University of Georgia Press.

Ryan, Judith. 2012. *The Novel after Theory*. New York: Columbia University Press.

Ryan, Marie-Laure. 1997. "Postmodernism and the Doctrine of Panfictionality." *Narrative* 5 (2): 165–87.

Savran, David. 1998. *Taking It Like a Man: White Masculinity, Masochism, and Contemporary American Literature*. Princeton, nj: Princeton University Press.

Schmitt, Arnaud. 2010. "Making the Case for Self-Narration against Autofiction." *a/b: Auto/Biography Studies* 25 (1): 122–37.

Scholes, Robert. 1968. "Double Perspective on Hysteria." *Saturday Review* 24 (August): 37.

———. 1975. *Structural Fabulation*. Notre Dame in: University of Notre Dame Press.

Schwenger, Peter. 1984. *Phallic Critiques: Masculinity and Twentieth-Century Literature*. London: Routledge and Kegan Paul.

Segura, Jonathan. 2011. "All Lies. pw Talks with Arthur Phillips." PublishersWeekly.com. February 28.

Self, Will. 2010. *Walking to Hollywood: Memories of Before the Fall*. New York: Grove Press.

Shostak, Debra. 1997. "The Diaspora Jew and the 'Instinct for Impersonation': Philip Roth's *Operation Shylock*." *Contemporary Literature* 38 (4): 726–54.

Shteyngart, Gary. 2006. *Absurdistan*. New York: Random House.

Siegle, Robert. 1986. *The Politics of Reflexivity: Narrative and the Constitutive Poetics of Culture*. Baltimore: Johns Hopkins University Press.

Silverman, Kaja. 1992. *Male Subjectivity at the Margins*. New York: Routledge.

Smart, Robert Augustin. 1985. *The Nonfiction Novel*. New York: University Press of America.

Smith, Sidonie, and Julia Watson. 2010. *Reading Autobiography: A Guide for Interpreting Life Narratives*. Minneapolis: University of Minnesota Press.

Spear, Thomas C. 1991. "Celeine and 'Autofictional' First-Person Narration." *Studies in the Novel* 23 (3): 357–70.

Spence, Donald P. 1982. *Narrative Truth and Historical Truth*. New York: Norton.

Stein, Gertrude. 1933. *The Autobiography of Alice B. Toklas*. New York: Harcourt, Brace.

Sukenick, Ronald. 1985. "Thirteen Digressions." In *In Form: Digressions on the Act of Fiction*, 16–33. Carbondale: Southern Illinois University Press.

——. 1999. *Up: A Novel*. Normal il: fc2. First published in 1968.

Talese, Gay. 1970. *Fame and Obscurity: A Book about New York, a Bridge, and Celebrities on the Edge*. New York: World.

Thompson, Hunter S. 1982. *The Great Shark Hunt*. New York: Warner.

——. 1998. *Fear and Loathing in Las Vegas*. New York: Vintage. First published in 1971.

Thoss, Jeff. 2015. *When Storyworlds Collide: Metalepsis in Popular Fiction, Film, and Comics*. Boston: Brill Rodopi.

Traber, Daniel S. 2007. *Whiteness, Otherness, and the Individualism Paradox from Huck to Punk*. New York: Palgrave Macmillan.

Turing, Alan. 1950. "Computing Machinery and Intelligence." *Mind* 54 (236): 433–60.

Varadharajan, Asha. 2008. "The Unsettling Legacy of Harold Bloom's Anxiety of Influence." *Modern Language Quarterly* 69 (4): 461–80.

Vees-Gulani, Susanne. 2003. "Diagnosing Billy Pilgrim: A Psychiatric Approach to Kurt Vonnegut's *Slaughterhouse-Five*." *Critique* 44 (2): 175–84.

Vickroy, Laurie. 2002. *Trauma and Survival in Contemporary Fiction*. Charlottesville: University of Virginia Press.

Vonnegut, Kurt. 1973. *Breakfast of Champions, or Goodbye Blue Monday*. New York: Random House.

——. 1994. *Slaughterhouse-Five, or The Children's Crusade*. New York: Delacorte Press. First published in 1969.

Wallace, David Foster. 2011. *The Pale King*. New York: Little, Brown.

Weber, Ronald. 1980. *The Literature of Fact: Literary Nonfiction in American Writing*. Athens: Ohio University Press.

Weingarten, Marc. 2006. *The Gang That Wouldn't Write Straight*. New York: Crown.

White, Hayden. 1976. "The Fictions of Factual Representation." In *The Literature of Fact*, edited by Angus Fletcher, 21–44. New York: Columbia University Press.

———. 1978. *Tropics of Discourse: Essays in Cultural Criticism*. Baltimore: Johns Hopkins University Press.

Whitehead, Anne. 2004. *Trauma Fiction*. Edinburgh: Edinburgh University Press.

"Who's Come a Long Way, Baby?" 1970. *Time*, August 31, 16–21.

Widiss, Benjamin. 2011. *Obscure Invitations: The Persistence of the Author in Twentieth-Century American Literature*. Stanford ca: Stanford University Press.

Wiegman, Robyn. 1999. "Whiteness Studies and the Paradox of Particularity." *boundary 2* 26 (3): 115–50.

Wimsatt, William K., and Monroe Beardsley. 1946. "The Intentional Fallacy." *Sewanee Review* 54 (3): 468–88.

Wolfe, Tom. 1968. *The Electric Kool-Aid Acid Test*. New York: Farrar, Straus and Giroux.

———. 1972. "The Birth of 'The New Journalism': Eyewitness Report by Tom Wolfe." *New York Magazine*, February 14, 44.

———. 1989. "Stalking the Billion-Footed Beast: A Literary Manifesto for the New Social Novel." *Harper's Magazine*, November, 45–56.

Wolfe, Tom, and E. W. Johnson, eds. 1973. *The New Journalism*. New York: Harper & Row.

"Women's Lib: A Second Look." 1970. *Time*, December 14, 50.

Woolf, Virginia. 1983. *The Diary of Virginia Woolf*. Vol. 4, *1931–35*. Edited by Anne Olivier Bell. Harmondsworth: Penguin Books.

———. 1995. *A Room of One's Own*. Cambridge: Cambridge University Press. First published in 1929.

Yagoda, Ben. 2009. *Memoir: A History*. New York: Riverhead Books.

Young, Elizabeth, and Graham Caveney. 1992. *Shopping in Space*. New York: Atlantic Monthly Press.

Index

Capote, Truman, 94, 98, 117
Caruth, Cathy, 127
Cha, Theresa, 194n15
Chabon, Michael, 132, 167; *Moonglow*, 167
Cohn, Dorrit, 152–53
Collins, Patricia Hill, 51
Colonna, Vincent, 10–11
Cooke, Dervila, 11, 193n6
Coover, Robert, 103
Couser, G. Thomas, 14–15, 148, 153, 154, 156–57, 162, 164, 178
Craps, Stef, 197n1
Crosthwaite, Paul, 129
Currie, Ron, Jr., 150, 157, 167, 168, 178; *Flimsy Little Plastic Miracles*, 150, 157–58

D'Amore, Jonathan, 77–78
death of the author. *See* Barthes, Roland
de Beauvoir, Simone, 32, 190n13
DeKoven, Marianne, 33
Derrida, Jacques, 17, 21, 73
Descartes, René, 32
Dickens, Charles, 14
Didion, Joan, 95, 110–11
dissociation, 136–37, 141
Don Quixote, 44, 74
Doubrovsky, Serge, 148–49, 187n4; and coinage of term "autofiction," 2, 6, 7, 8, 9–10, 13, 14–15; *Fils*, 6; on Lejeune's "Autobiographical Pact," 7–9

Eason, David L., 92, 94, 102, 105, 195n2, 195n5
Eggers, Dave, 78
Eliot, T. S., 108; impersonality and, 19, 31–32, 34, 35, 36, 45, 62, 63, 64, 98, 108, 149, 188n3
—Works: "The Love Song of J. Alfred Prufrock," 29–30; "Tradition and the Individual Talent," 31, 32, 33

Ellis, Bret Easton, 80, 121–22, 151, 165, 172
—Works: *Lunar Park*, 2, 3, 13, 81–82, 121–22, 150, 151, 165–66, 172–74, 175–76, 177, 178; *American Psycho*, 3, 173–74
Erikson, Kai, 127–28, 136
Everett, Percival, 84, 89–90, 91, 96, 194n16
Exley, Frederick, 76

Faludi, Susan, 29
Federman, Raymond, 17, 18, 62, 127, 132, 138–40; and surfiction, 2
—Works: *Aunt Rachel's Fur*, 139; *Return to Manure*, 17; *The Voice in the Closet*, 139
Felski, Rita, 25
feminism: first-wave, 28, 29; second-wave, 26–27, 29, 38–39, 40, 45–46
Ferrebe, Alice, 24
Ferreira-Meyers, Karen, 10–11
Fils, Leonora, 113
Fishkin, Shelley Fisher, 113
Fitzpatrick, Kathleen, 25, 27, 88, 91, 169
Fludernik, Monica, 54
Foer, Jonathan Safran, 126, 127, 132, 134, 135, 141–44
—Works: *Everything Is Illuminated*, 135, 141–44; *Extremely Loud and Incredibly Close*, 126
Forter, Greg, 32–33
Foucault, Michel, 21, 40, 69, 72–73, 77, 85; author-function, 63, 64, 70–71, 73, 77, 79, 83–84, 158, 165, 193n5; "What Is an Author?" 64, 69, 70–71
The French Lieutenant's Woman (Fowles), 52–53, 54, 56, 91
Frey, James, 157, 161–64, 164
Friedan, Betty, 190n13

To order or obtain more information on these or other University of
Nebraska Press titles, visit nebraskapress.unl.edu.